I0224423

Verse by Verse Commentary on

PSALMS
81-118

Enduring Word Commentary Series

By David Guzik

The grass withers, the flower fades,
but the word of our God stands forever.
Isaiah 40:8

Commentary on Psalms 81-118

Copyright ©2019 by David Guzik

Printed in the United States of America
or in the United Kingdom

Print Edition ISBN: 978-1-939466-93-8

Enduring Word

5662 Calle Real #184

Goleta, CA 93117

Electronic Mail: ewm@enduringword.com

Internet Home Page: www.enduringword.com

All rights reserved. No portion of this book may be reproduced in any form (except for quotations in reviews) without the written permission of the publisher.

Scripture references, unless noted, are from the New King James Version of the Bible, copyright ©1979, 1980, 1982, Thomas Nelson, Inc., Publisher.

Contents

Bibliography – Page 315
Author's Remarks – Page 317

Psalm 81 – Gathering God's People to Listen and Obey

The title of this psalm is **To the Chief Musician. On an instrument of Gath. A Psalm of Asaph.** *It indicates the audience of the psalm* (**the Chief Musician**)*, the author of the psalm* (**of Asaph**) *and the sound of the psalm* (**on the instrument of Gath**)*. This psalm is best connected with the Feast of Trumpets or the Feast of Tabernacles celebrated by the people of Israel.*

"This powerful psalm leaves no doubt of its festal character, and little doubt of the particular feast it was designed to serve: in a probability the Feast of Tabernacles. This commemorated the wilderness journey, and included a public reading of the law." (Derek Kidner)

A. A trumpet call to Israel.

1. (1-2) A call to praise God in song.

Sing aloud to God our strength;
Make a joyful shout to the God of Jacob.
Raise a song and strike the timbrel,
The pleasant harp with the lute.

a. **Sing aloud to God our strength**: Asaph knew it was good for God's people to hear the exhortation to **sing aloud**. We should honor God with singing, and our songs are sung **aloud**.

i. "It is to be regretted that the niceties of modern singing frighten our congregations from joining lustily in the hymns. For our part we delight in full bursts of praise, and had rather discover the ruggedness of a want of musical training than miss the heartiness of universal congregational song. The gentility which lisps the tune in wellbred whispers, or leaves the singing altogether to the choir, is very like a mockery of worship." (Spurgeon)

b. **Make a joyful shout**: There is a place for songs rich with awe, reverence, or contrition, but never to the exclusion of songs that **make a joyful shout to the God of Jacob**.

c. **Raise a song and strike the timbrel**: As the song unto God is raised, so should skillful music from instruments. Asaph listed three: **the timbrel**, **the pleasant harp**, and **the lute**.

> i. "The mention of the tambourine [**timbrel**] suggests that the people danced while singing praise." (VanGemeren)

> ii. "Franz Delitzsch, one of the great German commentators, points out that the summons in verse 1 is to the whole congregation; the summons in verse 2 is to the Levites, who were the appointed temple singers and musicians; and the summons in verse 3 is to the priests who had the specific task of blowing the trumpets." (Boice)

2. (3-5) The call to gather the people of God.

Blow the trumpet at the time of the New Moon,
At the full moon, on our solemn feast day.
For this *is* a statute for Israel,
A law of the God of Jacob.
This He established in Joseph *as* a testimony,
When He went throughout the land of Egypt,
***Where* I heard a language I did not understand.**

a. **Blow the trumpet**: The previous verse mentioned musical instruments, but the trumpet was not mentioned as an instrument to accompany praise. The purpose of this **trumpet** was to call God's people together for their **solemn feast day** at the **New Moon**.

> i. "The word for trumpet is shophar (*sopar*), the ram's horn such as sounded the attack at Jericho and in Gideon's battle, and which announced certain festal days." (Kidner)

> ii. "Here the reference to *the new moon*, or 'the new month' (New English Bible), points to the seventh month, which was the climax of the festal year and was ushered in with the sound of this horn." (Kidner)

> iii. "On the September new moon, the first day of the seventh month, was kept a great festival, called the 'feast of trumpets;' Leviticus 23:24, Numbers 29:1; which probably is here intended.... The tenth of the same month was the great day of atonement; and on the fifteenth was celebrated the feast of tabernacles." (Horne)

b. **This is a statute for Israel**: This stresses the *importance* of gathering God's people together. It was **a statute**, a **law**, and **established** as a **testimony** among God's people.

> i. One such **statute** is found in Numbers 10:10: *Also in the day of your gladness, in your appointed feasts, and at the beginning of your months, you shall blow the trumpets over your burnt offerings and over the sacrifices of your peace offerings; and they shall be a memorial for you before your God: I am the L*ORD *your God.*

> ii. "No time is amiss for praising God.... But some are times appointed, not for God to meet us (He is always ready) but for us to meet one another, that we may join together in praising God." (Henry, cited in Kidner)

c. **When He went throughout the land of Egypt**: Asaph thought of the great assembly of God's people as they came together to leave their slavery in Egypt. They gathered together for that initial deliverance, and it became the basis for their future assemblies and feasts.

> i. **I heard a language I did not understand**: "the Egyptian language, which at first was very ungrateful and unknown to the Israelites, Genesis 42:23, and probably continued so for some considerable time, because they were much separated both in place and conversation from the Egyptians, through Joseph's pious and prudent design." (Poole)

B. God speaks to His assembled people.

1. (6-7) God describes how He delivered and tested Israel.

"I removed his shoulder from the burden;
His hands were freed from the baskets.
You called in trouble, and I delivered you;
I answered you in the secret place of thunder;
I tested you at the waters of Meribah. Selah

a. **I removed his shoulder from the burden**: In the first part of the psalm, a call went to God's people to gather, suggested by their first gathering as a people as slaves in Egypt. Now God speaks to His gathered people and begins with reminding them of the great deliverance He gave them in setting them free from their slavery.

> i. "This psalm was a most appropriate 'invitation' to covenant renewal during the feast, when God's people reflected on all his acts in the past." (VanGemeren)

ii. "Let us remember, that we have been eased of far heavier burdens, delivered from severer task-masters, and freed from a baser drudgery; the intolerable load of sin, the cruel tyranny of Satan." (Horne)

b. **You called in trouble, and I delivered you**: God will hear those who cry out to Him. God heard the groaning of Israel under their burden of slavery in Egypt (Exodus 2:23-24). He brought deliverance to them through wonders and leaders like Moses.

i. "*The secret place of thunder* was Sinai, shrouded in smoke and terrible with the voice of God (Exodus 19:16ff.; 20:18ff.). It was education by encounter." (Kidner)

c. **I tested you at the waters of Meribah**: God not only delivered Israel, but He also trained them, and the testing at Meribah was an example of this. At Meribah, God miraculously provided water for a complaining and unbelieving Israel (Exodus 17:1-7).

i. "The story of Israel is only our own history in another shape. God has heard us, delivered us, liberated us, and too often our unbelief makes the wretched return of mistrust, murmuring, and rebellion." (Spurgeon)

2. (8-12) God's rejected call to Israel.

"Hear, O My people, and I will admonish you!
O Israel, if you will listen to Me!
There shall be no foreign god among you;
Nor shall you worship any foreign god.
I *am* the LORD your God,
Who brought you out of the land of Egypt;
Open your mouth wide, and I will fill it.
"But My people would not heed My voice,
And Israel would *have* none of Me.
So I gave them over to their own stubborn heart,
To walk in their own counsels.

a. **Hear, O My people**: Before God instructed His assembled people, He first called for their attention, telling them to **listen**.

i. "What a strange anomaly: a happy, joyfully worshipping congregation and a neglected and offended God." (Boice)

ii. "God looks for listeners as well as singers, on whom the sober lessons of the wilderness will not be lost." (Kidner)

b. **There shall be no foreign god among you**: Some 400 years of slavery in Egypt exposed Israel to the many pagan gods of Egypt. The command

God gave to Israel when the Israelites came out of Egypt is again stated to them in the days of Asaph. Coming from Egypt, Israel was commanded not to **worship any foreign god**, and the same command was for Israel in the land under their kings.

   i. "The problem is not that the world does not know God. How can we expect it to? The problem is that the people of God do not know God, or at least they do not act like they do. Instead of worshipping the Lord and him only, Christians seem to be worshipping the gods of the secular culture – gods of wealth, pleasure, fame, status, and self-absorption." (Boice)

c. **I am the LORD your God**: God's command to put away every foreign god was entirely reasonable. He was Yahweh (**the LORD**), the covenant God of Israel. He was the one who **brought** them **out of the land of Egypt**. No foreign god had done such things for Israel.

   i. "No other god had done anything for the Jews, and therefore they had no reason for paying homage to any other. To us the same argument will apply. We owe all to the God and Father of our Lord Jesus Christ: the world, the flesh, the devil, none of these have been of any service to us; they are aliens, foreigners, enemies, and it is not for us to bow down before them." (Spurgeon)

d. **Open your mouth wide, and I will fill it**: God made a promise to His faithful people. If they would in faith anticipate God's provision, God would provide. The reverse is also implied: God would not **fill** the closed mouth, the one with no anticipation of faith.

   i. "When the mother-bird brings food she never has to ask the little ones to open their mouths wide; her only difficulty is to fill the great width which they are quite sure to present to her: appetite and eagerness are never lacking, they are utterly insatiable…picture a nest of little birds reaching up their mouths, and all opening them as wide as they can." (Spurgeon)

   ii. This shows us that whatever we do open to God, He will fill. We can't open our mouths bigger than He can fill.

   - We open our mouths wide when we have a sense of need – when we are hungry.

   - We open our mouths wide when we ask for large things.

   - We open our mouths wide when we understand the greatness of the God we pray to.

- We open our mouths wide when we pray on Jesus' merits, not our own.

iii. "You may easily over-expect the creature, but you cannot over-expect God, 'Open thy mouth wide, and I will fill it;' widen and dilate the desires and expectations of your souls, and God is able to fill every chink to the vastest capacity. This honours God, when we greaten our expectation upon him; it is a sanctifying of God in our hearts." (Case, cited in Spurgeon)

iv. "That great saying teaches, too, that God's bestowals are practically measured by men's capacity and desire. The ultimate limit of them is His own limitless grace; but the working limit in each individual is the individual's receptivity, of which his expectancy and desire are determining factors." (Maclaren)

v. "Our cup is small, and we blame the fountain." (Spurgeon)

e. **But My people would not heed My voice**: This was the great tragedy. God was ready to fill the faith-filled open mouths of His people, but they would not obey Him. God said in sorrow, "**Israel would have none of Me.**" Rebellious Israel rejected God who had done so much for them *and* would have done much more.

f. **So I gave them over to their own stubborn heart**: This was God's judgment against His unbelieving people – to give **them over to their own stubborn heart**, to **walk in their own counsels**. One of the greatest judgments God can bring is to simply leave us alone to our own stubbornness and foolishness.

i. John Trapp thought it was as if God had "left them as a ship without a rudder; as a horse without reins, to go whither they would, and do what they would." (Trapp)

ii. "It reveals a constant method of God with His disloyal and disobedient children. When they will not go His way, He lets them go their way.... He permits them to learn by the bitter results of their own folly what He would have had them know by communion with Himself." (Morgan)

iii. "When we see men enabled, by wealth and power, to accomplish the inordinate desires of their hearts, and carry their worldly schemes into execution, without meeting any obstructions in their way, we are apt to envy their felicity; whereas such prosperity in wickedness is the surest mark of divine displeasure, the heaviest punishment of disobedience, both in individuals and communities." (Horne)

3. (13-16) God's sorrow over stubborn Israel.

"Oh, that My people would listen to Me,
That Israel would walk in My ways!
I would soon subdue their enemies,
And turn My hand against their adversaries.
The haters of the Lord would pretend submission to Him,
But their fate would endure forever.
He would have fed them also with the finest of wheat;
And with honey from the rock I would have satisfied you."

a. **Oh, that My people would listen to Me**: The tragedy is ironic. God could say of Israel, **My people**. They belonged to Him and He had claimed them. Yet they would not **listen** to Him; they would not **walk in** His ways. There is a sense of longing in these words: God's desire to bless His people and do good for them.

i. "The affectionate tone of these verses is also worth noting in the context of judgment: it is something of an Old Testament counterpart to the lament for Jerusalem (Matthew 23:37)." (Kidner)

b. **I would soon subdue their enemies**: This was an unclaimed blessing God wanted to give to a believing, obeying people. If God's people would only listen and obey, God would **subdue their enemies** and fight for them **against their adversaries**.

i. "Our enemies find the sharpest weapons against us in the armoury of our transgressions. They could never overthrow us if we did not first overthrow ourselves. Sin strips a man of his armour, and leaves him naked to his enemies." (Spurgeon)

c. **I would have satisfied you**: This psalm ends on a sad note, filled with the tragedy of missed opportunity and unfulfilled potential. God would have richly provided for them and **satisfied them** – *if* His people would have only listened and obeyed.

Psalm 82 – Earthly Judges Before the Great Judge

*This psalm is titled **A Psalm of Asaph**. The author **Asaph** was probably the great singer and musician of David and Solomon's era (1 Chronicles 15:17-19, 16:5-7, 25:6). 1 Chronicles 25:1 and 2 Chronicles 29:30 add that Asaph was a prophet in his musical compositions.*

"It takes us in a few words behind and beyond our present wrongs, to portray God's unbounded jurisdiction, his delegation of power, his diagnosis of our condition and his drastic intentions." (Derek Kidner)

A. God summons the judges.

1. (1-2) God questions the unjust judges.

God stands in the congregation of the mighty;
He judges among the gods.
How long will you judge unjustly,
And show partiality to the wicked? Selah

> a. **God stands in the congregation of the mighty**: Asaph gives us the picture of God in the midst of **the mighty**, standing in authority.

> > i. "**Standeth,** as a judge, diligently to observe all that is said or done there; and to give sentence accordingly. The judge sits when he heareth causes, but standeth up when he giveth sentence." (Poole)

> b. **He judges among the gods**: God's standing in the midst of these **mighty** ones is to bring judgment **among** them. The word **gods** here is *Elohim*, the plural for the generic word for *god* in Hebrew. The idea of God judging **gods** has led to several suggestions regarding the identity of these *elohim*, these **gods**.

> > • *Elohim* is often used to describe the true God, Yahweh. It is in the plural to describe both the majesty of His person, and to be a hint of the triune nature of God, being One God in Three Persons.

14

- *Elohim* is sometimes used as the plural of pagan deities, the false gods of the nations.
- *Elohim* is sometimes used in reference to angelic beings.
- *Elohim* is here best taken as a reference to human judges, who stand in the place of God in their ability to determine the fate of others.

    i. "Gathered around Him is an assembly of judges who are called elohim, because they are His delegates; they administer His will; they are His executive agents." (Morgan)

    ii. "The judges and magistrates are compared in this psalm to God, because they exercise something of His power in the right ordering of human society." (Meyer)

    iii. Martin Luther "pointed out that Psalm 82:1, 6 both establishes and limits the authority of princes. It establishes it, because it is God who appoints the authorities; it is he who calls them 'gods.' It limits their authority because they are accountable to him, as the psalm shows." (Boice)

    iv. "Earthly judicatories are the appointment of God. All magistrates act in his name, and by virtue of his commission. He is invisibly present at their assemblies, and superintends their proceedings. He receives appeals from their wrongful decisions; he will one day re-hear all causes at his own tribunal, and reverse every iniquitous sentence, before the great congregation of men and angels." (Horne)

    v. "Our Lord's reference to Psalm 82:6 in John 10:34-38 is, by the present writer, accepted as authoritatively settling both the meaning and the ground of the remarkable name of 'gods' for human judges." (Maclaren)

c. **How long will you judge unjustly?** As God calls together this assembly of judges, He did not do it to compliment them or pay them honor. He did it to confront them for judging **unjustly** and for showing **partiality to the wicked**. This confrontation shows that God Himself is the Judge at the ultimate Supreme Court.

    i. "The judges in mind have erred in that they have shown respect for the persons of the wicked, and thus departed from that strict justice which ever characterises the dealings of God to Whom they are all responsible." (Morgan)

    ii. "Will ye represent and express God to the world as a corrupt, crooked, and unrighteous judge?" (Trapp)

iii. "Our village squires and country magistrates would do well to remember this. Some of them had need go to school to Asaph till they have mastered this psalm. Their harsh decisions and strange judgments are made in the presence of him who will surely visit them for every unseemly act, for he has no respect unto the person of any, and is the champion of the poor and needy." (Spurgeon)

d. **Selah**: The idea of God calling the judges of the earth into special judgment is worthy of sober reflection.

i. **Selah**: "This gives the offenders pause for consideration and confession." (Spurgeon)

2. (3-4) God commands the unjust judges.

Defend the poor and fatherless;
Do justice to the afflicted and needy.
Deliver the poor and needy;
Free *them* from the hand of the wicked.

a. **Defend the poor and fatherless**: God's instruction to the judges of this earth is to do their duty in *defending* those who are often treated unjustly. In Asaph's day the **poor and the fatherless** were often the targets of unfair treatment. It was the job of the judges to **defend** them and to **do justice to the afflicted and needy**.

i. "You [judges] are their natural *protectors* under God. They are *oppressed: punish* their *oppressors*, however rich or powerful: and *deliver them*." (Clarke)

ii. "These...three verses, indeed the whole psalm, every prince should have painted on the wall of his chamber, on his bed, over his table, and on his garments. For here they find what lofty, princely, noble virtues their estate can practice, so that temporal government, next to the preaching office, is the highest service to God and the most useful office on earth." (Luther, cited in Boice)

b. **Free them from the hand of the wicked**: One characteristic of the **wicked** is that they prey upon **the poor and needy**. It was the divinely directed duty of judges to **free** the vulnerable from those who oppressed them.

i. "Law has too often been an instrument for vengeance in the hand of unscrupulous men, an instrument as deadly as poison or the dagger. It is for the judge to prevent such villainy." (Spurgeon)

ii. King Jehoshaphat of Judah gave similar wise instruction to judges in 2 Chronicles 19:6-7: *And said to the judges, "Take heed to what you are doing, for you do not judge for man but for the* LORD, *who is with you in the judgment. Now therefore, let the fear of the* LORD *be upon you; take care and do it, for there is no iniquity with the* LORD *our God, no partiality, nor taking of bribes."*

iii. "It is said of Francis the First, of France, that when a woman kneeled to him to beg justice, he bade her stand up; for, said he, Woman, it is justice that I owe thee, and justice thou shalt have; if thou beg anything of me, let it be mercy." (Price, cited in Spurgeon)

3. (5) God exposes the weakness of the unjust judges.

They do not know, nor do they understand;
They walk about in darkness;
All the foundations of the earth are unstable.

a. **They do not know, nor do they understand**: This should best be understood as a reference to the unjust judges themselves. Despite their high standing and higher opinion of themselves, they are often ignorant and easily overestimate their own understanding.

i. "They **know not,** to wit, the truth and right of the cause, nor the duty of their place. Men are oft said in Scripture *not to know* what they do not love and practise." (Poole)

ii. Adam Clarke had a much better opinion of the judges of his own time (1822), but he understood the application to the judges in Asaph's day: "They are ignorant and do not wish to be instructed. They will not learn; they cannot teach. Happy England! How different from Judea…in the days of Jehoshaphat! All thy judges are learned, righteous, and impartial. Never did greater men in their profession dignify any land or country." (Clarke)

b. **All the foundations of the earth are unstable**: When judges walk in the **darkness** of their arrogant pride, the lives of everyday people are uncertain and unstable, as if the ground that should be firm under their feet is shaking.

i. Boice mentioned three perils that are the destined doom for governments that forget God:
- Ignorance (**they do not know**).
- Inept action (**they walk about in darkness**).
- A society shaken (**all the foundations of the earth are unstable**).

ii. "There is nothing the world needs today more than the administration of strict and impartial justice." (Morgan)

iii. "When peasants may be horsewhipped by farmers with impunity, and a pretty bird is thought more precious than poor men, the foundations of the earth are indeed sinking like rotten piles unable to bear up the structures built upon them." (Spurgeon)

iv. "A community, whether ecclesiastical or civil, consisteth of great numbers; but its well-being dependeth on a few, in whose hands the administration is placed." (Horne)

B. God sentences the judges.

1. (6-7) God pronounces judgment on the unjust judges.

I said, "You *are* gods,
And all of you *are* children of the Most High.
But you shall die like men,
And fall like one of the princes."

a. **You are gods**: These human judges stood in the place of the gods above other people. They had the opportunity and the authority to change people's lives with a word, or sometimes even to end a life.

i. In John 10:34-39 Jesus quoted verse 6 in a debate with religious leaders when they accused Him of claiming to be God in a sinful, wrong way. Jesus reasoned, "If God gave these unjust judges the title 'gods' because of their office, why do you consider it blasphemy that I call Myself the 'Son of God' in light of the testimony of Me and My works?"

ii. Exodus 21:6 and 22:8-9 are other passages where God called earthly judges **gods**. In verse 6, **gods** translates the Hebrew word *elohim*. In Exodus 21:6 and 22:8-9 the same word *elohim* is translated "judges."

iii. "There must be some government among men, and as angels are not sent to dispense it, God allows men to rule over men, and endorses their office." (Spurgeon)

iv. "In his *Lex Rex,* Rutherford argues from this psalm that judges are not the creatures of kings, to execute their pleasure, and do not derive their power from the monarch, but are authorized by God himself as much as the king, and are therefore bound to execute justice whether the monarch desires it or no." (Spurgeon)

b. **And all of you are children of the Most High**: In still speaking to Israel's earthly judges, God reminded them that they – **and all** of humanity – **are children of the Most High**. This is true in the sense that every human being is made in the image of God and can be thought of as the *offspring* of God (Acts 17:28-29).

i. When these unjust judges denied protection and justice to the poor, fatherless, afflicted, and needy, the judges treated them as less than fully humans made in the image of God who should be regarded as God's creation, His offspring. The judges needed to remember this.

ii. There is another sense in which it *cannot* be said that all people are **children** of God. Some are children of God and others are children of their father the devil (John 8:44).

c. **You shall die like men**: The unjust judges of Israel needed to remember that others were greater than the judges thought, and they themselves were *less* than they thought. They were like **gods** only in a symbolic sense; they themselves would **die like men** and face judgment before the Judge of all the earth.

i. "**Like men;** or, *like ordinary men*, as the Hebrew word *adam* sometimes signifies, as it does in Psalm 49:12." (Poole)

ii. **You shall die like men**: "Ye shall wax old like others, then ye shall fall sick like others, then ye shall die like others, then ye shall be buried like others, then ye shall be consumed like others, then ye shall be judged like others, even like the beggars which cry at your gates." (Smith, cited in Spurgeon)

iii. **Fall like one of the princes**: "Our Henry VIII was told on his death bed that he should go to the place of princes; which was no great comfort, if the old proverb be true, that hell is paved with the crowns of princes and helmets of soldiers." (Trapp)

2. (8) A prayer for God to exercise His perfect judgment.

Arise, O God, judge the earth;
For You shall inherit all nations.

a. **Arise, O God, judge the earth**: Asaph closed the psalm with a plea to God to take *His* place as the ultimate Judge. The unjust judges of Israel had their own area of authority, but God's authority is over all **the earth**.

i. This prayer called upon God to do what the earthly judges would not do: properly **judge the earth**. Human judges had failed, so Asaph asked God to take judgment into His own hands.

b. **You shall inherit all nations**: This inheritance shows the greatness of God as judge. Earthly judges have their own greatness, but it is nothing compared to the Great Judge. This inheritance ultimately belongs to Jesus Messiah.

i. **For You shall inherit all nations**: "Does not this last verse contain a prophecy of our Lord, the calling of the Gentiles, and the prevalence of

Christianity over the earth? Thus several of the *fathers* have understood the passage. It is only by the universal spread of Christianity over the world, that the reign of righteousness and justice is to be established: and of whom can it be said that *he shall inherit all nations*, but of *Jesus Christ?*" (Clarke)

ii. "The last days shall see him enthroned, and all unrighteous potentates broken like potter's vessels by his potent sceptre. The second advent is still earth's brightest hope. Come quickly, even so, come, Lord Jesus." (Spurgeon)

iii. "It is great encouragement in missionary work to know that every nation is by right of gift and inheritance our Lord's. He sold His all to purchase it…. It is ours to make it His in fact." (Meyer)

Psalm 83 – A Prayer for Help When War Threatens

This psalm is titled **A Psalm of Asaph**. *The author* **Asaph** *was probably the great singer and musician of David and Solomon's era (1 Chronicles 15:17-19, 16:5-7, 25:6). 1 Chronicles 25:1 and 2 Chronicles 29:30 add that Asaph was a prophet in his musical compositions.*

Some commentators connect this psalm with 2 Chronicles 20:1-37 and the victory won in Jehoshaphat's time. Others see the collection of 10 enemies set against Israel as not referring to one specific occasion, but to the constant danger of extermination Israel lived under – relevant in both the ancient and modern world.

A. The appeal for help.

1. (1-4) Asking God to take action against those set on destroying Israel.

Do not keep silent, O God!
Do not hold Your peace,
And do not be still, O God!
For behold, Your enemies make a tumult;
And those who hate You have lifted up their head.
They have taken crafty counsel against Your people,
And consulted together against Your sheltered ones.
They have said, "Come, and let us cut them off from *being* **a nation,**
That the name of Israel may be remembered no more."

a. **Do not keep silent, O God**: Asaph sang this prayer in a time of national crisis. Enemies had come against Israel who were set on their national destruction. If God were to **keep silent** or hold His **peace** or **be still** on behalf of Israel, they would be destroyed.

i. **Do not keep silent**: "It is so difficult sometimes to go on living day by day without one authoritative word; and we are prone to rebuke Him for silence, that He is still, that He holds His peace.... But God has not kept silence. The Word was manifested. In Him the silence of eternity was broken." (Meyer)

21

b. **Your enemies make a tumult**: Asaph asked God to **behold** this crisis and to regard the enemies of Israel as His own **enemies**, as those who hated Him. Asaph was confident that if God did this, He would act on behalf of Israel.

i. "They are not only enemies to us thy people, but also to thy will, and name, and glory." (Poole)

c. **Come, and let us cut them off from being a nation**: This was the **crafty counsel** of the nations united against Israel. This desire of a confederation of nations to destroy Israel did not end in the days of Asaph. His prayer could be sung today as neighboring nations and the whole world community threaten Israel.

i. Adam Clarke paraphrased the words of verse 4: "Let us exterminate the whole race, that there may not be a record of them on the face of the earth." (Clarke)

ii. "In all the annals of recorded history there has never been a people so encircled by foes or as persecuted as the Jews have been. Yet surprisingly, the Jews have prospered. In 1836 a world census indicated that there were then three million Jews living in many countries. A century later, in 1936, in spite of severe persecutions in which many Jews were killed, particularly in Russia, a second census indicated that the Jewish world population had risen to sixteen million, an increase of thirteen million in a century. The Nazis killed more than six million Jews, but today there are more Jews in the world than before the Nazi era. The only explanation for this growth is that the hand of God has been on this people and that he has blessed them." (Boice)

iii. Israel has had its battles, ancient and modern. Christianity has also been opposed, and some have sought to completely **cut** Christians **off**.

One example was the Roman Emperor Diocletian (A.D. 284-305). Diocletian boasted that he had destroyed Christianity. He liked to think that he had defeated Christianity. He ordered a medal to be made with this inscription: "The name of Christianity being extinguished." Diocletian also set up at least two monuments on the frontier of the empire with these inscriptions:

Diocletian Jovian Maximian Herculeus Caesares Augusti for having extended the Roman Empire in the east and the west and for having extinguished the name of Christians who brought the Republic to ruin

Diocletian Jovian Maximian Herculeus Caesares Augusti for having everywhere abolished the superstition of Christ for having extended the worship of the gods

iv. Diocletian is dead and gone, comparatively a footnote on the pages of history. The fame and glory of Jesus Christ is spread over all the earth. God still takes care of His **sheltered ones**.

v. **Sheltered ones**: "The ten heathen nations conspired against Israel, but they could not really harm the chosen people, for God himself had hidden them as a hen hides her chickens under her wings when the kite hovers overhead, or as one who has found a treasure hides it away from the hands of the thief." (Spurgeon)

2. (5-8) The confederation of nations against Israel.

For they have consulted together with one consent;
They form a confederacy against You:
The tents of Edom and the Ishmaelites;
Moab and the Hagrites;
Gebal, Ammon, and Amalek;
Philistia with the inhabitants of Tyre;
Assyria also has joined with them;
They have helped the children of Lot. Selah

a. **They form a confederacy against You**: Asaph again emphasized that these enemies were not only against Israel, but against Yahweh, Israel's God.

i. **They form a confederacy**: Enemies often come together to attack God and His people. *That very day Pilate and Herod became friends with each other, for previously they had been at enmity with each other* (Luke 23:12).

ii. **Against You**: "The true antagonists are, not Israel and the world, but God and the world." (Maclaren)

iii. "What a motley group they were; a league against Israel is always attractive, and gathers whole nations within its bonds." (Spurgeon)

iv. "Let them come from east and west, south and north, and close round Israel; God alone is mightier than they." (Maclaren)

b. **The tents of Edom and the Ishmaelites**: The psalmist listed ten nations or peoples that were part of this **confederacy against** Israel and her God. It seems **the children of Lot** (specifically, **Moab** and **Ammon**) led this attack and the other eight nations **helped** them.

i. "The Hagarites (v. 6) were a tribe against whom the Transjordanian tribes of Reuben, Gad, and Manasseh fought at the time of the Jewish conquest of Palestine." (Boice)

ii. "*Gebal* is probably not the northern city of that name (better known as Byblos, and associated with Tyre: Joshua 13:5; 1 Kings 5:18) but a locality south of the Dead Sea." (Kidner)

iii. "The psalmist mentions ten different nations which had banded themselves together against God's chosen people Israel. Ten against one is long odds but then God was on the side of Israel." (Spurgeon)

iv. **Selah:** "There was good reason for a pause when the nation was in such jeopardy and yet it needs faith to make a pause, for unbelief is always in a hurry." (Spurgeon)

B. The cry for vengeance.

1. (9-12) Grant victory and deliverance as in the days of the Judges.

Deal with them as *with* Midian,
As *with* Sisera,
As *with* Jabin at the Brook Kishon,
Who perished at En Dor,
***Who* became *as* refuse on the earth.**
Make their nobles like Oreb and like Zeeb,
Yes, all their princes like Zebah and Zalmunna,
Who said, "Let us take for ourselves
The pastures of God for a possession."

a. **Deal with them as with Midian**: God's victory over **Midian** through Gideon is described in Judges 6, 7, and 8.

i. "Faith delights to light upon precedents, and quote them before the Lord; in the present instance, Asaph found a very appropriate one, for the nations in both cases were very much the same, and the plight of the Israelites very similar." (Spurgeon)

b. **As with Sisera**: God's victory over the Canaanite king **Jabin** and his general **Sisera**, through Deborah and Barak, is described in Judges 4.

i. **Who perished at En Dor**: "This refers to the defeat of the *Midianites* by *Gideon*, who were encamped in the valley of *Jezreel*, at the foot of Mount *Gilboa*, and near to *Tabor*, Judges 6:33; 7:1, and consequently in the environs of *En-dor*. There *Gideon* attacked and defeated them; and, in various places during their flight, they were destroyed." (Clarke)

ii. **Who became as refuse on the earth**: John Trapp noted that this means "they lay unburied, rotted above ground." This added to the defeat and disgrace of Israel's enemies.

c. **Make their nobles like Oreb**: **Oreb, Zeeb, Zebah** and **Zalmunna** were all princes of the Midianites, defeated by Gideon in Judges 7.

i. **Make their nobles**: "Smite the great ones as well as the common ruck. Suffer not the ringleaders to escape. As Oreb fell at the rock and Zeeb at the winepress, so do thou mete out vengeance to Zion's foes wherever thou mayest overtake them." (Spurgeon)

ii. "Oreb signifieth a crow, Zeeb a wolf, Zebah a cut-throat, Zalmunna a forbidder of shadow, or quiet, to his subjects; fit names for tyrants and persecutors of God's people." (Trapp)

d. **Let us take for ourselves the pastures of God for a possession**: Israel faced threats to her existence in the days of the Judges, and God delivered her. Asaph's prayer reminded Israel of God's previous rescue of Israel, using it as a reason to trust Him in the present crisis.

i. The phrase, **the pastures of God** reminds us again of what high regard God has for the land of Israel. He regards it as *His* **pastures**. "So the enemy's thoughts are re-phrased in the prayer, to bring out the truth about the territories they had coveted: these were *the pastures of God*, not simply the holdings of Israel." (Kidner)

ii. "The Midianites had despoiled the land of the crops and had caused great fear among the Israelites. This spoiling of Israel's crops is probably referred to in the bold claim 'Let us take possession of the pasturelands of God'." (VanGemeren)

2. (13-15) Bring them to destruction.

O my God, make them like the whirling dust,
Like the chaff before the wind!
As the fire burns the woods,
And as the flame sets the mountains on fire,
So pursue them with Your tempest,
And frighten them with Your storm.

a. **Like the chaff before the wind**: Asaph prayed that God would take these many enemies, determined to destroy Israel, and scatter them like **chaff before the wind** and the **whirling dust**. He prayed they would be consumed **like fire burns the woods**.

i. **Like the whirling dust**: "The word rendered 'whirling dust' in Psalm 83:13 is somewhat doubtful. It literally means a rolling thing, but what particular thing of the sort is difficult to determine." (Maclaren)

ii. "'Tumbleweed' (*galgal* lit., 'wheel') is a plant of the wild artichoke family (*Gundelia Tournefortii*), a plant with wheel-shaped stems and thistles." (VanGemeren)

b. **Pursue them with Your tempest**: To the ancient Hebrew, there was nothing more powerful than the **tempest** or the **storm**. The psalmist prayed that God would not only defeat Israel's enemies, but also **pursue** and **frighten them** with His great power.

3. (16-18) Bring these enemies to the knowledge of the true God.

Fill their faces with shame,
That they may seek Your name, O LORD.
Let them be confounded and dismayed forever;
Yes, let them be put to shame and perish,
That they may know that You, whose name alone *is* the LORD,
***Are* the Most High over all the earth.**

a. **Fill their faces with shame, that they may seek Your name**: Asaph ended this psalm with an unexpected turn. After praying for the destruction of Israel's enemies, he prayed that they would be thoroughly humbled (**fill their faces with shame**) so they would be led to **seek** Yahweh.

i. Asaph understood what we often forget: people will often only seek the LORD if they are first laid low before His power. There is a sense in which God must defeat us before He will save us.

ii. "But there is a deeper desire in the psalmist's heart than the enemies' destruction. He wishes that they should be turned into God's friends and he wishes for their chastisement as the means to that end." (Maclaren)

iii. "Shame has often weaned men from their idols, and set them upon seeking the Lord." (Spurgeon)

iv. "The punishments inflicted by heaven upon wicked men are primarily intended to humble and convert them." (Horne)

b. **That they may know that You...are the Most High**: This great humbling (**let them be put to shame and perish**) would lead to their surrender and submission to the God who is **Most High over all the earth.**

i. This psalm began with a plea that God would not remain silent, and ends with the idea of His fame and glory going out to all the earth. "When the silences of God are broken by His noises, men learn that the God of Grace is the Most High over all the earth." (Morgan)

Psalm 84 – The Pilgrim's Love and Longing for God and His House

The title of this psalm is **To the Chief Musician. On an instrument of Gath. A Psalm of the sons of Korah.** *These* **sons of Korah** *were Levites, from the family of Kohath. By David's time it seems they served in the musical aspect of the temple worship (2 Chronicles 20:19).*

Korah led a rebellion of 250 community leaders against Moses during the wilderness days of the Exodus (Numbers 16). God judged Korah and his leaders and they all died, but the sons of Korah remained (Numbers 26:9-11). Perhaps they were so grateful for this mercy that they became notable in Israel for praising God.

Charles Spurgeon said Psalm 84 was entitled "to be called The Pearl of Psalms. If the twenty-third be the most popular, the one-hundred-and-third the most joyful, the one-hundred-and-nineteenth the most deeply experiential, the fifty-first the most plaintive, this is one of the most sweet of the Psalms of Peace."

A. Longing for the House of God.

1. (1-2) Longing for God and His house.

How lovely *is* Your tabernacle,
O Lord of hosts!
My soul longs, yes, even faints
For the courts of the Lord;
My heart and my flesh cry out for the living God.

a. **How lovely is Your tabernacle**: One or more of the *sons of Korah* composed this psalm in the days of the **tabernacle**. It is also possible that the author referred to the temple in a historic, quaint way. The affection is clear; he *loved* the house of God, whether it was in a tent or a permanent building. He considered it beautiful, **lovely**.

i. "*How lovely* is more exactly 'How dear' or 'How beloved'; it is the language of love poetry." (Kidner)

27

ii. "He does not tell us how lovely they were, because he could not. His expressions show us that his feelings were inexpressible." (Spurgeon)

b. **My soul longs**: The psalmist's appreciation for God's house wasn't simply because it was beautiful. His **soul** longed for God's house, and **even faints** when denied the privilege of meeting with God among His people.

i. This was deep feeling. Not every love is so great as to make a longing. Not every longing is so great as to make a fainting.

ii. "I have rather – though the expression may seem harsh to some – called this the 'appetite for God' than 'the love of God'.... [The appetite for God] has all the cheerful spontaneity of a natural, even a physical, desire." (Lewis, cited in VanGemeren)

c. **My heart and my flesh cry out for the living God**: The house of God was dear and desired by the psalmist because it was where he met God. Everything within him – **heart** and **flesh** – longed for God and His house.

i. **Cry out**: "The word in question indicates a loud cry, not necessarily a joyful one (cf. Psalm 17:1; Lamentations 2:19)." (Kidner)

ii. "Crieth aloud, as a child when hungry crieth every whit of him, hands feet, face, all cry; and then the mother flings by all, then she flies and outruns herself; so here." (Trapp)

iii. This speaks to those who are leaders in God's house today. More than offering programs, social connections, entertainment, excitement, or self-improvement, they must make places and meetings in which people meet **the living God**.

iv. This speaks to all who come to the house of God today. They must come without primary focus upon programs, social connections, entertainment, excitement, or self-improvement; they must come with the primary focus and expectation of meeting with **the living God**.

v. The emphasis on meeting **the living God** prevents regarding the tabernacle or temple in the wrong way. The temple as a place could be viewed incorrectly (as in Acts 7:48, 7:54). The psalmist considers it here in its best sense: the place to meet with **the living God**.

vi. "There was no superstition in this love. He loved the house of God because he loved the God of the house. His heart and flesh cried out, not for the altar and the candlestick, but for his God." (Spurgeon)

vii. **The living God**: "That Name is more than a contrast with the gods of the heathen. It lays bare the reason for the psalmist's longings." (Maclaren)

2. (3-4) Satisfaction in the house of God.

Even the sparrow has found a home,
And the swallow a nest for herself,
Where she may lay her young—
Even **Your altars, O LORD of hosts,**
My King and my God.
Blessed *are* **those who dwell in Your house;**
They will still be praising You. Selah

a. **Even the sparrow has found a home**: Perhaps the psalmist saw birds – the **sparrow** and the **swallow** – that had made a **nest**, living at the house of God, in view of the altar itself. He considered those birds blessed, living at the tabernacle.

i. "The writer of this Psalm had peculiar familiarity with the Temple. He had watched it with loving eyes, and seen the birds finding rest and refuge there." (Morgan)

ii. Boice offered that the sparrow is an example of a bird of small significance and the swallow is a picture of restlessness. Likewise, the insignificant can find his place in the house of God, and the restless man can find his rest (**nest**) there – near God's altar.

iii. "It is evidently the design of this passage to intimate to us, that in the house, and at the altar of God, a faithful soul findeth freedom from care and sorrow, quiet of mind, and gladness of spirit; like a bird that had secured a little mansion for the reception and education of her young." (Horne)

iv. "You and I, dear friends, will be wise if we do as this sparrow did; for she found a house for herself because she looked for it, she found it because it was there all ready for her, and she found it by appropriating it so that it became her very own. Thus may we appropriate the Lord Jesus Christ, by an act of faith, and so make him our very own!" (Spurgeon)

v. **My King and my God**: "The double 'my' is very precious; he lays hold upon his God with both his hands, as one resolved not to let him go till the favour requested be at length accorded." (Spurgeon)

b. **Blessed are those who dwell in Your house**: The psalmist went from envying the birds living at the tabernacle to envying the priests who had rooms at the **house** of God. He felt they could live a life of constant praise (**they will still be praising You**).

i. **Still be praising**: "It is not enough to praise him, it must be a praising *him still,* before it will make a blessedness; and though to praise God

be an easy matter, yet *to praise him still,* will be found a busy work."
(Baker, cited in Spurgeon)

B. Finding strength for the pilgrim's journey.

1. (5-7) Strength for the one away from the house of God.

Blessed *is* the man whose strength *is* in You,
Whose heart *is* set on pilgrimage.
***As they* pass through the Valley of Baca,**
They make it a spring;
The rain also covers it with pools.
They go from strength to strength;
Each one appears before God in Zion.

a. **Blessed is the man whose strength is in You**: The man who finds his **strength** in God is also the one **whose heart is set on pilgrimage**. He does not rely on self or the world for strength, but considers himself a visitor, a traveler, a pilgrim in this world. His true strength and treasure are in the world to come.

i. This strength and heart of a pilgrim are displayed by the love for the house of God. There he meets with God, along with other pilgrims, and they gain strength in God together as they meet.

ii. The love and longing for the house of God are not meant as an escape from the world, but as a preparation for life *in* the world.

iii. **Strength is in You**: "If he cannot be at Zion, he can be with God; if he cannot enjoy sweetness he can find strength." (Kidner)

b. **As they pass through the Valley of Baca**: The heart for God's house provided wisdom and strength for the life lived away from God's house. A difficult place (such as **the Valley of Baca**) was transformed into **a spring**, complete with **rain** and **pools** of water.

i. The sense or meaning of **the Valley of Baca** is uncertain. Commentators usually suggest that **Baca** speaks of tears and weeping, or of drought and dryness. Thoughts of difficulty and trouble are present in either.

ii. **Baca** is a "noun derived from a verb which signifies to 'weep'." (Horne) Horne went on to explain, "This present world is to us this valley of weeping; in our passage through it we are refreshed by the streams of divine grace, flowing down from the great fountain of consolation."

iii. Kidner gives the other sense: "*Baca*…is thought to indicate a tree or shrub which grows in arid places; hence New English Bible, 'the thirsty valley'."

iv. "*The valley of tears*, as this valley might be called, for the trouble or vexation which travellers found there by reason of drought, or otherwise." (Poole)

c. **They go from strength to strength**: With the blessedness expressed by plenty of water in an otherwise dry place, the pilgrim lives in **strength** and goes to more **strength**. The rich relationship with God is a never-ending supply of strength for the journey, even in difficult seasons.

i. On a normal journey (especially a difficult one), the usual pattern is to go from strength to weakness or fatigue. Not so with those whose strength is in God – **they go from strength to strength**.

ii. "The farther they travel onward in that way, instead of being faint and weary, as travellers in such cases [should] be, they grow stronger and stronger." (Poole)

iii. "They proceed from one degree of grace to another, gaining Divine virtue through all the steps of their probation." (Clarke)

d. **Each one appears before God in Zion**: The journey has a destination – **Zion**, the city of God. The love and longing for the house of God will bring **each one** to his destination, appearing **before God in Zion**.

i. "Not merely to be in the assembly, but to appear before God was the object of each devout Israelite. Would to God it were the sincere desire of all who in these days mingle in our religious gatherings. Unless we realise the presence of God we have done nothing; the mere gathering together is nothing worth." (Spurgeon)

2. (8) The pilgrim's prayer.

O Lord God of hosts, hear my prayer;
Give ear, O God of Jacob! Selah

a. **God of hosts, hear my prayer**: This song from the sons of Korah was more than a declaration; it was also a **prayer**. It was a plea for the plenty spoken of by the supply of water. It was a supplication for the strength that continues and builds.

b. **Give ear, O God of Jacob**: The psalmist **grounded** his plea in the long history of God's dealing with His covenant people. That same God who blessed and was faithful to **Jacob** will also be faithful to His people today. This is worthy of meditation – thus the insertion of the psalm's second **Selah**.

C. The surpassing greatness of God and His house.

1. (9) Asking for God's attention.

O God, behold our shield,
And look upon the face of Your anointed.

> a. **O God, behold our shield**: We take **shield** here as a reference to a literal **shield**, which was the main means of defense for Israel. The psalmist asked God to **behold** what Israel wisely did to defend itself.

> b. **Look upon the face of Your anointed**: We take **Your anointed** as a reference to the King of Israel, who was specially anointed for his office. Though the psalmist had first in mind David (or possibly Solomon), it also points toward the *Messiah*, the ultimate **anointed** One.

2. (10-12) The greatness of God and His house.

For a day in Your courts *is* better than a thousand.
I would rather be a doorkeeper in the house of my God
Than dwell in the tents of wickedness.
For the LORD God *is* a sun and shield;
The LORD will give grace and glory;
No good *thing* will He withhold
From those who walk uprightly.
O LORD of hosts,
Blessed *is* the man who trusts in You!

> a. **A day in Your courts is better than a thousand**: The psalmist began with love and longing for the house of God, and now he returns to the thought. Time spent at God's house was better and more valuable than time spent elsewhere.

> > i. "A declaration comparable to Paul's 'all things but loss' (Phil. 3:8, KJV), or to Asaph's 'Whom have I in heaven but thee?' (Ps. 73:25)." (Kidner)

> b. **I would rather be a doorkeeper in the house of my God**: This was another expression of the psalmist's love and longing regarding **the house** of **God**. Living a luxurious life in the fancy **tents of wickedness** meant nothing to him; he would rather humbly serve in God's house.

> > i. "We sometimes read this as though there were something heroic about the choice, some touch of sacrifice in the decision. There is nothing of the kind. The singer was a man of profoundest commonsense." (Morgan)

ii. "To bear burdens and open doors for the Lord is more honour than to reign among the wicked. Every man has his choice, and this is ours. God's worst is better than the devil's best." (Spurgeon)

iii. **Doorkeeper**: "As the Korahites were, to whom this psalm was committed; and for whose encouragement this might be spoken. A doorkeeper is first in, last out." (Trapp)

iv. "There may be a reference to the Korahites' function of door keepers, in that touchingly beautiful choice of the psalmist's, rather to lie on the threshold of the Temple than to dwell in the tents of wickedness." (Maclaren)

v. "Who *now* prefers the worship of God to genteel, gay, honourable, and noble company, to mirthful feasts, public entertainments, the stage, the oratorio, or the ball! Reader, wouldst thou rather be in thy *closet*, wrestling in prayer, or reading the Scriptures on thy knees, than be at any of the above places?" (Clarke)

c. **For the LORD God is a sun and shield**: The psalmist explains the goodness and blessing that come to those pilgrims who love and long for the house of God. They enjoy God as the source of blessing (**sun**) and defense (**shield**). They receive His generous **grace and glory**.

i. "This is the only place in the Bible where God is explicitly called 'a sun.' It is because he shines on us and is the brightness of our days." (Boice)

ii. "A sun for happy days and a shield for dangerous ones. A sun above, a shield around. A light to show the way and a shield to ward off its perils." (Spurgeon)

iii. "How God suits Himself to our need! In darkness, He is a Sun; in the sultry noon, a Shield; in our earthly pilgrimage He gives grace; when the morning of heaven breaks, He will give glory. He suits Himself to every varying circumstance in life. He becomes what the exigency of the moment requires." (Meyer)

d. **The LORD will give grace and glory**: The connection between God's grace and His glory was later on the mind of the Apostle Paul: *We have peace with God through our Lord Jesus Christ, through whom also we have access by faith into this grace in which we stand, and rejoice in hope of the glory of God* (Romans 5:1-2).

i. To say, **will give grace** puts it in the future tense. It means that there is more grace for God to give and more grace for us to receive. It also means that grace is something that God will **give**, and not sell.

ii. Grace is God's first gift, and glory is His last gift. "Glory never comes without grace coming first, but grace never comes without glory coming last; the two are bound together, and 'what God hath joined together, let not man put asunder.'" (Spurgeon)

e. **No good thing will He withhold**: A promise is made to **those who walk uprightly** – they will receive every good thing God has for them. The nature of this promise is appropriate under the Old Covenant, where God promised direct blessings for obedience and curses for disobedience. Under the New Covenant, the believer receives God's good things on the basis of Jesus' goodness, and *then* goes on to **walk uprightly**.

i. "What does the text say? It does not say, 'I will force all my children to enjoy every good thing.' No, but, 'No good thing will he withhold.' There are thousands of mercies that we do not enjoy, not because they are withheld, but because we do not take them." (Spurgeon)

ii. "Because God is what He is, and gives what He gives, it is the highest wisdom to take Him for our true good, and never to let Him go." (Maclaren)

f. **Blessed is the man who trusts in You**: God's greatness and goodness lead the psalmist to experience and declare the blessedness of trusting in God.

i. "The essence of godliness is in submissiveness to the Great King, who will grant his blessings to those who find their refuge in him." (VanGemeren)

Psalm 85 – Praying for Revival and Restoration

This psalm is titled **To the Chief Musician. A Psalm of the sons of Korah.** *These* **sons of Korah** *were Levites, from the family of Kohath. By David's time it seems they served in the musical aspect of the temple worship (2 Chronicles 20:19).*

Like several psalms, Psalm 85 (in some ways) seems to fit the period of Israel's return from exile; in other ways it does not. Alexander Maclaren noted, "The book of Nehemiah supplies precisely such a background as fits the psalm. A part of the nation had returned indeed, but to a ruined city, a fallen Temple, and a mourning land, where they were surrounded by jealous and powerful enemies." Even if this psalm belongs to an earlier period (such as the end of Saul's reign), God's people find themselves in this place from time to time, and this beautiful Psalm is appropriate.

A. Gratitude for favor and restoration.

1. (1-2) Brought back from captivity and sin.

Lord, You have been favorable to Your land;
You have brought back the captivity of Jacob.
You have forgiven the iniquity of Your people;
You have covered all their sin. Selah

> a. **You have been favorable to Your land**: The psalmist finds relief in God's care for His land. Notably, the territory of Israel is called **Your land**. The Bible understands that all the earth belongs to the Lord (Psalm 24:1), and yet there is an undeniable way in which Israel is His special possession, with God having a special regard for His **land**.

> b. **You have brought back the captivity of Jacob**: Many think this phrase means this psalm was written after the Babylonian captivity. This is possible, and some psalms clearly date to this period (such as Psalm 79). Yet the idea of Israel being in some kind of **captivity** also suits some other periods, such as the period of Philistine domination in the later years of Saul's reign (1 Samuel 28-31).

i. "Israel is not pining for past glories, which are often an optical illusion…but remembering past mercies. This is realistic; it is also stimulating: it leads to prayers rather than dreams." (Kidner)

c. **You have forgiven the iniquity of Your people**: The psalmist was not only interested in the land, but more importantly in *relationship* with God. The **iniquity** that once hindered relationship was now taken away. The idea was so important and precious to the psalmist that he repeated it in different words according to the style of Hebrew poetry.

i. **Forgiven, covered**: "He uses two significant words for pardon, both of which occur in Psalm 32:1-11. In Psalm 85:2a, sin is regarded as a weight pressing down the nation, which God's mercy lifts off and takes away; in Psalm 85:2b, it is conceived of as a hideous stain or foulness, which His mercy hides, so that it is no longer an offence to heaven." (Maclaren)

ii. **Forgiven their iniquity**: "*Thou hast borne*, or *carried away, the iniquity*. An allusion to the ceremony of the *scapegoat*." (Clarke)

iii. **All their sin**: "All of it, every spot, and wrinkle, the veil of love has covered all. Sin has been divinely put out of sight." (Spurgeon)

2. (3) Rescued from God's righteous anger.

You have taken away all Your wrath;
You have turned from the fierceness of Your anger.

a. **You have taken away all Your wrath**: The psalmist found peace in the satisfaction of God's **wrath**. Once they were the righteous subjects of God's judgment, and now they were delivered from it. There is special beauty in the words **all Your wrath**, speaking of a complete work.

i. As with the previous verse (*covered all their sin*), this looks forward to the complete work of Jesus on the cross, where He satisfied God's righteous requirement to the full with a *once-for-all* sacrifice (Hebrews 7:27, 9:12, 10:10).

ii. "Some of the strongest salvation language in Scripture is present in these verses. 'Covered their sins' describes what is meant by *atonement*. 'Set aside your wrath' is what is meant by the word *propitiation*." (Boice)

b. **You have turned from the fierceness of Your anger**: There is great relief in knowing God's **anger** has passed. This is especially true when considering the **fierceness** of His anger.

B. Prayer for continued favor and restoration.

1. (4-5) A prayer for restoration.

Restore us, O God of our salvation,
And cause Your anger toward us to cease.
Will You be angry with us forever?
Will You prolong Your anger to all generations?

a. **Restore us, O God of our salvation**: The psalmist began by thanking God for return and restoration. In light of that past goodness, the psalmist now prays for continued and present restoration.

b. **Will You be angry with us forever?** Verse 3 thanked God for the turning of His fierce anger. That work in the past was the basis of this prayer, "Lord do it again."

2. (6-7) A prayer for revival.

Will You not revive us again,
That Your people may rejoice in You?
Show us Your mercy, LORD,
And grant us Your salvation.

a. **Will You not revive us again**: This is a simple and wonderful prayer for revival. It recognizes that revival is not man-made, but given by God. Yet it also recognizes that one may and should *pray* for revival, and pray with godly expectation.

i. This prayer for revival "…implies that the people were alive once, have died in a spiritual sense, and now need to be given spiritual life again. This is what the church almost always needs, and it is how revivals come." (Boice)

ii. The context tells us *when* to pray for revival.

- We should pray for revival when we remember the great things God has done in the past (as in verses 1-3).

- We should pray for revival when we sense we are under a cloud of divine displeasure or an evident lack of blessing (as in verses 4-5).

iii. The context tells us *who* to pray for.

- In praying for revival, pray for the pastor. Ask God to personally revive him, to strengthen him against temptation and discouragement, and to fill him with faith. Ask God to bless the pastor's work with great spiritual power. James McGrady is an example of a man who made the most of getting his congregation to pray for him. He was the man so ugly that he attracted attention. McGrady came over the Allegheny Mountains to minister on the frontier of Kentucky. He had three little box-like

Presbyterian churches. McGrady described the work during the winter of 1799 as "…for the most part weeping and mourning with the people of God." He promoted a once-a-month *concert* of prayer with other churches, but he asked his people to pray for him when the sun set on Saturday for half an hour and when the sun rose on Sunday for half and hour. McGrady was no specimen as a preacher – he had a bad voice and people noticed his awkward gestures in preaching. But in 1800 there came a flood of blessing, with meetings as large as 25,000 people.

- In praying for revival, pray for the congregation. Pray for a great outpouring of the Holy Spirit upon the *congregation*, not only on the preacher.

- In praying for revival, pray for other churches in your community.

- In praying for revival, pray for the community in general, that Jesus would answer the promise of John 16:7-8, sending the Holy Spirit to convict the world of sin.

b. **That Your people may rejoice in You**: Praying for revival means praying that God's work among His people would cause them to find their joy in nothing else than in Him. So we pray:

- Full of confidence, knowing that God can revive.
- Full of boldness, pleading with God for revival.
- Full of humility, desiring God's glory and praise.

    i. "The words before us teach us that gratitude has an eye to the giver, even beyond the gift – 'thy people may rejoice in *thee*.' Those who were revived would rejoice not only in the new life but in the Lord who was the author of it." (Spurgeon)

c. **Show us Your mercy**: Revival is a work of God's **mercy**. It isn't earned or deserved. God graciously grants true revival.

d. **Grant us Your salvation**: True revival demonstrates that **salvation** is God's work. Jonah saw a great work of revival in Nineveh, flowing from his embrace of the great principle: *Salvation is of the LORD* (Jonah 2:9).

C. Confidence in God's response.

1. (8-9) Hearing God's word of peace.

I will hear what God the LORD will speak,
For He will speak peace
To His people and to His saints;

But let them not turn back to folly.
Surely His salvation *is* near to those who fear Him,
That glory may dwell in our land.

a. **I will hear what God the LORD will speak**: In the last section of this psalm, the psalmist expressed surrender and submission to God. The proper attitude of the believer praying for revival is to surrender to the authority of God's word.

i. "'I will be silent. I have spoken to him; now I will hear what his answer is. I will hold my ear attentive to listen to his voice.' O my dear hearers, when you are willing to hear God, there are good times coming to you!" (Spurgeon)

b. **For He will speak peace**: The psalmist was confident in the goodness of God, and that God would **speak peace** to His humble, surrendered **people and to His saints**.

i. "The gospel is accordingly styled by St. Peter 'the word which God sent unto the children of Israel, preaching peace by Jesus Christ.' Acts 10:36." (Horne)

ii. "He that will not hear the gospel of peace, shall never know the peace of the gospel. If you will not hear the Holy Spirit when he warns you of your sin, neither shall you hear him revealing peace through pardon." (Spurgeon)

c. **But let them not turn back to folly**: Humility and surrender are proper attitudes for God's people. They should turn to Him in true repentance, and **not turn back to folly**.

d. **His salvation is near to those who fear Him**: The humble and surrendered people of God enjoy the nearness of **His salvation**. As God moves among His people this way, **glory may dwell in our land**.

2. (10-13) The good righteousness of God.

Mercy and truth have met together;
Righteousness and peace have kissed.
Truth shall spring out of the earth,
And righteousness shall look down from heaven.
Yes, the LORD will give *what is* good;
And our land will yield its increase.
Righteousness will go before Him,
And shall make His footsteps *our* pathway.

a. **Mercy and truth have met together**: In beautiful terms the psalmist describes the salvation God brings to His people. It might seem that **mercy** and **truth** are set against each other, with **mercy** looking to grant pardon and truth determined to condemn. In God's great work of salvation, **mercy and truth have met together**.

> i. **Mercy and truth have met together**: The word here translated **mercy** is the great Hebrew word *hesed*, which often has the idea of *grace* or *loyal love*. This verse may have been the inspiration for what John later wrote: *And the Word became flesh and dwelt among us, and we beheld His glory, the glory as of the only begotten of the Father, full of grace and truth* (John 1:14). *For the law was given through Moses, but grace and truth came through Jesus Christ* (John 1:17).

b. **Righteousness and peace have kissed**: Even as mercy and truth meet, so **righteousness and peace** greet each other warmly. It might seem that **righteousness** would condemn me and prevent God's *shalom* (**peace**) from ever reaching me. In God's great work of salvation, His **righteousness and peace** are the best of friends.

> i. "These four divine attributes parted at the fall of Adam, and met again at the birth of Christ.... Mercy was ever inclined to save man, and Peace could not be his enemy; but Truth exacted the performance of God's threat, 'The soul that sinneth, it shall die'; and Righteousness could not but give to every one his due." (Horne)

> ii. "Now, *Where* did these meet? In Christ Jesus. *When* were they reconciled? When he poured out his life on Calvary." (Clarke)

> iii. Paul later expressed this idea in Romans 3:26: *That He might be just and the justifier of the one who has faith in Jesus.* At the cross, God demonstrated His righteousness by offering man *justification* (a legal verdict of "not guilty"), while remaining completely *just* (because the righteous penalty of sin had been paid at the cross). God could be only just, and simply send every guilty sinner to hell, as a just judge would do. Only God could find a way to be both *just and the justifier of the one who has faith in Jesus.*

c. **Truth shall spring out of the earth, and righteousness shall look down from heaven**: God pours out His **truth** and **righteousness**. They seem to spring forth from creation itself. Prophetically, we may say this refers not only to the reconciliation started at the cross, but also has in view its completion at the end of the age, when *creation itself also will be delivered from the bondage of corruption into the glorious liberty of the children of God* (Romans 8:21).

> i. "The devil is the great disrupter. He has brought disharmony to the universe. God brings harmony. In these verses four great attributes of

God meet together…and then, like conquering generals, they march side by side to a victory that is the sure and certain hope of God's people." (Boice)

d. **Righteousness will go before Him**: Righteousness so marks God that it goes before Him, as the tail of a comet goes behind the comet. God's **righteousness** is so rich that it also makes **His footsteps our pathway** – the pathway of His people.

i. "The psalmist began with a reflection of God's past acts of salvation and leaves a canonical hope in the progression of redemption, as God's 'righteousness' advances his kingdom." (VanGemeren)

ii. **His footsteps our pathway**: "God's march…will leave a track wherein his people will joyfully follow." (Spurgeon)

Psalm 86 – Help from the Great God

The title of this psalm is simply **A Prayer of David**. *We can't place it at a specific time in David's life, because there are too many possible points where this could connect with his general circumstances. This psalm is notable because David uses the Hebrew word Adonai ("Master") seven times when referring to God.*

"There are four other psalms each called by the name Tephillah, or 'prayer,' but this deserves to be distinguished from the rest and known as 'the prayer of David,' even as the ninetieth Psalm is known as 'the prayer of Moses.' It savours of David. The man of sincerity, of ardor, of trials, of faults, and of great heart, pleads, sobs, and trusts through all the verses of this psalm." (Charles Spurgeon)

A. A plea for help with reasons given.

1. (1) Help me because of my great need.

Bow down Your ear, O LORD, hear me;
For I *am* poor and needy.

a. **Bow down Your ear**: David used expressive language to speak of his need. The idea – figurative, of course – is that God in heaven bows His head to earth to hear David's plea for help – David's cry, "**Hear me.**"

i. "When our prayers are lowly by reason of our humility, or feeble by reason of our sickness, or without wing by reason of our despondency, the Lord will bow down to them, the infinitely exalted Jehovah will have respect unto them." (Spurgeon)

ii. After the request, David then gave God some reasons *why* his prayer should be answered. David thought carefully in his prayer, and presented both requests and reasons to God. "The psalm is unique in its method of urging a petition upon the ground of some known fact." (Morgan)

b. **For I am poor and needy**: This was the first of several reasons *why* God should answer the request of the first line. David here appealed to God's sympathy, to His compassion. A hard-hearted God wouldn't care for a **poor and needy** man, or worse yet might despise him. Yet David knew that God was full of love and compassion and would be moved by the fact that David was, and knew himself to be, **poor and needy**.

> i. It is significant that David *began* his plea with this. His understanding of the love and compassion of God was foundational.

> ii. David was not afraid to be humble, as we ae sometimes. "To confess that we are poor and needy seems demeaning. To be a servant seems unworthy. We want to be people who deserve something from God because of who we are." (Boice)

2. (2) Help me because I am connected to You.

Preserve my life, for I *am* holy;
You are my God;
Save Your servant who trusts in You!

> a. **Preserve my life**: David's problem was desperate; he felt that without God's help he could perish. Considering the many people set against him (as seen in verse 14), he had reason to be this concerned.

> > i. Beyond this, we aren't told the nature of David's need. We know it was severe, and he felt it to be life-threatening. Yet we don't know if it was danger from Saul, or the Philistines, or from assassins, or from a dozen other things. *This is good*, because it allows us to see our need in David's need. It allows us to know that we can approach God on the same basis for whatever our need is.

> b. **For I am holy**: This wasn't a claim to absolute holiness. David knew he was a sinner; that he had and would sin. Yet he also knew that as a man among other men – and especially next to those who were against him – he was a **holy** man.

> c. **You are my God; save Your servant who trusts in You**: David based this plea on three similar ideas, all rooted in the fact that he was connected to God.

> > • **I am holy**: "I am connected to You morally God; I embrace Your holiness in my own life."

> > • **You are my God**: "I am connected to You with worship and honor."

> > • **Save Your servant who trusts in You**: "I am connected to You in trust and faith."

> > > i. In all this we see how *intelligent* and *well-thought-out* David's prayer was. When he came to the throne of God, he came with careful thought.

3. (3-4) Help me because I cry unto You.

Be merciful to me, O Lord,
For I cry to You all day long.
Rejoice the soul of Your servant,
For to You, O Lord, I lift up my soul.

a. **Be merciful to me...For I cry to You all day long**: David asked for mercy because he was completely dependent upon God. He cried to God **all day long** because he could not or would not rely on anyone else for help.

i. "Lest any should, by the former words (I am holy), suspect him to be a merit-monger, he beggeth mercy, with instancy and constancy of request." (Trapp)

ii. To take this same figure, many of us would **cry to** God for a period of time and then figure out another way to address our need. Not David; he relied on God and God alone.

iii. **O Lord**: This is the first of seven uses of *Adonai* in this psalm. Many translators use smaller letters to indicate the translation of *Adonai* (Lord), as opposed to all capital letters of some kind to translate *Yahweh* (LORD or Lord). "The name of God which dominates is Adonahy, or Lord, which indicates absolute Lordship, and by the use of which the singer shows his sense of submission and loyalty." (Morgan)

b. **Rejoice the soul of Your servant, for to You...I lift up my soul**: The *reason* is much the same as in the previous verse; an expression of reliance and trust in God (**to You...I lift up my soul**). But the *request* is beautifully stated: **Rejoice the soul of Your servant**. David felt that he could only find joy in his soul as God met his need.

4. (5) Help me because You are a gracious God.

For You, Lord, *are* good, and ready to forgive,
And abundant in mercy to all those who call upon You.

a. **For You, Lord, are good, and ready to forgive**: David based this plea on the graciousness of God, knowing that He is **good** and **ready to forgive**. Far too many people who should know better doubt both the goodness of God and His readiness to forgive.

i. "Whereas most men, though they will forgive, yet they are not *ready* to forgive, they are hardly brought to it, though they do it at last. But God is *'ready to forgive.'*" (Caryl, cited in Spurgeon)

ii. "We are blinded by sin, and cannot believe that God is ready to forgive. We think that we must induce Him to forgive, by tears, promises of amendment, religious observances.... Oh, clasp this word to your heart! Say it over and over again – 'Ready to forgive, ready to forgive!'" (Meyer)

iii. Many wait to repent and ask forgiveness because they think that *time* might make God *more* forgiving. That isn't possible. He is ready to forgive *now*.

iv. "You have fallen a hundred times, and are ashamed to come to God again; it seems too much to expect that He will receive you again. But He will, for He is ready to forgive." (Meyer)

b. **Abundant in mercy to all those who call upon You**: As David called upon God for help, he expected **abundant mercy** from God. This expectation spoken in faith would be answered.

5. (6-7) The confidence of an answer to this plea for help.

Give ear, O LORD, to my prayer;
And attend to the voice of my supplications.
In the day of my trouble I will call upon You,

For You will answer me.

a. **Give ear...attend to the voice of my supplications**: Again, David simply asked for God to *hear* him. He was confident that if the loving, merciful God heard his plea, He would answer favorably.

i. David here repeated the idea from verse 1, but the repetition had a purpose. "He repeats and multiplies his requests, both to ease his own troubled mind, and to prevail with God, who is well-pleased with his people's importunity [persistence] in prayer." (Poole)

b. **In the day of my trouble I will call upon You, for You will answer me**: This demonstrates David's wonderful confidence in God. He knew that God was not a fair-weather friend; instead, God could be counted on even in the **day of trouble**.

i. Adam Clarke put the emphasis on **my** and **me** in verses 6-7. "Attend to *me*. Millions call upon thee for help and mercy; but who has more need than myself?"

ii. **You will answer me**: "Our experience confirms us in the belief that Jehovah the living God really does aid those who call upon him, and therefore we pray and mean to pray, not because we are so fascinated by prayer that for its own sake we would continue in it if it proved to be mere folly and superstition, as vain philosophers assert; but because we really, indeed, and of a truth, find it to be a practical and effectual means of obtaining help from God in the hour of need." (Spurgeon)

B. Depending on the great God who helps His people.

1. (8-10) The greatness of God.

Among the gods *there is* none like You, O Lord;
Nor *are there any works* like Your works.
All nations whom You have made
Shall come and worship before You, O Lord,
And shall glorify Your name.
For You *are* great, and do wondrous things;
You alone *are* God.

a. **Among the gods there is none like You**: David's understanding of who God is in this psalm – listening, holy, worthy of trust, merciful, good, ready to forgive – stands in contrast to the contemporary understanding of many of the pagan gods, such as Baal, Ashtoreth, or Dagon. Many of these gods were understood to be bitter, vengeful, cunning, and sexually depraved. David knew that the LORD God was different.

i. "I am not now calling upon a deaf and impotent idol, for then I might cry my heart out, and all in vain, as they did, 1 Kings 18:26-29; but upon the Almighty and most gracious God." (Poole)

b. **Nor are there any works like Your works**: David knew that when *God* did something, it was glorious. It had the imprint of His glorious character upon it, and could not be compared to the works of man.

i. "*Works* probably mean here the things God has made, rather than the deeds He has done (which come later, 10a)." (Kidner)

c. **All nations whom You have made shall come and worship before You**: David recognized that God was creator and master over **all nations**, not merely Israel. In a day when most gods were considered to be only national or regional deities, David knew that his God – the living God, the true God – was different.

d. **For You are great, and do wondrous things; You alone are God**: David understood that the LORD was not one God among many gods, or even the best God among many gods. He **alone** is **God**, and none other.

i. "*Wondrous things*, variously translated in the Psalms, is a frequent term for God's miracles of salvation." (Kidner)

ii. It is **do**, not *did* (though *did* would be true also). "Note that the verb *doest* is in the present, the Lord is doing wondrous things, they are transpiring before our eyes." (Spurgeon)

2. (11-12) Whole-life dependence on the great God.

Teach me Your way, O LORD;
I will walk in Your truth;
Unite my heart to fear Your name.
I will praise You, O Lord my God, with all my heart,
And I will glorify Your name forevermore.

a. **Teach me Your way, O LORD**: Because David knew who God is – not perfectly, of course, but with great understanding – his natural reaction was to submit himself to this great, gracious God and to ask Him to **teach** him.

i. Again, this shows that David understood that this amazing God *cared for him*. This same majestic God, whom all nations will worship and glorify, will hear the plea from one *poor and needy* man (verse 1) who asks, "**Teach me Your way, O LORD.**"

ii. This verse also shows a subtle shift in the psalm. In the first section (verses 1-7) David desperately cried out for help. In doing so, he thought deeply about who God is and what He does. Those thoughts did not make David retract his plea for help, but it did make him say, "I need to learn from this great God. **Teach me Your way, O LORD.**"

iii. We could even say that David's great need showed him his need to be taught. It brought him to say, "Don't give me *my way*, Lord; teach me *Your way*."

iv. "Most of us, when we pray, are concerned about deliverance and help and guidance and such things. But we are not nearly as concerned to be taught God's way and to be helped to serve him with an undivided heart." (Boice)

b. **I will walk in Your truth**: This determination gave integrity to David's request. He wanted to be taught so that he could live – so that he could **walk** in God's **truth**. This wasn't merely to satisfy intellectual curiosity or to win arguments; it was to live.

i. "*Walking*, in the Scripture, takes in the whole of our conversation or conduct: and to walk *in* anything, intends a fulness of it. For a man to *walk in* pride, is something more than to be proud: it says, that pride is his way, his element; that he is wholly under the influence of it." (Jay, cited in Spurgeon)

c. **Unite my heart to fear Your name**: David knew he could only walk in God's truth with a *united heart*. A divided heart – divided among different loyalties and different deities – could never walk in God's truth.

i. "Our minds are apt to be divided between a variety of objects, like trickling streamlets which waste their force in a hundred runnels;

our great desire should be to have all our life-floods poured into one channel and to have that channel directed towards the Lord alone." (Spurgeon)

ii. **Unite my heart**: "*Join* all the purposes, resolutions, and affections of my heart *together*, to fear and to glorify thy name. This is a most important prayer. A *divided* heart is a great curse; *scattered* affections are a miserable plague. When the *heart* is not at *unity* with itself, the work of religion cannot go on. *Indecision* of *mind* and *division* of *affections* mar any work. The *heart* must be *one*, that the *work* may be *one*. If this be wanting, all is wrong. This is a prayer which becomes the mouth of every Christian." (Clarke)

iii. We could say that the united heart is the goal; the way to the goal is "**teach me Your way, O LORD**" and "**I will walk in Your truth**." David therefore indicated that this couldn't happen in his own self-effort. Instead, he asked God to **unite** his **heart** as he was taught and as he walked in the truth. Since Yahweh is God alone (verse 10), David wanted his heart to be towards God alone.

iv. At the same time, the idea of a unified heart is one of the Old Testament promises of the New Covenant, as in Ezekiel 11:19: *Then I will give them one heart*. As part of this New Covenant, we have reason to pray confidently for God to work a unified heart in us.

d. **Way...truth...unite**: He is our way, our truth, and our life (John 14:6). He is our *way*; we say, "**Teach me Your way**." He is our *truth*; we say, "**I will walk in Your truth**." He is our *life*; we say, "**Unite my heart to fear Your name**."

e. **I will praise You, O Lord my God, with all my heart**: This is what David wanted to do with his united heart – he wanted to **praise** God with it. As noted earlier in the psalm, David knew God was worthy of such praise; but he knew he could only praise God as he should with God uniting his heart.

i. David wanted to do this *with* his united heart; but perhaps he also understood that **praise** is one way to **unite** the **heart**. When we consciously focus the attention of our mind, emotions, and affections upon who God is and what He has done for us, our heart is marvelously united.

ii. "Here is a God-given beginning (and practical means) to the answer of his prayer: his *whole heart* absorbed in praise." (Kidner)

iii. "Though nothing can add to God's essential glory, yet praise exalts him in the eyes of others. When we praise God, we spread his fame and renown, we display the trophies of his excellency." (Watson, cited in Spurgeon)

iv. **O Lord my God**: "This is the second time in the Psalm that David calls the Lord 'my God,' the first time he was in an agony of prayer (verse 2), and now he is in an ecstacy of praise." (Spurgeon)

- He is our God in times of trouble – we rely upon Him.
- He is our God in times of rejoicing – we praise Him.

3. (13-15) Depending on the graciousness of God.

For great *is* Your mercy toward me,
And You have delivered my soul from the depths of Sheol.
O God, the proud have risen against me,
And a mob of violent *men* have sought my life,
And have not set You before them.
But You, O Lord, *are* a God full of compassion, and gracious,
Longsuffering and abundant in mercy and truth.

a. **For great is Your mercy toward me, and You have delivered my soul from the depths of Sheol**: David thought about God's *past* deliverance in his life. The merciful God who rescued him before would rescue him again.

i. **Great is Your mercy**: "Mercy" here is *hesed*, the great word for covenant love, love that is promised in a covenant relationship.

ii. "As for the rescue *from the depths of Sheol*, it is possible to take this as either past or future." (Kidner)

b. **The proud have risen against me, and a mob of violent men have sought my life**: David lived such a long life of danger and adventure that we can't precisely place this event in his life. It could have come at several points. Obviously, the danger was clear and real.

c. **And have not set You before them**: For David it was clear. **Proud** men, **violent** mobs, are not surrendered to God. If these **proud** and **violent** men had set God before them, they would have shared some of His **compassion**, graciousness, **longsuffering**, **mercy**, **and truth**.

d. **You, O Lord, are a God full of compassion**: David knew that the evil of man did not negate the goodness of God. God is **full of compassion, and gracious, longsuffering and abundant in mercy and truth**, despite the pride and violence of men.

i. **But You**: "What a contrast! We get away from the hectorings and blusterings of proud but puny men to the glory and goodness of the Lord." (Spurgeon)

ii. Compare the words of this psalm with the phrasing of Exodus 34:6-7, the great revelation of God to Moses: *The LORD, the LORD God, merciful and gracious, longsuffering, and abounding in goodness and truth, keeping mercy for thousands, forgiving iniquity and transgression and sin.*

iii. It seems that twice in this psalm David quoted the words and ideas from Moses' encounter with God recorded in Exodus 34:6-7. We see this in verse 5: *For You, Lord, are good, and ready to forgive, and abundant in mercy.* Also, it is seen here in verse 15: **But You, O Lord, are a God full of compassion, and gracious, longsuffering and abundant in mercy and truth**.

iv. "David seems to have stood in the cleft of the rock with Moses, and to have heard the name of the Lord proclaimed even as the great lawgiver did, for in two places in this Psalm he almost quotes *verbatim* the passage in Exodus 34:6." (Spurgeon)

v. We could say that David read his Bible, and learned who God is. Then he took that knowledge to prayer, and asked God to answer his prayer because of who He revealed Himself to be in the Scriptures.

4. (16-17) A hopeful plea for help.

Oh, turn to me, and have mercy on me!
Give Your strength to Your servant,
And save the son of Your maidservant.
Show me a sign for good,
That those who hate me may see *it* **and be ashamed,**
Because You, LORD, have helped me and comforted me.

a. **Turn to me, and have mercy on me**: Through it all, David never approached God on the basis of what he *deserved*. Anything he received from God, he would receive on the basis of **mercy**.

b. **Give Your strength to Your servant**: This answer to this plea of David is confirmed by the later exhortation of Paul: *Be strong in the Lord and in the power of His might* (Ephesians 6:10). God does **give** His **strength** to His **servant**!

c. **Save the son of Your maidservant**: We aren't told much in 1 or 2 Samuel about David's mother, but this brief mention suggests that she was a godly woman who served God and who could be called "**Your maidservant**."

i. In a few places (such as Genesis 14:14 and Jeremiah 2:14) the Bible gives the idea of a *home-born* slave – someone who is a slave because his mother was a slave, and he was born into servitude. That may be

David's idea here; to express how completely he belongs to God, he pleads as **the son of Your maidservant.**

d. **Show me a sign for good**: David seems to say, "Lord, I do not expect the whole answer right now. Yet, **show me a sign for good** – give me some indication of Your help and power – so **that those who hate me may see it and be ashamed.**"

i. Here David is wonderful for his *humility* – not demanding all the answer from God right now. He is also wonderful for his *humanity* – asking for **a sign for good** at the moment.

ii. In some cases, it is wrong to ask God, "**Show me a sign for good.**" It is wrong when our attitude is, "God, prove to me that You love me" or "I will believe if You **show me a sign**, but if You do not, then I will not believe You." Yet there are some proper times when we can cry out to God, "**Show me a sign for good.**"

- Answers to prayer are a **sign for good** (verse 1, *Bow down Your ear, O LORD, hear me*).

- Preservation of character is a **sign for good** (verse 2, *for I am holy*).

- Deliverance from trouble is a **sign for good** (verse 2, *Save Your servant who trusts in You!*).

- Joy in a surrendered life is a **sign for good** (verse 4, *Rejoice the soul of Your servant, for to You, O Lord, I lift up my soul*).

- A sense of forgiveness is a **sign for good** (verse 5, *You, Lord, are good, and ready to forgive*).

- Confidence in God is a **sign for good** (verse 7, *For You will answer me*).

- Knowing and declaring the greatness of God is a **sign for good** (verse 10, *For You are great, and do wondrous things*).

- With proud and violent men as enemies, it is a **sign for good** (verse 14, *the proud have risen against me, and a mob of violent men have sought my life*).

iii. Some – such as Adam Clarke – take this expression differently. "'*Make* with me a sign.' Fix the honourable mark of thy name upon me, that I may be known to be thy servant. There seems to be an allusion here to the *marking of a slave*, to ascertain whose property he was." Perhaps we could say, "Put Your mark of goodness on me, so that all can see that I am Yours and You will deliver me."

e. **Because You, L**ORD**, have helped me and comforted me**: Once again David bases his current expectation on God's prior help. Every past experience of God's goodness to us is a promise of His continued blessing.

Psalm 87 – Citizens of Zion

This psalm is simply titled **A Psalm of the sons of Korah. A Song**. *These* **sons of Korah** *were Levites, from the family of Kohath. By David's time it seems they served in the musical aspect of the temple worship (2 Chronicles 20:19).*

Charles Spurgeon observed, "This 'Psalm or song' was either composed by the sons of Korah, or dedicated to them: as they kept the doors of the house of the Lord, they could use this beautiful composition as a Psalm within the doors, and as a song outside."

A. The greatness of Jerusalem.

1. (1-2) Zion beloved by God.

His foundation *is* in the holy mountains.
The LORD loves the gates of Zion
More than all the dwellings of Jacob.

> a. **His foundation is in the holy mountains**: Yahweh is not a local deity; the whole earth belongs to the LORD (Exodus 9:29, Psalm 24:1). Yet He has a special regard for Jerusalem, which is described as **in the holy mountains**.

>> i. "The city owes all its stability and sanctity to him: the first word of the psalm is literally 'His establishment' – an abrupt and emphatic opening – and its hills are (lit.) 'hills of holiness' because he is there; it is not the other way round. He is there simply because he *loves* the place." (Kidner)

>> ii. "The psalmist's fervent love for Jerusalem is something more than national pride. It is the apotheosis [elevation] of that emotion, clarified and hallowed into religion. Zion is founded by God Himself. The mountains on which it stands are made holy by the Divine dwelling." (Maclaren)

> b. **His foundation**: God's **foundation** is in Jerusalem, the center of His redemptive work. Since God's work happens in time and space, it had to

happen somewhere, and God chose Jerusalem as the place where much of it happened.

- There Melchezidek, king and priest of God Most High, reigned and served.
- There Abraham was willing to offer Isaac on the mount of the Lord where His perfect sacrifice would be provided.
- There David, Israel's greatest earthly king, reigned and made it the kingdom's capital.
- There the tabernacle of God found its fulfillment and permanence in the great temple David designed and Solomon built.
- There the institutions of sacrifice, worship, and priestly service were established for centuries.
- There Jesus recognized and honored the city and observed the feasts and temple rituals.
- There Jesus died for our sins, was buried, and rose from the dead.
- There the church was born in a day at Pentecost.
- There the apostles served and sent out the Gospel.
- There God will establsih the physical, geographic center of His ultimate kingdom upon earth.

c. **The LORD loves the gates of Zion**: For all these reasons and more, God has special love for Jerusalem, regarding it even more than the rest of His Holy Land (Zechariah 2:12) and more than the territory of Israel in general (**more than all the dwellings of Jacob**).

i. "As the dwellings of Jacob in the promised land were beloved by him more than the dwellings of other nations, so he 'loved the gates of Sion more than the dwellings of Jacob.'" (Horne)

2. (3) Zion praised.

Glorious things are spoken of you,
O city of God! Selah

a. **Glorious things are spoken of you**: The psalmist praised Jerusalem by noting what others said about the city. Many spoke **glorious things** about the city.

- Glorious faith was exercised in Jerusalem.
- Glorious things happened in Jerusalem.
- Glorious things were taught in Jerusalem.
- Glorious worship was offered in Jerusalem.

- Glorious atonement was made in Jerusalem.

- Glorious anointing was poured out in Jerusalem.

- God's glorious presence was evident in Jerusalem.

- A glorious future awaits Jerusalem.

b. **O city of God**: God's special regard for Jerusalem does not take away from the fact that He is Lord and God over all the earth. Still, there is a special way in which Zion can be called the **city of God**, because out of all the places He could have chosen, God chose *that place* to center His redemptive work for the whole world.

i. According to Boice, this line from verse 3 was the inspiration of the title and concept of Augustine's great work, *The City of God*.

B. The blessedness of the citizens of Zion.

1. (4) Boasting over the citizens of Zion.

"I will make mention of Rahab and Babylon to those who know Me; Behold, O Philistia and Tyre, with Ethiopia: 'This *one* was born there.'"

a. **I will make mention of Rahab and Babylon**: After a focus on Jerusalem itself, God spoke of the Gentile nations on every side of Israel, who were their rivals and often enemies. God promised that even among the rivals there would be **those who know Me** – those who have true relationship with Him.

i. "Rahab is Egypt, and so called for its strength and pride. Babel, the chief city of the Babylonians. These were deadly enemies to Jerusalem, which was ground between them as between a pair of millstones." (Trapp)

ii. "Tyre is the type of godless luxury and inflated material prosperity, and, though often in friendly alliance with Israel, as being exposed to the same foes which harassed her, she was as far from knowing God as the other nations were. Cush, or Ethiopia, seems mentioned as a type of distant peoples, rather than because of its hostility to Israel." (Maclaren)

iii. **Who know Me**: "A translation of the Hebrew verb *yadah*, which has a rich variety of meanings. It can mean 'know,' 'acknowledge,' 'understand,' 'be sure,' 'know about,' 'experience,' and other variations.... Here it means more than merely admitting that there is such a God as Jehovah or even acknowledging him as the one true God. It means coming to him in a saving relationship, bowing before him, and seeking to know him better." (Boice)

b. **This one was born there**: This is both a promise and an invitation to the Gentile world. *They* could be accounted by God as the privileged **one** who **was born there** in Zion. They could be regarded as citizens of Jerusalem and be registered among God's people.

i. This reminds us that even though God made His ancient covenant with Abraham, Isaac, Jacob, and their descendants, *relationship* with Him was not based on genetics. Anyone from the Gentile world was welcome to honor the God of Israel, surrender to His Lordship, and be reckoned among God's people. This was true of Melchizedek, true of Rahab, true of Ruth, and true of Naaman.

ii. It is also a prophetic picture of what God would do in and through the Gospel, bringing Gentiles into true and real relationship with Him through a new birth. In a spiritual sense, it can be said of the one who is born again, **this one was born there**.

iii. "Thus, in a very short space, the psalmist indicates that in the day of God's future blessing all the nations of the world (or at least representatives of all the nations of the world) will come to know and praise the true God." (Boice)

iv. The confident words **this one was born there** are even more wonderful because the citizen referred to here does not say it of himself; *God* says it of him or her.

v. This also speaks of God's love and attention for the *individual*. "Man by man will the Lord reckon them, for they are each one precious in his sight; the individual shall not be lost in the mass, but each one shall be of high account." (Spurgeon)

2. (5-6) God records the register of His people.

And of Zion it will be said,
"This *one* and that *one* were born in her;
And the Most High Himself shall establish her."
The LORD will record,
When He registers the peoples:
"This *one* was born there." Selah

a. **Of Zion it will be said, "This one and that one were born in her"**: The psalmist repeated the thought from the previous verse and expanded it. The identification with Zion, the City of God, would be so wonderful and precious that it would be cherished to say, "**This one was born there.**"

i. If a city is regarded as great or important, people enjoy identifying with that city. When we appreciate the high regard God has for **Zion**, the city of Jerusalem, we see the value in being regarded as her citizen, the city established by **the Most High Himself**.

ii. **Of Zion it will be said**: Kidner and others note that the Septuagint renders it something like this: *and Zion shall be called a mother*. Paul had this verse directly in mind in Galatians 4:26: *but the Jerusalem above is freem which is the mother of us all.*

b. **The Lord will record, when He registers the peoples**: This citizenship and birthright is declared and recorded by God. It is **He** who **registers the peoples**.

i. The Bible clearly speaks of God's special regard towards the land of Israel, and for Jerusalem specifically. Yet the idea of being a citizen of Zion and being registered as a born-citizen of His City is *also* a spiritual concept. The New Testament speaks of a *heavenly* Zion and our registration there: *But you have come to Mount Zion and to the city of the living God, the heavenly Jerusalem, to an innumerable company of angels, to the general assembly and church of the firstborn who are registered in heaven* (Hebrews 12:22-23). Paul also noted, *the Jerusalem above is free, which is the mother of us all* (Galatians 4:26).

ii. In Jesus Christ, every believer can have the privilege of registration in Zion, of being a citizen of the heavenly City of God. This does not eliminate the special regard God has had, presently has, and will have for the literal land of Israel and Jerusalem, but it surpasses it.

iii. "Foreign nations are here described not as captives or tributaries, not even as doing voluntary homage to the greatness and glory of Zion, but as actually incorporated and enrolled, by a new birth, among her sons." (Perowne, cited by Spurgeon)

iv. *We* can have the honor, the security, the confidence, the assurance that comes from it being said of us, **this one was born there**. "It will be an honour to any person to have been born in Zion. But how great is the honour to be *born from above*, and be a citizen of the Jerusalem that is from above! To be children of God, by faith in Christ Jesus!" (Clarke)

v. "Jehovah's census of his chosen will differ much from ours; he will count many whom we should have disowned, and he will leave out many whom we should have reckoned. His registration is infallible." (Spurgeon)

3. (7) The blessedness of Zion's citizens.

Both the singers and the players on instruments *say,*
"All my springs *are* **in you."**

a. **Both the singers and the players on instruments say**: This point was so important that both the **singers** and **instruments** of Israel emphasized it. It's possible that **instruments** here refers to *dancers*.

i. "The crowds in the earthly Jerusalem are celebrating with music, song, and possibly even dance. The verbal phrase 'make music' [**players of instruments**] is better translated as 'dancing'." (VanGemeren)

b. **All my springs are in you**: The **springs** refer to the spontaneously flowing sources of water and to the life, refreshment, and to the goodness they bring to a dry land. These **springs are in you**, and according to Kidner, grammatically "**you**" can refer to Zion as a place or to God Himself. It is better to see it as a reference to God: **All my springs are in You** [God].

i. The goodness of God often comes to us like water from a spring. It seems to bubble up from a hidden, secret source.

ii. "What all these references are saying is that 'every good and perfect gift is from above' – that is, from God. All we are or hope to be, all we have or ever hope to have, all we attain or ever hope to attain is from him. The people of God acknowledge this and praise God for it." (Boice)

iii. "If all my springs are in God, then *let all my streams flow to God*. All the rivers run into the sea, because they all came from the sea. It was from the sea that the sun drew up the clouds which fed the thousand rills which fall into the rivers, and so the rivers run back to the sea. Let us do the same. What we have had from God must go to God." (Spurgeon)

Psalm 88 – A Desperate Prayer from Deep Affliction

This psalm is titled **A Song. A Psalm of the sons of Korah. To the Chief Musician. Set to "Mahalath Leannoth." A Contemplation of Heman the Ezrahite.**

This psalm is **A Song**, *yet a remarkably sad song, and is often regarded as the saddest psalm in the entire collection.* **Mahalath Leannoth** *seems to refer to the musical instrument upon which the song was composed. Psalm 53 also mentions the* **Mahalath**.

Psalm 88 is one of the thirteen psalms called **A Contemplation**, *which according to James Montgomery Boice might be better understood as "instruction."*

As for the author and singer of the psalm, **Heman the Ezrahite**, *there are many mentions of a Heman in the days of David and Solomon. Assuming that they all refer to the same man, he was noted for:*

- His great wisdom (1 Kings 4:31).
- His being a Kohathite, among the sons of Korah (1 Chronicles 6:33).
- His musical ability and service (1 Chronicles 6:33, 15:17-19, 16:41-42, 25:1; 2 Chronicles 5:12, 35:15).
- His many and exceptional sons and daughters (1 Chronicles 25:5-6).
- His service to the king (1 Chronicles 25:6).

The identity of the singer of this dark song helps us to understand it. It came from a wise, talented, accomplished, and blessed man.

"A doleful ditty, beginning and ending with complaints; and therefore sung in the primitive times, among other penitential psalms, as the public confession of persons excommunicated." (John Trapp)

"In this Psalm, Heman makes a map of his life's history, he puts down all the dark places through which he has traveled. He mentions his sins, his sorrows, his hopes (if

he had any), his fears, his woes, and so on. Now, that is real prayer, laying your case before the Lord." (Charles Spurgeon)

A. Prayer from the one under great affliction.

1. (1-2) Asking God to hear prayer in affliction.

O LORD, God of my salvation,
I have cried out day and night before You.
Let my prayer come before You;
Incline Your ear to my cry.

> a. **O LORD, God of my salvation**: The opening line would lead us to expect a much more optimistic psalm. When the psalmist begins by extolling Yahweh as the **God of my salvation**, we expect that he experienced that rescue, that deliverance in the moment. This was not the case. This title was both in past remembrance and clinging to a future hope. It is one of the small glimmers of light in an otherwise dark psalm.

> > i. "The only ray of comfortable light which shines throughout the Psalm. The writer has salvation, he is sure of that, and God is the sole author of it. While a man can see God as his Saviour, it is not altogether midnight with him." (Spurgeon)

> > ii. "To address God as the God of his salvation, to discern His hand in the infliction of sorrows, is the operation of true though feeble faith. 'Though He slay me, yet will I trust in Him,' is the very spirit of this psalm." (Maclaren)

> > iii. "From beginning to end there is no trace of bitterness, no desire for revenge on enemies, no angry reflections on the goodness of God. Rather, the references to God reveal a remarkable sense of His grace and goodness." (Morgan)

> b. **Let my prayer come before You**: The prayer was passionate (**cried out**) and constant (**day and night**). The psalmist was desperate for God to bend towards Him to hear and answer his prayer.

> > i. **I have cried out**: "The prayer is a deeply piercing shout. Though *rinnāh* may denote a shout of joy in other contexts (cf. 47:1; 105:43), it is here a loud cry for divine help. The psalmist shouts loudly to the Lord, hoping that he will hear." (VanGemeren)

> > ii. No matter how deep and dark Heman's affliction was, he could still talk to God about it. "Despair sometimes strikes men dumb, and sometimes makes them eloquent." (Maclaren)

iii. "He did not cast out brutish and wild complaints and moans in misery, as it is natural for people to do, but poured forth his soul into God's blessed bosom, and now prayeth an answer." (Trapp)

2. (3-5) The depth of affliction.

For my soul is full of troubles,
And my life draws near to the grave.
I am counted with those who go down to the pit;
I am like a man *who has* no strength,
Adrift among the dead,
Like the slain who lie in the grave,
Whom You remember no more,
And who are cut off from Your hand.

a. **My soul is full of troubles**: The agony was not superficial. It went down deep to the soul. It was inward in the **soul** and outward, threatening his physical life (**my life draws near to the grave**). Others expected the psalmist to die (**I am counted with those who go down to the pit**).

i. "The emotions and suffering expressed by the psalmist are close in spirit to those of Psalm 22. In the tradition of the church, these psalms were linked together in the Scripture reading on Good Friday." (VanGemeren)

ii. **My soul is full of troubles**: "The psalmist has found the quickest argument before his God. There is nothing that so quickly makes the bell ring in heaven as the touch of a troubled hand." (Meyer)

iii. "He had his house full and his hands full of sorrow; but, worse than that, he had his heart full of it. Trouble in the soul is the soul of trouble." (Spurgeon)

b. **Adrift among the dead**: The psalmist was so weak and afflicted that he felt, and others regarded him, as practically dead already. Death seemed to pull on him as he was passively **adrift** and **like the slain**.

c. **Whom You remember no more**: The singer dreaded death, fearing that it would mean being cut off not only from earthly relationships, but also from his relationship with God.

i. As with Psalm 6 and other passages, it is wrong to take these agonized words as evidence that there is no life beyond death. The Old Testament has a shadowy understanding of the world beyond. Sometimes it shows a clear confidence (Job 19:25), and sometimes it has the uncertainty shown here.

ii. "Such thoughts are in startling contrast with the hopes that sparkle in some psalms (such as Psalm 16:10, etc.), and they show that clear, permanent assurance of future blessedness was not granted to the ancient Church. Nor could there be sober certainty of it until after Christ's resurrection. But it is also to be noticed that this psalm neither affirms nor denies a future resurrection." (Maclaren)

iii. The book of Psalms and the Old Testament in general do not present a comprehensive theology of the world beyond. The book of Psalms expresses the agony, fear, and uncertainty of death's doorstep. The singers in the psalms often *know* they can remember God and give Him thanks now, but don't have the same certainty about the world beyond.

iv. "At rare moments the Psalms have glimpses of rescue from Sheol, in terms that suggest resurrection, or a translation like that of Enoch or Elijah (*cf.* 16:10; 17:15; 49:15; 73:24)." (Kidner)

v. 2 Timothy 1:10 says that Jesus *brought life and immortality to light through the gospel.* The understanding of the after-life was murky at best in the Old Testament; but Jesus let us know more about heaven and hell than anyone else could. Jesus could do this because He had first-hand knowledge of the world beyond.

B. The Divine source of affliction.

1. (6-7) You, God, have brought me low.

You have laid me in the lowest pit,
In darkness, in the depths.
Your wrath lies heavy upon me,
And You have afflicted *me* with all Your waves. Selah

a. **You have laid me in the lowest pit**: Boldly, the psalmist tells God what he feels and experiences – that *God Himself* has caused His downfall, setting him **in darkness, in the depths.**

b. **Your wrath lies heavy upon me**: It seemed that the source of the affliction was the righteous **wrath** of God. The psalmist had a deep sense of his own sinfulness. Even as he felt himself sinking under **all Your waves,** he did not protest that God's wrath was unfair.

i. "The wrath of God is the very hell of hell, and when it weighs upon the conscience a man feels a torment such as only that of damned spirits can exceed." (Spurgeon)

ii. "Yet the most important similarity [with Job] is that God had caused Job's suffering, if not directly, at least by permitting Satan to afflict him – Job was unable to imagine why – and this is what the psalmist is claiming too. These similarities are so great, including even certain echoes of language that Franz Delitzsch has suggested that Job and the psalm might even be by the same author, Heman the Ezrahite." (Boice)

iii. **Selah**: "There was need to rest. Above the breakers the swimmer lifts his head and looks around him, breathing for a moment, until the next wave comes. Even lamentation must have its pauses." (Spurgeon)

2. (8-9a) You, God, have made me alone.

You have put away my acquaintances far from me;
You have made me an abomination to them;
***I am* shut up, and I cannot get out;**
My eye wastes away because of affliction.

a. **You have put away my acquaintances far from me**: In his affliction, his former friends wanted nothing to do with him. This also was seen as God's doing.

i. "His situation resembles that of Job, as his friends did not understand him. More than that, our Lord's suffering on earth was such that his own disciples forsook him (cf. Luke 23:49)." (VanGemeren)

ii. **You have made me an abomination to them**: "If taken literally, it points to some loathsome disease, which had long clung to him, and made even his friends shrink from companionship, and thus had condemned him to isolation. All these details suggest leprosy, which, if referred to here, is most probably to be taken, as sickness is in several psalms, as symbolic of affliction." (Maclaren)

iii. "Even more telling than the metaphors of dungeons and deep waters is the remembered look on the faces of his fellow men, a revulsion which isolates him in the narrow prison of himself." (Kidner)

b. **I am shut up, and I cannot get out**: Perhaps worst of all, the psalmist felt that there was *no escape*. Life was draining from him and if God did not respond, there seemed to be no remedy.

C. **The urgent prayer from the afflicted one.**

1. (9b-12) I need Your help in the land of the living.

LORD, I have called daily upon You;
I have stretched out my hands to You.
Will You work wonders for the dead?
Shall the dead arise *and* praise You? Selah
Shall Your lovingkindness be declared in the grave?

Or Your faithfulness in the place of destruction?
Shall Your wonders be known in the dark?
And Your righteousness in the land of forgetfulness?

a. **I have called daily upon You**: The psalmist reminded God of his constant prayer, made in the familiar Hebrew posture of **stretched out** hands to God.

b. **Will You work wonders for the dead?** Because the psalmist was uncertain of the world beyond, he diligently asked God to answer his prayer and meet his need soon, when he knew that he could receive God's **wonders** and speak of the **lovingkindness** and **faithfulness** of God.

i. The way these verses refer to the world beyond is a good illustration of the uncertainty that the Old Testament writers often demonstrated regarding what lay beyond this life:

- The dead.
- The grave.
- The place of destruction.
- The dark.
- The land of forgetfulness.

ii. *We* know that the world beyond is not these things, but the psalmist did not yet have that revelation.

2. (13-15) I need You to break the silence.

But to You I have cried out, O L**ORD****,**
And in the morning my prayer comes before You.
L**ORD****, why do You cast off my soul?**
Why **do You hide Your face from me?**
I *have been* **afflicted and ready to die from** *my* **youth;**
I suffer Your terrors;
I am distraught.

a. **To You I have cried out**: After a brief focus on the terror and uncertainty of the grave, the psalmist once again set his focus on the LORD. Like David, he sought God **in the morning** (Psalm 5:3, 55:17, 59:16).

i. **In the morning**: "Early, come to thee, before the ordinary time of morning prayer, or before the dawning of the day, or the rising of the sun. The sense is, Though I have hitherto got no answer to my prayers, yet I will not give over praying nor hoping for an answer." (Poole)

ii. **In the morning my prayer comes before You**: "The secret of it is that with determination he keeps himself in touch with God, crying

to Him, and going out to meet Him at the break of each new day."
(Morgan)

b. **Why do You hide Your face from me?** The sad idea from earlier in the
psalm is repeated. The worst of the psalmist's afflictions was the sense that
God had in some way forsaken him, that his **soul** was **cast off** from God.
He simply sang: **I suffer Your terrors; I am distraught.**

3. (16-18) I need You to rescue me from Your wrath.

Your fierce wrath has gone over me;
Your terrors have cut me off.
They came around me all day long like water;
They engulfed me altogether.
Loved one and friend You have put far from me,
***And* my acquaintances into darkness.**

a. **Your fierce wrath has gone over me:** Continuing the thought from
the previous lines, the psalmist understood that in some way God was the
source of his present affliction. If he suffered terrors, he could say to God
they were "**Your terrors.**" Even in his affliction, the psalmist believed in
God. This was a crisis, but it was a crisis of *faith*, not of unbelief.

   i. **Your fierce wrath:** "In Psalm 88:16 the word for wrath is in the
   plural, to express the manifold outbursts of that deadly indignation.
   The word means literally heat; and we may represent the psalmist's
   thought as being that the wrath shoots forth many fierce tongues of
   licking flame, or, like a lava stream, pours out in many branches."
   (Maclaren)

b. **They engulfed me altogether:** Afflicted and alone (**loved one and
friend You have put far from me**), the psalmist felt overwhelmed, as if he
were about to drown in his misery. The psalm here ends, with no answer
but a continued cry to God, who alone can rescue from such distress and
despair.

   i. "The happy ending of most psalms of this kind is seen to be a bonus,
   not a due; its withholding is not a proof of either God's displeasure or
   his defeat." (Kidner)

c. **And my acquaintances into darkness:** Many take this phrase in
a different sense, such as the NIV: *the darkness is my closest friend.* The
agonized cry of this psalm, together with its absence of anger or bitterness
against God, shows that there is a real sense in which the psalmist's darkness
has been a friend. It has – in a deep and even terrible way – brought him
into closer trust and relationship with God.

i. When Paul Simon began the song *Sound of Silence* with the phrase, *Hello darkness, my old friend*, he was not the first to express the idea. This seems to be Heman's sense. "'*And mine acquaintance into darkness,*' or better still, *my acquaintance is darkness*. I am familiar only with sadness, all else has vanished. I am a child crying alone in the dark. Will the heavenly Father leave his child there?" (Spurgeon)

ii. When we remember that Heman wrote this psalm, who lived a blessed life in many ways (see notes on this psalm's title), we realize that God used even this painful season for good.

iii. "This supposedly Godforsaken author seems to have been one of the pioneers of the singing guilds set up by David, to which we owe the Korahite psalms (43–49; 84f.; 87f.), one of the richest veins in the Psalter. Burdened and despondent as he was, his existence was far from pointless. If it was a living death, in God's hands it was to bear much fruit." (Kidner)

iv. "We thank God that there is one such song as this, with its revelation of what results in character when a soul, in the midst of the most appalling suffering, still maintains the activity of practiced relationship with God. We have also met such souls, and their witness to the power of the Divine grace is more potent than any theoretical expositions." (Morgan)

Psalm 89 – The Incomparable God and His Covenant to David

The title of this psalm is **A Contemplation of Ethan the Ezrahite.** *There are several men named* **Ethan** *in the Hebrew Scriptures, but this man is mentioned specifically in 1 Kings 4:31 as someone who was famous for his wisdom — yet surpassed by Solomon's greater wisdom. This means he was likely a contemporary of Solomon and was also alive during the reign of David.*

"Ethan is probably identical with Jeduthun, who founded one of the three choirs (cf. 1 Chronicles 15:19; 2 Chronicles 5:12). Ethan shared with Heman a reputation for wisdom." (Derek Kidner)

A. The incomparable God and His covenant to David.

1. (1-2) Forever mercy and faithfulness.

I will sing of the mercies of the LORD forever;
With my mouth will I make known Your faithfulness to all generations.
For I have said, "Mercy shall be built up forever;
Your faithfulness You shall establish in the very heavens."

> a. **I will sing of the mercies of the LORD:** Ethan began this psalm with a declaration of praise in song, focused on the **mercies** (from the word *hesed*, sometimes thought of as covenant love or loyal love) of Yahweh. The great lovingkindness of God lasts forever, so the praise of Him should also be sung **forever**.

> > i. This is a psalm with a lot of trouble, but the presence of trouble didn't silence the psalmist's praise; he sang of God's **mercies.** "We have not one, but many *mercies* to rejoice in, and should therefore multiply the expressions of our thankfulness." (Spurgeon)

> > ii. "We think when we are in trouble we get ease by complaining; but we do more, we get joy, by praising. Let our complaints therefore be turned into thanksgiving." (Matthew Henry, cited in Spurgeon)

b. **Will I make known Your faithfulness**: Ethan not only experienced the **mercies** and **faithfulness** of God; he also wanted to **make** them **known** to others. This was for their benefit, that they might also experience God's faithfulness and mercy. More importantly he wanted to spread the glory and fame of God as broadly as possible.

i. Ethan knew something of how good God was; it was fitting that others also know, and he was determined to tell them.

c. **Mercy shall be built up forever; Your faithfulness You shall establish**: Ethan **said** this to declare the goodness of God. He noted the permanent, enduring character of God's **mercy** and **faithfulness**, and how *God* had **established** these things.

i. **Mercy shall be built up forever**: The word **mercy** is "…another of the key words in 2 Samuel 7, with its play on the theme of the house David would have built for God, and the living house God would build instead for David." (Kidner)

ii. "A building is an orderly thing as well as a fixed thing. There is a scheme and design about it. Mercy shall be built. God has gone about blessing us with designs that only his own infinite perfections could have completed." (Spurgeon)

2. (3-4) God's covenant with David.

"I have made a covenant with My chosen,
I have sworn to My servant David:
'Your seed I will establish forever,
And build up your throne to all generations.'" Selah

a. **I have made a covenant**: As an expression of the *mercies* and *faithfulness* mentioned in the previous verses, Ethan noted the covenant God made with David as described in 2 Samuel 7. There, God promised to build and establish the house of David.

i. Ethan's mention of the covenant shows that it was public knowledge in the days of David and Solomon. People knew what God promised to David, and they understood that Solomon fulfilled it only partially.

b. **Your seed I will establish forever**: God promised David, *I will set up your seed after you, who will come from your body, and I will establish his kingdom* (2 Samuel 7:12). This promise was partially fulfilled in Solomon, the direct son of David and immediate heir to his throne. It would be most perfectly fulfilled in the One known as the *Son of David* – the Messiah, Jesus Christ (Matthew 12:23).

i. "We have an incontestable proof, that the covenant with David had Messiah for its object; that Solomon was a figure of him; and that the Scripture hath sometimes a double sense." (Horne)

c. **And build up your throne to all generations**: God promised David, *I will establish the throne of his kingdom forever* (2 Samuel 7:13). Again, this was fulfilled in an immediate and partial way with Solomon, but in a full and perfect way with Jesus the Messiah.

i. "The pledge to David is also extended to his descendants (v.4) and thereby to the future generation of subjects. The Lord himself will secure the rule of the Davidic dynasty." (VanGemeren)

d. **Selah**: Ethan believed that the wonderful generosity and faithfulness of God in such a promise was worthy of emphasis and meditation, so he instructed the musical pause **Selah**.

3. (5-10) God praised for His faithfulness and might.

And the heavens will praise Your wonders, O LORD;
Your faithfulness also in the assembly of the saints.
For who in the heavens can be compared to the LORD?
***Who* among the sons of the mighty can be likened to the LORD?**
God is greatly to be feared in the assembly of the saints,
And to be held in reverence by all *those* around Him.
O LORD God of hosts,
Who *is* mighty like You, O LORD?
Your faithfulness also surrounds You.
You rule the raging of the sea;
When its waves rise, You still them.
You have broken Rahab in pieces, as one who is slain;
You have scattered Your enemies with Your mighty arm.

a. **The heavens will praise Your wonders, O LORD**: Ethan was probably familiar with David's words in Psalm 19: *The heavens declare the glory of God.* God was not only to be praised for His **faithfulness…in the assembly of the saints**, but for His staggering work of creation.

i. Several commentators regard the reference to **the saints, the sons of the mighty**, and **the assembly of the saints** to mean angelic beings. If so, Ethan the psalmist brought together all creation to recognize the greatness and majesty of God.

ii. "Earth and heaven are one in admiring and adoring the covenant God: Saints above see most clearly into the heights and depths of divine love, therefore, they praise its wonders; and saints below, being conscious of their many sins and multiplied provocations of the Lord, admire his faithfulness." (Spurgeon)

iii. "Did not 'the heavens praise the wonders of Jehovah,' when a choir of angels descended from above, to sing an anthem, at the birth of Christ? And how must the celestial courts have resounded with the hallelujahs of those blessed spirits, when they again receive their King, returning in triumph from the conquest of his enemies?" (Horne)

iv. **Your wonders...Your faithfulness**: "They praise God's 'wonder' (which here means, not so much His marvellous acts, as the wonderfulness of His Being, His incomparable greatness and power), and His Faithfulness, the two guarantees of the fulfilment of His promises." (Maclaren)

b. **Who in the heavens can be compared to the LORD?** God's greatness means that He is also *incomparable*. He is not to be measured on the scale used to measure the greatness of men or even angels (if **sons of the mighty** refers to angelic beings).

i. God's incomparability is an aspect of His *holiness*. *Holy* means apartness; God is incomparably greater than all created things.

c. **God is greatly to be feared in the assembly of the saints**: Understanding the incomparability (holiness) of God should bring forth a sense of awe and praise from His people, especially as they meet together. He is **to be held in reverence by all those around Him**.

i. "Irreverence is rebellion. Thoughts of the covenant of grace tend to create a deeper awe of God." (Spurgeon)

d. **Who is mighty like You, O LORD?** Ethan continued his meditation on the incomparability of God with attention to His might, expressed in His ability to control unruly creation. This unruly creation is described as **the raging of the sea** and the defeat of **Rahab**.

i. "The extent of the ocean, the multitude of the waves, and their fury when excited by a storm, render it, in that state, the most tremendous object in nature." (Horne)

ii. "The ruling of the raging of the sea, the stilling of the stormy waves, and the breaking and scattering of the might of Egypt are used by the psalmist to illustrate the omnipotence of Jehovah, before which the mightiest monarchy on earth had no more power than if it had been a corpse." (Spurgeon)

e. **You have broken Rahab in pieces, as one who is slain**: **Rahab** is often taken as a personification of proud and strong Egypt. This may be true in this context, yet there is also a fascinating connection to the Canaanite mythology of that time, transforming and using that connection to glorify God as in the Incomparable One.

i. The name **Rahab** means *proud one*, and in Canaanite mythology the sea god *Yam* was subdued, and the sea serpent Rahab was killed at creation. Here, as in Job 26:12-13 (which perhaps Ethan had in mind), this Canaanite mythology is transformed and used to teach.

ii. Later the prophet Isaiah would use the same imagery and tone in speaking of Yahweh's great victory over Rahab: *Are You not the arm that cut Rahab apart, and wounded the serpent?* (Isaiah 51:9)

iii. In the ancient Middle East, there were many legends about the gods who fought other gods in creating the earth. Ethan, Asaph, Job, and Isaiah may have known those stories and used them to draw attention to the true God, Yahweh. It is Yahweh who rules **the raging of the sea**, even though ancient legends said that Tiamat (the Deep) was the chaotic goddess defeated by the hero god Marduk (Bel), or that Yam (the Sea) was defeated by Baal. It is Yahweh who cuts **Rahab in pieces**, not Marduk or Baal.

iv. There is the possibility that there is a grain of historical truth communicated in these ancient mythologies and legends. Ancient rabbinic mythologies suggest that an evil serpent was in the primeval sea resisting creation, and that God killed the serpent and brought order to the world as described in Genesis 1:1-2.

v. Satan is often represented as a dragon or a serpent (Genesis 3; Revelation 12 and 13), and the sea is thought of as a dangerous or threatening place in the Jewish mind (Isaiah 57:20; Mark 4:39; Revelation 21:1). It's possible that Rahab is another serpent-like manifestation of Satan, who was the original *proud one* (**Rahab**). It is also possible that *Leviathan* refers to the same creature (as in Job 3:8, Job 41:1, Psalm 74:14, and Isaiah 27:1).

vi. It is important to note that the Hebrew Scriptures do not simply believe or adopt this Canaanite mythology; they take it and transform it, using it to exalt Yahweh in a way that the Canaanite myths never did. Elmer B. Smick notes this in the *Expositor's Bible Commentary* on Job: "Here the sea that God subdues is not the deity Yam. Job depersonalized Yam by using the definite article (the sea), thus expressing his innate monotheistic theology.... Further, by his own wisdom, skill, and power he 'cut Rahab to pieces' and 'pierced the gliding serpent,' unlike Marduk who depended on the enablement of the father-gods."

vii. "A study of the Old Testament names for the well-known Canaanite mythological sea monsters like Rahab shows how purposefully the Old Testament authors used the language to enrich their own poetic conceptions of the supremacy of the one and only true God." (Smick)

4. (11-14) The glory and strength of God in heaven and on earth.

The heavens *are* Yours, the earth also *is* Yours;
The world and all its fullness, You have founded them.
The north and the south, You have created them;
Tabor and Hermon rejoice in Your name.
You have a mighty arm;
Strong is Your hand, *and* high is Your right hand.
Righteousness and justice *are* the foundation of Your throne;
Mercy and truth go before Your face.

a. **The heavens are Yours, the earth also is Yours; the world and all its fullness**: In the previous verses, the psalmist Ethan transformed a Canaanite myth to show that Yahweh, the covenant God of Israel, performs all things and no other god had that power. In these verses, he stated the same principle in different words, proclaiming that no other god or gods created or maintains the **heavens** or the **earth**. The **fullness** of the entire world, **the north and the south**, all belong to God.

i. "Turn to all points of the compass, and behold the Lord is there. The regions of snow and the gardens of the sun are his dominions: both the land of the dawning and the home of the setting sun rejoice to own his sway." (Spurgeon)

b. **Strong is Your hand, and high is Your right hand**: The skill and strength of men are often expressed in the arm and hands, especially the **right hand**. Ethan applied this principle in a metaphor to God, expressing His skill and strength.

i. **You have a mighty arm**: The psalmist knew this; we have greater reason to know it. The psalmist knew it because of God's might in creation and in Israel's deliverance from Egypt. We know those same things, but we can also see God's **mighty arm** in much greater work of Jesus Messiah and what He did in His life, teaching, sacrificial death, and triumphant resurrection.

c. **Righteousness and justice are the foundation of Your throne**: The psalmist praised the incomparable might of God, but he did not ignore God's *moral* greatness. Yahweh has the right to reign merely because of His omnipotence, but His nature demands that **righteousness and justice** mark His rule; the **foundation** of His **throne** and **mercy and truth go before** His **face**.

i. **Mercy and truth go before Your face**: "These shall be the *heralds* that shall announce the coming of the Judge. His *truth* binds him to fulfill all his declarations; and his *mercy* shall be shown to all those who have fled for refuge to the hope that is set before them in the Gospel." (Clarke)

5. (15-18) The blessedness of those who know the incomparable God.

Blessed *are* the people who know the joyful sound!
They walk, O LORD, in the light of Your countenance.
In Your name they rejoice all day long,
And in Your righteousness they are exalted.
For You *are* the glory of their strength,
And in Your favor our horn is exalted.
For our shield *belongs* to the LORD,
And our king to the Holy One of Israel.

a. **Blessed are the people who know the joyful sound**: Those who know the joyful sound of this truth – of God in His incomparable might, His righteousness and justice, and His mercy and truth – are a **blessed** people, and blessed in many ways.

- They enjoy the favor and fellowship of God's face: **They walk, O LORD, in the light of Your countenance.**

- They **rejoice all day long** in the **name** – the character and nature – of the incomparable God.

- They find their strength in God, especially in His **favor**: **You are the glory of their strength**.

- They enjoy God's protection: **Our shield belongs to the LORD.**

  i. **You are the glory of their strength**: "It is the duty of Christians, as it was that of Israelites, to ascribe all their strength, their success, and their glory, whether in matters temporal or spiritual, to Jehovah alone." (Horne)

b. **And our king to the Holy One of Israel**: A further blessing is that God takes a particular interest in their **king**. The following lines of the psalm suggest that this **king** was David.

B. The vision to God's holy one regarding the covenant with David.

1. (19-24) God's help to the king.

Then You spoke in a vision to Your holy one,
And said: "I have given help to *one who is* mighty;
I have exalted one chosen from the people.
I have found My servant David;
With My holy oil I have anointed him,
With whom My hand shall be established;
Also My arm shall strengthen him.
The enemy shall not outwit him,
Nor the son of wickedness afflict him.
I will beat down his foes before his face,
And plague those who hate him.
But My faithfulness and My mercy *shall be* with him,
And in My name his horn shall be exalted."

a. **I have given help to one who is mighty**: The previous lines (verse 18) spoke of God's special interest in the ruler of His people. Here some of the result of that interest is described. Speaking **in a vision** to the king (**Your holy one**), God promised to strengthen and **help** the ruler.

i. Spurgeon thought the **holy one** in this context was Nathan the prophet, not David. "The holy one here meant may be either David or Nathan the prophet, but most probably the latter, for it was to him that the word of the Lord came by night (2 Samuel 7:4-5)." (Spurgeon)

b. **I have exalted one chosen from the people**: The son of Jesse – **David** – was not from a noble or especially influential family, but **from the people**. Nevertheless, God **found** him and regarded him as His **servant**.

i. "Here was no self-made king and empire-builder, carving out a career for himself." (Kidner)

ii. Spurgeon pointed out three similarities to Jesus from the phrase, **I have exalted one chosen from the people**:

- Jesus was *extracted* from the people.
- Jesus was *elected* by God from among the people.
- Jesus was *exalted* above the people.

c. **I have found My servant David**: In this section of the psalm, God described the many blessings He placed upon David, the man after His own heart (1 Samuel 13:14).

- The blessing of help (**I have given help**).
- The blessing of exaltation (**I have exalted**).
- The blessing of election (**one chosen from the people**).

- The blessing of anointing (**I have anointed him**).
- The blessing of security (**with whom My hand shall be established**).
- The blessing of God's own strength (**My arm shall strengthen him**).
- The blessing of protection (**the enemy shall not outwit him, nor the son of wickedness afflict him**).
- The blessing of vindication (**I will beat down his foes before his face, and plague those who hate him**).
- The blessing of ongoing faithfulness and mercy (**My faithfulness and My mercy shall be with him**).
- The blessing of exalted strength (**in My name his horn shall be exalted**).

   i. **I have anointed**: "More important than any crown was the fact of being *anointed*, and so set apart for sacred office; it was this that gave rise, in due course, to the title Messiah or Christ." (Kidner)

   ii. **I will beat down his foes before his face**: "These verses complement Psalm 2, where the Lord's anointed receives full authority to subjugate all resistance of God's enemies on earth. The real source of David's power and authority lies in the Lord's presence and purpose." (VanGemeren)

   iii. "None of his enemies shall be able to prevail against him. It is worthy of remark that David was never overthrown; he finally conquered every foe that rose up against him. Saul's persecution, Absalom's revolt, Sheba's conspiracy, and the struggle made by the partisans of the house of Saul after his death, only tended to call forth David's skill, courage, and prowess, and to seat him more firmly on his throne." (Clarke)

2. (25-29) More blessings to the king.

Also I will set his hand over the sea,
And his right hand over the rivers.
He shall cry to Me, 'You *are* my Father,
My God, and the rock of my salvation.'
Also I will make him *My* firstborn,
The highest of the kings of the earth.
My mercy I will keep for him forever,
And My covenant shall stand firm with him.
His seed also I will make *to endure* forever,
And his throne as the days of heaven."

   a. **I will set his hand over the sea, and his right hand over the rivers**: This promised a dominion that David never seemed to fulfill. As the previous section spoke of the blessings God promised to David, the promises gradually become of a nature in which their perfect fulfillment was only in David's greater Son, the *Seed* of David (verses 4, 29, 36).

b. **You are my Father**: This was true for David, but even more true for Jesus the Messiah, who did all things looking to and in dependency on God the Father (John 5:19, 8:28).

c. **I will make him My firstborn**: This was true of David in the sense that even though he was the youngest of many brothers (1 Samuel 16:11), God gave him the prominence and favor associated with the **firstborn**. That prominence and favor was even truer of Jesus, the Son of David – made **the highest of the kings of the earth** (1 Timothy 6:15, Revelation 19:16).

   i. "*First-born* is not always to be understood *literally* in Scripture. It often signifies simply a *well-beloved*, or *best-beloved son*; one preferred to all the rest, and distinguished by some eminent prerogative. Thus God calls Israel *his son*, his *first-born*, Exodus 4:22." (Clarke)

d. **My mercy I will keep for him forever**: This **mercy** to David's house was promised in the **covenant** God made with him (2 Samuel 7:15).

   i. **My covenant shall stand firm**: "With Jesus the covenant is ratified both by blood of sacrifice and by oath of God; it cannot be cancelled or altered, but is an eternal verity, resting upon the veracity of one who cannot lie." (Spurgeon)

   ii. "Never forget that, when once God has entered into covenant with a soul, He will stand to it, till the heavens be no more." (Meyer)

e. **His seed also I will make to endure forever, and his throne as the days of heaven**: This promise from the Davidic covenant (2 Samuel 7:16) is only fulfilled in the **forever** reign of the Messiah, Jesus Christ.

3. (30-37) The promises of the Davidic covenant repeated.

"If his sons forsake My law
And do not walk in My judgments,
If they break My statutes
And do not keep My commandments,
Then I will punish their transgression with the rod,
And their iniquity with stripes.
Nevertheless My lovingkindness I will not utterly take from him,
Nor allow My faithfulness to fail.
My covenant I will not break,
Nor alter the word that has gone out of My lips.
Once I have sworn by My holiness;
I will not lie to David:
His seed shall endure forever,

And his throne as the sun before Me;
It shall be established forever like the moon,
Even *like* the faithful witness in the sky." Selah

a. **If his sons forsake My law**: All of those in David's royal line had some part of this Davidic covenant. Some of these were disobedient kings, and God brought considerable correction to both the kings and the kingdom.

i. **I will punish their transgression with the rod**: "Not with the sword, not with death and destruction; but still with a smarting, tingling, painful rod." (Spurgeon)

b. **Nevertheless My lovingkindness I will not utterly take from him**: As described in the Davidic covenant, Yahweh would never completely take His *hesed*, His covenant love, from the house of David (2 Samuel 7:14-16). Yahweh would remain faithful to His **covenant** and His **word**.

i. **I have sworn by My holiness**: "God here pledges the crown of his kingdom, the excellent beauty of his person, the essence of his nature. He does as good as say that if he ceases to be true to his covenant he will have forfeited his holy character. What more can he say? In what stronger language can he express his unalterable adherence to the truth of his promise?" (Spurgeon)

c. **His throne as the sun before Me; it shall be established forever like the moon**: God's promises to David regarding his royal house and the reigning Messiah to come from that house were constant, like the sun and the moon, the **faithful witness in the sky**.

i. **His throne as the sun before Me**: "Splendid and glorious! Dispensing light, heat, life, and salvation to all mankind." (Clarke)

C. The covenant and the crisis.

1. (38-45) The feeling that God had forsaken His covenant promises to David.

But You have cast off and abhorred,
You have been furious with Your anointed.
You have renounced the covenant of Your servant;
You have profaned his crown *by casting it* to the ground.
You have broken down all his hedges;
You have brought his strongholds to ruin.
All who pass by the way plunder him;
He is a reproach to his neighbors.
You have exalted the right hand of his adversaries;
You have made all his enemies rejoice.
You have also turned back the edge of his sword,
And have not sustained him in the battle.

You have made his glory cease,
And cast his throne down to the ground.
The days of his youth You have shortened;
You have covered him with shame. Selah

a. **But You have cast off and abhorred**: The first 37 verses of this psalm soared with confidence in God's incomparable greatness and in His covenant to David. Here, the tone suddenly shifted as Ethan considered some present crisis, which seemed to be all the worse when contrasted with his understanding of God's greatness and faithfulness to the covenant with David.

i. Because we don't know the exact time Ethan wrote, we don't know the crisis that prompted this desperate cry.

- It might have been Absalom's rebellion (2 Samuel 15-18).
- It might have been the spiritual decline of Solomon (1 Kings 11).
- It might have been the rapid and radical decline of the kingdom after Solomon's death (1 Kings 12).
- It might have been a crisis no recorded in the Bible.

ii. "With an honesty found consistently in the psalms but often lacking in ourselves, it also describes a situation in which God has not seemed to be faithful, and it asks, 'Where is your faithfulness?'" (Boice)

iii. "But these glorious promises are set in sharpest contrast with a doleful present, which seems to contradict them." (Maclaren)

iv. "Taken as a whole, this song is one of the finest in the collection as a revelation of how the man of faith is compelled to view calamity." (Morgan)

b. **You have renounced the covenant of Your servant; You have profaned his crown by casting it to the ground**: Ethan's words here seem a shocking contradiction to what he wrote earlier in the psalm, in which he demonstrated the full confidence of faith and the true report of his feelings. Ethan *knew* God had not **renounced the covenant**, but in the present crisis it *felt* like it.

i. "*Renounced* may be too decisive a word for this rare verb, whose meaning has to be guessed from its parallel terms, *i.e.* 'defiled' (Psalm 89:39b) and 'scorned' (Lamentations 2:7a). Perhaps 'disdained' or 'held cheap' would be more accurate. It is in any case the language of experience, not an accusation of bad faith." (Kidner)

ii. **You have**: "Yet all this is spoken of as the work of Jehovah. The key phrase to this portion is, 'Thou hast.'" (Morgan)

iii. To think that God has allowed such disaster is painful. However, it's even more painful to think that God had nothing to do with it, and we are at the mercy of random events, fate, and luck.

c. **The days of his youth You have shortened; you have covered him with shame**: The king himself – David, Solomon, or a later king – was personally affected and weakened by the crisis. The promises of God through the Davidic covenant *seemed* empty at the time.

i. **Selah**: "*Selah.* The interceding poet takes breath amid his lament, and then turns from describing the sorrows of the kingdom to pleading with the Lord." (Spurgeon)

2. (46-48) A plea for speedy rescue.

How long, LORD?
Will You hide Yourself forever?
Will Your wrath burn like fire?
Remember how short my time is;
For what futility have You created all the children of men?
What man can live and not see death?
Can he deliver his life from the power of the grave? Selah

a. **How long, LORD?** Ethan couldn't bear the idea that the crisis would last much longer. He poured out his plea to God, who seemed to be hiding and angry with Israel and her king.

b. **Remember how short my time is**: Perhaps Ethan prayed this on behalf of the weary king, or perhaps he longed to see the king and kingdom vindicated in his life, perhaps in his old age. The mention of shortness of time and the **futility** of life add a sense of urgency and even desperation to the request.

c. **Can he deliver his life from the power of the grave?** The answer to this rhetorical question is of course, *no*. No mere man can deliver **his** own life from the grave and its power. Men often wish to forget their complete dependence upon God regarding the life to come, but the psalmist urged us to remember it often, emphasizing it with **Selah**.

i. There has only been One with the power to **deliver his life from the power of the grave** – Jesus Christ. Jesus promised to raise his own body after three days in the grave (John 2:19).

ii. "All men at their best estate are mortal and miserable, kings and people must unavoidably die by the condition of their natures; and therefore, Lord, do not increase our affliction, which of itself is more than enough." (Poole)

iii. "The problems of verses 47f. cry out for the gospel's answer." (Kidner)

3. (49-51) A prayer for restoration of previous mercies.

Lord, where *are* Your former lovingkindnesses,
***Which* You swore to David in Your truth?**
Remember, Lord, the reproach of Your servants—
***How* I bear in my bosom *the reproach of* all the many peoples,**
With which Your enemies have reproached, O Lord,
With which they have reproached the footsteps of Your anointed.

a. **Lord, where are Your former lovingkindnesses?** Ethan again made honest, heartfelt inquiry from a season of crisis. The request shows that he would not allow himself to stay in the belief that God had cast them off or renounced His covenant. He could still appeal to God on the basis of what God promised to David, what He **swore to David in** His **truth**.

b. **Remember, Lord, the reproach of Your servants**: Ethan asked God to notice their low and despised state, and to act mercifully in light of the seeming triumph of God's own **enemies**, who were also enemies of God's **anointed** king.

i. **They have reproached the footsteps of Your anointed**: "Finally, the prayer…begins to accustom our eyes to the combination of *servant* (Psalm 89:50) and Messiah (*anointed*, Psalm 89:51), the recipient of God's promises and man's *insults*." (Kidner)

4. (52) A conclusion of praise.

Blessed *be* the Lord forevermore!
Amen and Amen.

a. **Blessed be the Lord forevermore**: The psalmist concludes this song with a hard-fought declaration of praise. This came from a man who knew God's promises and trusted them, all the while honestly pouring out his pain before God in his present distress.

i. "He ends where he began; he has sailed round the world and reached port again. Let us bless God before we pray, and while we pray, and when we have done praying, for he always deserves it of us. If we cannot understand him, we will not distrust him." (Spurgeon)

b. **Amen and Amen**: Ethan the Ezrahite invited the people of God to join him in his confident, hard-fought declaration of praise.

i. This particular ending makes many think that Psalm 89:52 was added as an exclamation at the end of Book Three of Psalms. "This is the doxology with which the third Book of Psalms ends." (Morgan)

ii. "This doxology belongs alike to all the Psalms of the Third Book, and ought not to be treated as if it were merely the last verse of the Psalm to which it adjoins." (Binnie, cited in Spurgeon)

Psalm 90 – The Prayer of Moses in the Wilderness

This psalm is titled **A Prayer of Moses the man of God**. *Some commentators think this was not the same famous and familiar Moses, but the evidence is much stronger for believing that this was indeed the great leader of Israel. This is the only song of Moses in the psalms, but there are two other songs in the Pentateuch (Exodus 15 and Deuteronomy 32), as well as the blessing of the tribes of Israel in Deuteronomy 33.*

If we connect it with any particular time in the life of Moses, the best suggestion is the time described in Numbers 20. "The historical setting is probably best understood by the incidents recorded in Numbers 20: (1) the death of Miriam, Moses' sister; (2) the sin of Moses in striking the rock in the wilderness, which kept him from entering the Promised Land; and (3) the death of Aaron, Moses' brother." (James Montgomery Boice)

Charles Spurgeon wrote of the phrase, **The man of God***: "Moses was peculiarly a man of God and God's man; chosen of God, inspired of God, honoured of God, and faithful to God in all his house, he well deserved the name which is here given him."*

A. Finding refuge in the eternal God.

1. (1) Yahweh the refuge and protection of His people.

Lord, You have been our dwelling place in all generations.

a. **Lord, You have been our dwelling place**: This *prayer of Moses* was almost certainly written during the wilderness years on the way to Canaan. In all those years Israel lived in constant need of refuge, shelter, and protection. More than their tents and their armies, Israel had God as their **dwelling place**, their refuge and their protection.

i. **Lord**: The psalm "begins with this great affirmation concerning the relation of man to God. Addressing Him, not as Elohim the Mighty One, nor as Jehovah, the Helper, but as Adonai, the Sovereign Lord, the singer declares that He has been the dwelling-place, the habitation, the home of man in all generations." (Morgan)

ii. **Our dwelling place**: "The Hebrew word for 'dwelling place' may also be translated 'refuge,' which is how it appears in Deuteronomy 33:27, one of the other songs of Moses." (Boice)

b. **Our dwelling place in all generations**: Moses understood that Yahweh's help to His people did not begin with the exodus from Egypt. From their pilgrim beginnings under their patriarch Abraham to the days of Moses, God had been their **dwelling place**, their refuge and protection.

i. It isn't a good thing to refer to anyone as *homeless*. Spiritually speaking, that never needs to be the state of the believer. We have our home in Him, and home should be a place where we rest, where we can be ourselves, where love and happiness dominate. All this should mark our relationship with God.

ii. "In this Eternal One there is a safe abode for the successive generations of men. If God himself were of yesterday, he would not be a suitable refuge for mortal men; if he could change and cease to be God he would be but an uncertain dwelling-place for his people." (Spurgeon)

iii. "He that dwelleth in God cannot be unhoused, because God is stronger than all; neither can any one take another out of his hands, John 10:29. Here, then, it is best for us…to seek a supply of all our wants in God alone." (Trapp)

2. (2) The eternal origin of Yahweh.

Before the mountains were brought forth,
Or ever You had formed the earth and the world,
Even from everlasting to everlasting, You *are* God.

a. **Before the mountains were brought forth**: In the wilderness on the slow route to Canaan, Moses saw **mountains** on the horizon and reflected on the truth that God existed before those **mountains**. It was God who **formed the earth and the world**.

b. **Even from everlasting to everlasting, You are God**: Before anything existed, God was. From eternity past through eternity future (**everlasting to everlasting**), He exists, independent of all His creation.

i. "This is the highest description of the *eternity* of God to which human language can reach." (Clarke)

ii. "The Psalmist, about to describe man's fleeting and transitory state, first directs us to contemplate the unchangeable nature and attributes of God." (Horne)

3. (3) The judgment of the eternal God.

You turn man to destruction,
And say, "Return, O children of men."

a. **You turn man to destruction**: Moses had seen the judgment of God **turn man to destruction**. He saw it with wicked Egypt and disobedient Israel. The eternal God who created all things was and is a God to be appropriately feared and respected by man. God takes interest in the affairs of men and exercises His holy judgment.

b. **Return, O children of men**: This was not a call to repentance; it was a command of man to return to the dust from which he came, an echo of Genesis 3:19: *For dust you are, and to dust you shall return.*

i. "Although *dust* is a different word from that of Genesis 3:19 ('you are dust, and to dust you shall return'), the idea of returning to it (*Turn back*) almost certainly alludes to the curse of Adam, and uses the same verb." (Kidner)

ii. "If we had no Scripture at all to prove this, daily experience before our eyes makes it clear how all men, even the wisest, the strongest, the greatest and the mightiest monarchs and princes in the world, be but miserable men, made of red earth, and quickly turn again to dust." (Smith, cited in Spurgeon)

B. Man before the God of judgment.

1. (4-6) God's perception of time and our perception of time.

For a thousand years in Your sight
***Are* like yesterday when it is past,**
And *like* a watch in the night.
You carry them away *like* a flood;
***They are* like a sleep.**
In the morning they are like grass *which* grows up:
In the morning it flourishes and grows up;
In the evening it is cut down and withers.

a. **For a thousand years in Your sight are like yesterday when it is past**: Having introduced the idea of God's eternal being, living outside of time with no beginning or end, Moses poetically repeated the idea. For the eternal God, a **thousand years** seems like a single day, and a single day in the **past**, not the present.

i. "He is raised above Time, and none of the terms in which men describe duration have any meaning for Him. A thousand years, which to a man seem so long, are to Him dwindled to nothing, in comparison with the eternity of His being. As Peter has said, the converse must also be true, and 'one day be with the Lord as a thousand years.'" (Maclaren)

b. **You carry them away like a flood**: From God's eternal perspective, the days and the years and each millennium pass quickly. For Moses and Israel in the wilderness, time seemed to pass slowly, but Moses knew this was not God's perspective. From God's perspective, a thousand years passes quickly **like a sleep**.

c. **Like grass which grows up**: Moses used many poetic pictures to describe God and time. In God's sight a thousand years was like yesterday, like a watch in the night, like a flood, like a night of sleep. He added this picture: a thousand years is like grass which **grows up** in the **morning** and in **the evening it is cut down and withers**. God's perspective of time's passing is very different from ours.

2. (7-8) God's judgment on their open and secret sins.

For we have been consumed by Your anger,
And by Your wrath we are terrified.
You have set our iniquities before You,
Our secret *sins* in the light of Your countenance.

a. **For we have been consumed by Your anger**: In the first section of this psalm, Moses connected the idea of God's eternal nature with His judgment upon man. In this section the two ideas are repeated. The God who stands over time and sees a thousand years as yesterday certainly has the right and the authority to judge mankind, especially His own people.

i. In the wilderness Moses and the people of Israel felt **consumed** by God's anger and **terrified** by His **wrath**. It must have been crushing for Moses to see a whole generation melt away in the wilderness, dying away under the judgment of God.

ii. "This was specially the case in reference to the people in the wilderness, whose lives were cut short by justice on account of their waywardness; they failed, not by a natural decline, but through the blast of the well-deserved judgments of God." (Spurgeon)

iii. "**Consumed**; either naturally, by the frame of our bodies; or violently, by extraordinary judgments. Thou dost not suffer us to live so long as we might by the course of nature." (Poole)

b. **You have set our iniquities before You**: The judgment of God came against His people because of their **iniquities**. When the eternal, holy God saw and considered them, His response was **anger** and **wrath**. Moses understood that God's anger against His people was not unreasonable or unearned.

i. "We do not understand the full blessedness of believing that God is our asylum, till we understand that He is our asylum from all that is destructive...nor do we know the significance of the universal experience of decay and death, till we learn that it is not the result of our finite being, but of sin." (Maclaren)

c. **Our secret sins in the light of Your countenance**: It was not only their obvious **iniquities** but also their **secret sins** that God saw. Such sins were not **secret** before God and His judgment.

3. (9-11) Man's frailty understood against the eternity of God.

For all our days have passed away in Your wrath;
We finish our years like a sigh.
The days of our lives *are* seventy years;
And if by reason of strength *they are* eighty years,
Yet their boast *is* only labor and sorrow;
For it is soon cut off, and we fly away.
Who knows the power of Your anger?
For as the fear of You, *so is* Your wrath.

a. **All our days have passed away in Your wrath**: With poetic power, Moses compared the eternal nature of the holy God with the frail, temporary nature of sinful man. God stands forever, but long days **have passed away in Your wrath** and **we finish our years like a sigh**.

i. "It was toward the close of the desert wanderings that Moses wrote this sublime psalm, all the imagery of which is borrowed from the wilderness. The watch around the campfire at night; the rush of the mountain flood; the grass that sprouts so quickly after the rain, and is as quickly scorched; the sigh of the wearied pilgrim." (Meyer)

b. **The days of our lives are seventy years**: Moses lived 120 years according to Deuteronomy 31:2 and 34:7. He did not say **seventy years** as either a promise or a limit, but as a poetic estimate of a lifespan. The emphasis is on the futility of life; even if one should live past the norm of **seventy years** and live **eighty years**, the end of it all is **only labor and sorrow**.

i. **Seventy years**: "Which time the ancient heathen writers also fixed as the usual space of men's lives." (Poole)

c. **For it is soon cut off, and we fly away**: Moses described the short and often futile sense of this life. The deep cry of Moses seems to anticipate important themes in Ecclesiastes.

d. **Who knows the power of Your anger?** Moses connected the ideas of a relatively short and frustrating life to the fact of God's righteous judgment. Moses especially saw and lived this in the wilderness.

i. "Moses saw men dying all around him; he lived among funerals, and was overwhelmed at the terrible results of the divine displeasure. He felt that none could measure the might of the Lord's wrath." (Spurgeon)

C. A prayer in light of who God is and how He deals with man.

1. (12) Praying for wisdom.

So teach *us* to number our days,
That we may gain a heart of wisdom.

a. **So teach us to number our days**: When Moses considered the frail nature of humanity and the righteous judgment of God, it made him ask God for the wisdom to understand the shortness of life.

i. "*To number our days*; to consider the shortness and miseries of this life, and the certainty and speediness of death, and the causes and consequences thereof." (Poole)

ii. "Of all arithmetical rules this is the hardest – to *number our days*. Men can number their herds and droves of oxen and of sheep, they can estimate the revenues of their manors and farms, they can with a little pains number and tell their coins, and yet they are persuaded that their days are infinite and innumerable and therefore do never begin to number them." (Tymme, cited in Spurgeon)

iii. "To live with dying thoughts is the way to die with living comforts." (Trapp)

iv. **So teach us** means that this wisdom must be *learned*. It isn't automatic. Most people live with little awareness that life is short, and their **days** should be **numbered**. Young people especially often think their days have no number and give little thought to what lies beyond this life.

b. **That we may gain a heart of wisdom**: Learning to **number our days** will give us **a heart of wisdom**. This is wisdom not only for the mind, but for the **heart** as well.

i. "Let us deeply consider our own frailty, and the shortness and uncertainty of life, that we may live for eternity, acquaint ourselves with thee, and be at peace; that we may die in thy favour and live and reign with thee eternally." (Clarke)

2. (13-17) Praying for mercy and blessing.

Return, O Lord!
How long?
And have compassion on Your servants.
Oh, satisfy us early with Your mercy,

That we may rejoice and be glad all our days!
Make us glad according to the days *in which* **You have afflicted us,**
The years *in which* **we have seen evil.**
Let Your work appear to Your servants,
And Your glory to their children.
And let the beauty of the LORD **our God be upon us,**
And establish the work of our hands for us;
Yes, establish the work of our hands.

a. **Return, O L**ORD: This psalm of Moses carefully considered the judgment of God, and yet his prayerful response to that consideration was a plea to God for His presence, for His **compassion**, and for His **mercy** – the *hesed* of Yahweh, His loyal covenant love.

i. In verse 3 God spoke to mankind in judgment, telling him to *return* to destruction (or, to dust). Now, in prayer, Moses asked God to **return**. It was as if Moses said to God's people, "If you continue in sin, you will return to the dust; your only hope is for God to **return** to you."

b. **How long?** This was a meaningful question. Moses asked God not to delay in bringing His presence, **compassion**, and **mercy** to His people. It was a bold question, as if accusing God of being late in His help.

i. "When men are under chastisement they are allowed to…ask 'how long?' Our fault in these times is not too great boldness with God, but too much backwardness in pleading with him." (Spurgeon)

c. **Satisfy us early with Your mercy**: Moses understood that true satisfaction was not rooted in money, fame, romance, pleasure, or success. It was satisfied with God's **mercy**, His faithful, covenant goodness to His people.

i. "Alexander Maclaren said, 'The only thing that will secure life-long gladness is a heart satisfied with the experience of God's love.' This means that nothing will satisfy the human heart ultimately except God." (Boice)

ii. This **mercy** should be sought **early**. "There is no hour like that of morning prime for fellowship with God. If we would dare to wait before Him for satisfaction *then*, the filling of that hour would overflow into all other hours." (Meyer)

iii. "The renewal of his love is associated with "the morning" (cf. Psalm 30:5; 49:14; 143:8; Lam 3:23), as the light of day is contrastive with the darkness (gloom) of the night. Thus the psalmist prays for

a new beginning, which the Lord alone can open up for his people."
(VanGemeren)

d. **Make us glad according to the days in which You have afflicted us**:
Many were the days of their affliction; Moses asked that the days of their
gladness would also be many. He hoped the days of gladness would be so
long that God's **glory** would be evident even **to their children**.

i. "The New Testament, incidentally, will outrun verse 15's modest
prayer for joys to balance sorrows, by its promise of 'an eternal weight
of glory beyond all comparison' (2 Cor. 4:17)." (Kidner)

ii. "The time of our pilgrimage upon earth is a time of sorrow; we
grieve for our departed friends and our surviving friends must soon
grieve for us; these are days wherein God afflicteth us." (Horne)

iii. "Lord, if we must die in this desert, if this whole generation (except
Caleb and Joshua) must pass away in the wilderness, then, at any
rate, give us the fullness of Thy favor now, that we may spend all our
remaining days, whether they be too few or many, in gladness and
rejoicing." (Spurgeon)

iv. **According to the days**: "The good Lord measures out the dark and
the light in due proportions, and the result is life sad enough to be safe,
and glad enough to be desirable." (Spurgeon)

e. **Let the beauty of the LORD our God be upon us**: Earlier in this psalm
Moses spoke of God's people being *consumed* and *terrified*. He prayed that
the gracious God would exchange that misery for His own **beauty**.

i. The **beauty of the LORD our God** is great beauty. It is impossible to
think of a higher level of beauty or goodness.

ii. **The beauty of the LORD**: "His favourable countenance, and gracious
influence, and glorious presence." (Poole)

iii. "The faithful beseech God to let his 'beauty,' his splendor, the light
of his countenance, his grace and favour, be upon them." (Horne)

f. **And establish the work of our hands for us**: The final aspect of blessing
Moses prayed for was for the permanence of the **work** of God's people.
Without this blessing in our lives, our work and its effectiveness pass
quickly and are of little impact.

i. Essentially, Moses asked that God would work with man. "Fleeting
as our days are, they are ennobled by our being permitted to be God's
tools." (Maclaren)

ii. "Good men are anxious not to work in vain. They know that without
the Lord they can do nothing, and therefore they cry to him for help

in the work, for acceptance of their efforts, and for the establishment of their designs." (Spurgeon)

iii. "Satisfaction, gladness, success in work must all come from the right relation of man in his frailty to the eternal Lord." (Morgan)

Psalm 91 – The Assurance Given to those Who Trust in God

This psalm has no title, and therefore the author remains unknown. Because it shares some of the themes of Psalm 90, some think Moses was the author. Because it shares some of the themes and phrases of Psalms 27 and 31, some think the author was David. "Some of its language, of strongholds and shields, reminds us of David, to whom the LXX [Septuagint] ascribes it; other phrases echo the Song of Moses in Deuteronomy 32, as did Psalm 90; but it is in fact anonymous and timeless, perhaps all the more accessible for that." (Derek Kidner)

Many have noted the wonderful character of this psalm: "This psalm is one of the greatest possessions of the saints." (G. Campbell Morgan)

"In the whole collection there is not a more cheering Psalm, its tone is elevated and sustained throughout, faith is at its best, and speaks nobly." (Charles Spurgeon)

"It is one of the most excellent works of this kind which has ever appeared. It is impossible to imagine anything more solid, more beautiful, more profound, or more ornamented." (de Muis, cited in Spurgeon)

A. The assurance of God's protection.

1. (1-2) The protection, comfort, and care of Yahweh.

He who dwells in the secret place of the Most High
Shall abide under the shadow of the Almighty.
I will say of the LORD, "He is my refuge and my fortress;
My God, in Him I will trust."

> a. **He who dwells in the secret place of the Most High**: God has a **secret place** for His own (Psalm 27:5, 31:20), and it is a place to *live in*. Those who dwell there **abide under the shadow of the Almighty**, knowing His protection, comfort, and care.

> > i. In Psalm 90:1, Moses spoke of God as the dwelling place of His people. The opening lines of Psalm 91 seem to take that idea further.

91

"Moses spoke of God as the dwelling-place, the habitation, the home of man. This singer seems to accept that great idea, and then to speak of the most central chamber of the dwelling-place, referring to it as the Secret Place, and describing its complete security." (Morgan)

ii. There are many followers of Jesus Christ who seem to know very little of **the secret place of the Most High** or what it is to **abide under** His **shadow**. Many seem to regard this as only a thing for mystics or the super-spiritual. Yet David, if he wrote this, was a warrior and man well acquainted with the realities of life. It is true that the life of the spirit seems to come more easily for some than for others, but there is an aspect of **the secret place of the Most High** that is for everyone who puts his trust in Him.

iii. "Every child of God looks towards the inner sanctuary and the mercy-seat, yet all do not *dwell* in the most holy place; they run to it at times, and enjoy occasional approaches, but they do not habitually reside in the mysterious presence." (Spurgeon)

iv. **The shadow of the Almighty**: "This is an expression which implies great nearness. We must walk very close to a companion, if we would have his shadow fall on us." (Duncan, cited in Spurgeon)

v. Spurgeon (borrowing from Frances Ridley Havergal) suggested four ways the Scripture speaks of **the shadow of the Almighty**.

- The shadow of the rock (Isaiah 32:2).
- The shadow of the tree (Song of Solomon 2:3).
- The shadow of His wings (Psalm 63:7).
- The shadow of His hand (Isaiah 49:2).

vi. These first two verses of Psalm 91 use four wonderful titles or names for God:

- **Most High**: *Elyon.*
- **Almighty**: *Shadday.*
- **The Lord**: *Yahweh.*
- **My God**: *Elohay.*

b. **He is my refuge and my fortress**: The one who lives intimately with God knows the greatness of His protection. God Himself becomes like a mighty **refuge** and **fortress** for the believer.

i. **My refuge**: "Have you ever said definitely, 'O Lord, thou art my refuge'? Fleeing from all other, have you sheltered in Him from the windy storm and tempest, from the harrow by day, and pestilence by night, from man and devil? You must avow it. Do not only think it, but say it." (Meyer)

c. **My God, in Him I will trust**: This close relationship with God and all the benefits that come from it are for those who know Yahweh as **God**, and who truly **trust** in Him. As a believer receives His protection, comfort, and care, he trusts God all the more, and increasingly knows Him as **God**.

i. "Men are apt enough to proclaim their doubts, and even to boast of them, indeed there is a party nowadays of the most audacious pretenders to culture and thought, who glory in casting suspicion upon everything; hence it becomes the duty of all true believers to speak out and testify with calm courage to their own well-grounded reliance upon their God." (Spurgeon)

ii. Spurgeon suggested many different Biblical examples of people who had their own expression of the phrase **My God**.

- *My God* is the young convert's confession (Ruth, as in Ruth 1:16).
- *My God* is the individual Christian's belief (Thomas, as in John 20:28).
- *My God* is the declaration of the believer when opposed (Micaiah, as in 1 Kings 22:14).
- *My God* is the secret vow of the believer in consecration (Jacob, as in Genesis 32:28-30).
- *My God* is the deepest comfort to God's children in great woe (Jesus, as in Matthew 27:46).
- *My God* is the celebration for the victorious believer (Miriam, as in Exodus 15:21).

2. (3-4) How God brings His protection, comfort, and care.

Surely He shall deliver you from the snare of the fowler
***And* from the perilous pestilence.**
He shall cover you with His feathers,
And under His wings you shall take refuge;
His truth *shall be your* shield and buckler.

a. **Surely He shall deliver you from the snare of the fowler**: Following the general statement of the first two verses, now the psalmist describes the specific ways God protects and cares for His people – beginning with rescue from those who would trap God's people as the **fowler** snares birds.

i. These are "…metaphors for the plots which would entangle our affairs (Psalm 140:1–5) or compromise our loyalty (Psalm 119:110)." (Kidner)

ii. "We are foolish and weak as poor little birds, and are very apt to be lured to our destruction by cunning foes, but if we dwell near to God, he will see to it that the most skilful deceiver shall not entrap us." (Spurgeon)

iii. The devil and his agents often work as **the fowler** works.

- The fowler works in secret.
- The fowler changes his trap and methods.
- The fowler often entices with pleasure or profit.
- The fowler often uses a bad example, a decoy.

iv. "The most striking feature of this section (and the one following) is the use of the singular *you* throughout, which is a way of saying that these truths are for each person individually. They are for you if you will truly trust or abide in God." (Boice)

b. **And from the perilous pestilence**: God also protects His people in times of plague and disease. The psalmist, inspired by the Holy Spirit, did not intend this as an absolute promise, that every believer would be delivered from every **snare** or every **pestilence**. Instead, the idea is that the psalmist could point to many times when God did just that for His trusting people.

i. "This does not mean that those who trust God never die from infectious diseases or suffer from an enemy's plot, of course. It means that those who trust God are habitually delivered from such dangers. What Christian cannot testify to many such deliverances?" (Boice)

ii. "Lord Craven, a Christian, was a nobleman who was living in London when plague ravaged the city in the fifteenth century. In order to escape the spreading pestilence Craven determined to leave the city for his country home, as many of his social standing did. He ordered his coach and baggage made ready. But as he was walking down one of the halls of his home about to enter his carriage, he overheard one of his servants say to another, 'I suppose by my lord's quitting London to avoid the plague that his God lives in the country and not in town.' It was a straightforward and apparently innocent remark. But it struck Lord Craven so deeply that he canceled his journey, saying, 'My God lives everywhere and can preserve me in town as well as in the country.

I will stay where I am.' So he stayed in London. He helped the plague victims, and he did not catch the disease himself." (Boice)

iii. There is also a spiritual understanding and application of this. "The soul hath likewise her enemies, ready to attack and surprise her at all hours." (Horne)

iv. "Children of God are not always immune from physical plague and pestilence; but they are ever guarded from destructive spiritual forces as they dwell in the secret place of the Most High." (Morgan)

c. **He shall cover you with His feathers**: In a metaphor, God is represented as a bird, sheltering young chicks **under His wings** – as David previously described in Psalm 61:4.

i. "The mother eagle, spreading her…wing over her eaglets, is a wonderful symbol of the union of power and gentleness." (Maclaren)

ii. "Saith Luther; it is faith which maketh thee the little chicken, and Christ the hen; that thou mayest hide, and hope, and hover, and cover under his wings; for there is health in his wings." (Trapp)

iii. Boice connected Matthew 23:37 to verse 4: "Jesus would have saved and sheltered Jerusalem and its inhabitants, but the people were not willing. They would not come to him. They would not 'dwell' in the shelter of the Most High. They cried out for his crucifixion instead." (Boice)

d. **His truth shall be your shield and buckler**: The pictures of God's protection continue with **His truth** represented as the smaller, often round **shield** and the larger, often rectangular shield, the **buckler**.

i. "As for God's care, it combines the warm protectiveness of a parent bird with the hard, unyielding strength of armour." (Kidner)

ii. **Shield and buckler**: "Double armour has he who relies upon the Lord. He bears a shield and wears an all-surrounding coat of mail." (Spurgeon)

iii. Boice on **buckler**: "The Hebrew word signifies something that is wrapped around a person for his or her protection; hence, it can mean 'buckler,' 'armor,' or, as in the NIV, a 'rampart' or fortress."

3. (5-6) The result of God's protection and care.

You shall not be afraid of the terror by night,
***Nor* of the arrow *that* flies by day,**
***Nor* of the pestilence *that* walks in darkness,**
***Nor* of the destruction *that* lays waste at noonday.**

a. **You shall not be afraid**: Having God as a shelter and refuge gives strength and courage to the people of God. When God's people are stuck deep in fear, it is an indication that they fall short of proper trust in God as protector and comforter.

> i. "Not to be afraid is in itself an unspeakable blessing, since for every suffering which we endure from real injury we are tormented by a thousand griefs which arise from fear only." (Spurgeon)

> ii. "In life the Lord may permit many terrible things to happen to his children (cf. Job), as he did to his own Son, our Lord. But his children know that no power is out of God's control." (VanGemeren)

b. **Of the terror by night, nor of the arrow that flies by day**: The psalmist represented all kinds of destruction that could come in all kinds of circumstances. It could come **by night** or **by day**, **in darkness** or **at noonday**. It could come as **terror** or by **arrow**, as a **pestilence** or as **destruction**. Whenever or however it comes, God is able to defend His people.

> i. "The assaults of enemies and the devastations of pestilence are taken in Psalm 91:5-6 as types of all perils." (Maclaren)

4. (7-8) Assurance for the believer.

A thousand may fall at your side,
And ten thousand at your right hand;
***But* it shall not come near you.**
Only with your eyes shall you look,
And see the reward of the wicked.

a. **A thousand may fall at your side**: The psalmist described how God's protection could conquer any odds or probabilities. God's protection and care could be so specifically focused that it can preserve one in **ten thousand**.

> i. "It is impossible that any ill should happen to the man who is beloved of the Lord; the most crushing calamities can only shorten his journey and hasten him to his reward. Ill to him is no ill, but only good in a mysterious form. Losses enrich him, sickness is his medicine, reproach is his honour, death is his gain. No evil in the strict sense of the word can happen to him, for everything is overruled for good." (Spurgeon)

b. **See the reward of the wicked**: In contrast to the protection of His chosen, God has also appointed a **reward** for the **wicked**. God's people are encouraged to **look** at this truth and carefully consider it.

B. The assurance repeated twice over.

1. (9-13) Repeating the promise of deliverance and assurance of victory.

Because you have made the LORD, *who is* **my refuge,**
Even **the Most High, your dwelling place,**
No evil shall befall you,
Nor shall any plague come near your dwelling;
For He shall give His angels charge over you,
To keep you in all your ways.
In *their* **hands they shall bear you up,**
Lest you dash your foot against a stone.
You shall tread upon the lion and the cobra,
The young lion and the serpent you shall trample underfoot.

a. **Because you have made the LORD...your dwelling place**: The principles and promises in verses 10 through 16 are directed towards those who trust in the LORD, making Him their **dwelling place** – their source of life and satisfaction.

b. **No evil shall befall you**: The previous promises (verses 5-8) of security and safety even in a time of **plague** are repeated. Again, this is not regarded as an absolute promise for every believer in every circumstance, because beloved people of God *have* fallen to evil or died in plague. It is the happy expectation of the psalmist and a general expression of God's protection, comfort, and care for His people.

i. "Martin Luther wrote that this refers to 'one who really dwells and does not merely appear to dwell and does not just imagine that he dwells' in God." (Boice)

ii. "This and such-like promises are not to be understood absolutely and universally, as if no truly good man could be cut off by the plague or other common calamities, which is confimed both by other plain texts of Scripture, and by unquestionable experience." (Poole)

iii. "For it may befall a saint to share in a common calamity; as the good corn and weeds are cut down together, but for a different end and purpose." (Trapp)

iv. "God doth not say no afflictions shall befall us, but no evil." (Watson, cited in Spurgeon)

c. **Nor shall any plague come near your dwelling**: Charles Spurgeon gave remarkable testimony to a specific fulfillment of this promise:

i. "In the year 1854, when I had scarcely been in London twelve months, the neighbourhood in which I laboured was visited by Asiatic cholera, and my congregation suffered from its inroads. Family after family summoned me to the bedside of the smitten, and almost every day I was called to visit the grave. I gave myself up with youthful ardour to the visitation of the sick, and was sent for from all corners of the district by persons of all ranks and religions. I became weary in body and sick at heart. My friends seemed falling one by one, and I felt or fancied that I was sickening like those around me. A little more work and weeping would have laid me low among the rest; I felt that my burden was heavier than I could bear, and I was ready to sink under it. As God would have it, I was returning mournfully home from a funeral, when my curiosity led me to read a paper which was wafered up in a shoemaker's window in the Dover Road. It did not look like a trade announcement, nor was it, for it bore in a good bold handwriting these words: '*Because thou hast made the Lord, which is my refuge, even the most High, thy habitation; there shall no evil befall thee, neither shall any plague come nigh thy dwelling.*' The effect upon my heart was immediate. Faith appropriated the passage as her own. I felt secure, refreshed, girt with immortality. I went on with my visitation of the dying in a calm and peaceful spirit; I felt no fear of evil, and I suffered no harm. The providence which moved the tradesman to place those verses in his window I gratefully acknowledge, and in the remembrance of its marvellous power I adore the Lord my God." (Spurgeon)

d. **For He shall give His angels charge over you**: This describes another way God may send His protection and care unto His people – through **His angels**, commanding them to **keep** and **bear...up** His people.

i. "The *angels of God* shall have an especial charge to accompany, defend, and preserve thee; and against their power, the influence of evil spirits cannot prevail. These will, when necessary, turn thy steps out of the way of danger; ward it off when it comes in thy ordinary path." (Clarke)

ii. "Charge; charge is a strict command, more than a bare command; as when you would have a servant do a business certainly and fully, you lay a charge upon him, I charge you that you do not neglect that business; you do not barely tell what he should do, prescribe him his work, but you charge him to do it. So says the Lord unto the angels." (Bridge, cited in Spurgeon)

iii. "Not one guardian angel, as some fondly dream, but all the angels are here alluded to.... They have received commission from their Lord and ours to watch carefully over all the interests of the faithful." (Spurgeon)

iv. "How angels thus keep us we cannot tell. Whether they repel demons, counteract spiritual plots, or even ward off the subtler physical forces of disease, we do not know. Perhaps we shall one day stand amazed at the multiplied services which the unseen bands have rendered to us." (Spurgeon)

v. "Let us remember that it is GOD, whose these angels are; HE gives them charge – from HIM they receive their commission – to HIM they are responsible for their charge. From God thou art to expect them; and for their help he alone is to receive the praise. It is expressly said, *He shall give his angels charge*; to show that they are not to be *prayed to* nor *praised*; but GOD *alone*, whose *servants* they are." (Clarke)

e. **For He shall give His angels charge over you**: The promise in verses 11 and 12 was quoted and twisted by Satan in His temptation of Jesus in the wilderness (Matthew 4:5-7, Luke 4:9-12). Satan tempted Jesus to create an artificial crisis by throwing Himself from a high point on the temple mount, and Satan quoted Psalm 91:11-12 as a promise of protection if Jesus were to do this.

i. As Matthew 4 records, Satan's quotation of Psalm verses 11 and 12 is a pattern of how he twists the Word of God.

- Verses 11 and 12 were *falsely quoted*, because the devil left out the words **to keep you in all your ways**. To test God in this way was *not* Jesus' way; it was not the way of the Savior. "God had never promised, nor ever given, any protection of angels in sinful and forbidden ways." (Poole on Matthew 4)

- This text is *wrongly applied*, because it was not used to teach or encourage, but intended instead to deceive: "…making this word a promise to be fulfilled upon Christ's neglect of his duty; extending the promise of special providence as to dangers into which men voluntarily throw themselves." (Poole on Matthew 4)

ii. In a strange way we are grateful for Satan's attempt in Matthew 4, because it helps us better understand Psalm 91. We see that it does not give absolute promises for every believer in every circumstance, but beautiful promises of God's protection, comfort, and care that are specifically received and applied in the believer by the Holy Spirit.

iii. The angels were there to help Jesus in His temptation, just not in the way the devil suggested (Matthew 4:11).

f. **You shall tread upon the lion and the cobra**: The protection of God to His people extends beyond the general deliverance from harm; it also speaks of a general granting of victory to His people, even over opponents as strong as the **young lion** and the **cobra**.

i. These words are "…depicting God's servants not merely as survivors but as victors, who *trample* deadly enemies *under foot.*" (Kidner)

ii. There is another interesting connection with the temptation of Jesus in the wilderness. "The Lord's trust in his Father also resulted in Satan's defeat, another part of the psalm the devil omitted." (Boice)

2. (14-16) God's promise to and blessing over the one who loves Him.

"Because he has set his love upon Me, therefore I will deliver him;
I will set him on high, because he has known My name.
He shall call upon Me, and I will answer him;
I *will be* with him in trouble;
I will deliver him and honor him.
With long life I will satisfy him,
And show him My salvation."

a. **Because he has set his love upon Me**: These last three verses are set in the first person as God speaks promise and blessing over His people. He speaks specifically over those who **set** their **love upon** Him. It has been wonderfully noted that the last words of this psalm are not spoken *by* God's people, but *to* God's people.

i. **He has set his love upon Me**: This "…is used elsewhere in contexts of setting one's heart on somebody or on some enterprise. As man's commitment to God it comes only here." (Kidner)

ii. To **set** one's **love upon** God means to do it by choice. He does not wait for the feeling of love to come, but simply chooses to think and act towards God in ways that express and build love. This would include:

- Spending time with God.
- Listening to God.
- Reading what God has written to us.
- Speaking to God.
- Thinking of God in unoccupied moments.
- Adoring God.
- Speaking of God to others.
- Giving to God and making glad sacrifices to Him and for Him.

iii. Our present culture often thinks of love as something that happens to people, not something chosen. The phrase **because he has set his love on Me** reminds us that a significant aspect of love is indeed a choice, and this describes in part the love we should give unto God.

b. **Therefore I will deliver Him**: The promises and principles stated previously in this psalm are repeated again, but this time from the perspective of God Himself. God will protect His beloved and **set him on high** – and do it **because he has known My name**, having a real relationship with God.

i. **I will set him on high**: "I will place him *out of the reach* of all his enemies. I will *honour* and *ennoble* him, *because he hath known my name* – because he has loved, honoured, and served me, and rendered me that worship which is my due. He has *known* me to be the God of infinite mercy and love." (Clarke)

ii. "There are blessings that some believers miss out on, simply because they are always fretting and do not trust God as they should. Here the psalmist quotes God as saying that the blessings are for those who love God and acknowledge his name (verse 14), call upon him (verse 15), and seek satisfaction in what he alone can provide." (Boice)

c. **He shall call upon Me, and I will answer him**: God promises to answer the prayer of the one who loves Him, and the one who genuinely knows Him.

d. **I will be with him**: In the last lines of the psalm, God spoke personal and wonderful blessings over the one who loves and knows Him:

- The blessing of His presence: **I will be with him in trouble.**
- The blessing of His protection: **I will deliver him.**
- The blessing of His promotion: **I will...honor him.**
- The blessing of His prosperity: **With long life I will satisfy him.**
- The blessing of His preservation: **And show him My salvation.**

i. **I will be with him**: "So, no man need add solitude to sadness, but may have God sitting with him, like Job's friends, waiting to comfort him with true comfort." (Maclaren)

ii. **I will be with him in trouble**: "Again God speaks and acts like a tender-hearted mother towards a sickly child. When the child is in perfect health she can leave it in the hands of the nurse; but when it is sick she will attend it herself; she will say to the nurse, 'You may attend a while to some other business, I will watch over the child myself.'" (Dawson, cited in Spurgeon)

Psalm 92 – The Goodness of Giving Thanks to the LORD

This psalm is titled **A Psalm. A Song for the Sabbath day**. *It is the only psalm so titled and was perhaps a song to be sung and meditated on the Sabbath. Derek Kidner observed: "This Song for the Sabbath is proof enough, if such were needed, that the Old Testament sabbath was a day not only for rest but for corporate worship ('a holy convocation,' Lev. 23:3), and intended to be a delight rather than a burden."*

"The Jews have for a long while used this Psalm in the synagogue-worship on their Sabbath, and very suitable it is for the Sabbath-day; not so much in appearance, for there is little or no allusion to any Sabbatic rest in it, but because on that day above all others, our thoughts should be lifted up from all earthly things to God himself." (Charles Spurgeon)

A. Giving thanks.

1. (1-3) The manner of giving thanks.

It is good to give thanks to the LORD,
And to sing praises to Your name, O Most High;
To declare Your lovingkindness in the morning,
And Your faithfulness every night,
On an instrument of ten strings,
On the lute,
And on the harp,
With harmonious sound.

> a. **It is good to give thanks to the LORD:** This Sabbath psalm begins with a simple yet profound statement. It is a **good** thing **to give thanks** to Yahweh, the covenant God of Israel and the Maker of heaven and earth.

> • It is good because thanks to our Creator is appropriate.

> • It is good because thanks to our Covenant Redeemer is fitting.

- It is good because thanks to the One who blesses and delivers us is right.
- It is good because thanks to the One who is all-good is always good.
- It is good because thanks to God does us benefit.
- It is good because thanks to God sets an example for others to do the same.
- It is good because a mere attitude of thankfulness is not enough.

i. Giving thanks to God is more than *right*; it is also **good**: "…good, no doubt, in the sense that, in love, he values it, as he valued his creation; but also in the sense that it uplifts and liberates us." (Kidner)

ii. "The statement seems an obvious one; no one will be inclined to contradict it. Yet how little we know of this highest function of worship, that of offering the pure sacrifice of praise." (Morgan)

iii. "Go carefully and thoroughly through the ordinary services of our churches, whether the form be liturgical or what we designate free, or extempore, and note how small a part of them is devoted to the giving of thanks." (Morgan)

iv. "The devout heart feels that worship is 'good,' not only as being acceptable to God and conformable to man's highest duty, but as being the source of delight to the worshipper." (Maclaren)

b. **And to sing praises to Your name, O Most High**: Hebrew poetry often uses parallelism, repeating an idea with similar words. This is an example of this, with the second phrase repeating the essential idea of the first. Therefore, for the psalmist, to **sing praises** to God's **name** is very much like giving **thanks to the LORD**. Singing is a valid and wonderful expression of gratitude to God.

i. "It is good to give thanks in the form of vocal song. Nature itself teaches us thus to express our gratitude to God; do not the birds sing, and the brooks warble as they flow?" (Spurgeon)

ii. "Our personal experience has confirmed us in the belief that it is good to sing unto the Lord; we have often felt like Luther when he said, '*Come,* let us sing a Psalm, and drive away the devil.'" (Spurgeon)

c. **To declare Your lovingkindness in the morning**: Proclaiming God's **lovingkindness** (*hesed*, the great word for God's loyal, covenant love) and **faithfulness** is another way to give thanks to the LORD. This declaration is not only to be made on the good days or nights, but **every night**.

i. "The 'mercy' of God in promising salvation, and his 'faithfulness' in accomplishing it, are inexhaustible subjects for 'morning and evening' praises." (Horne)

ii. "Eagerly and promptly should we magnify the Lord; we leave unpleasant tasks as long as we can, but our hearts are so engrossed with the adoration of God that we would rise betimes to attend to it. There is a peculiar freshness and charm about early morning praises; the day is loveliest when it first opens its eyelids, and God himself seems then to make distribution of the day's manna, which tastes most sweetly if gathered ere the sun is hot." (Spurgeon)

iii. This kind of heartfelt praise gives honor to God. "We talk as if, really, we were to be pitied for living, as if we were little better off than toads under a hallow, or snails in a tub of salt. We whine as if our lives were martyrdoms, and every breath a woe. But it is not so. Such conduct slanders the good Lord." (Spurgeon)

iv. **Your faithfulness every night**: "We have a day's more experience than we had in the morning; therefore we have more power to sing of God's faithfulness." (Spurgeon)

d. **On an instrument**: Worship and honor to God may be expressed in music, with a variety of instruments. However, it should be done **with harmonious sound**, meaning that those who dedicate their music to serving God and His people should endeavor to be **harmonious** and excellent in their presentation of the music.

i. "I know that there is a tradition in the church that opposes the use of musical instruments in worship, but I do not see how it can stand in the light of these and other Bible passages." (Boice)

ii. The first three verses of this psalm show that worshipping and honoring God have many different aspects and expressions. We should worship God in any available and honoring way.

- It may be thanksgiving, singing, or declaration.
- It may be because of who He is (**the Lord, Most High**) or because of what He has done (expressed in acts of **lovingkindness** and **faithfulness**).
- It may be done at day or night.
- It may be done with singing and with instrumental music.

2. (4) The reason for giving thanks.

For You, Lord, have made me glad through Your work;
I will triumph in the works of Your hands.

a. **For You, Lord**: The emphasis is on God's personal work. This is what *He Himself* has done.

b. **Have made me glad through Your work**: Sometimes God's servants grumble about His works and ways. The way of the psalmist is far better, to be **made glad** through the **work** of God.

i. "The acts of God are not to be separated from his nature ('love,' 'faithfulness'; cf. v. 2), because his "deeds" are expressive of his nature." (VanGemeren)

c. **I will triumph in the works of Your hands**: The focus is entirely on God, and not on self. The **triumph** is found not in what we do for God, but on what God has done with his own **hands**.

B. God's works for His people and His enemies.

1. (5-6) God's great thoughts.

O Lord, how great are Your works!
Your thoughts are very deep.
A senseless man does not know,
Nor does a fool understand this.

a. **How great are Your works**: Having brought up the idea of God's works in the previous lines, the psalmist now declares **how great** those works are.

i. **How great are Your works**: "They are multitudinous, stupendous, and splendid: *and thy thoughts* – thy designs and counsels, *from* which, *by* which, and *in reference* to which, they have been formed; *are very deep* – so profound as not to be fathomed by the comprehension of man." (Clarke)

ii. "The struggles of faith with unbelief...are ended for this singer. He bows in trustful adoration before the greatness of the works and the unsearchable depth of the purpose of God which directs the works." (Maclaren)

iii. "But how doth the regenerate soul exult and triumph, at beholding that 'work' of God's 'hand' whereby he hath created all things anew in Christ Jesus!" (Horne)

b. **Your thoughts are very deep**: First among God's **works**, the psalmist spoke of the great intelligence of God. God's knowledge is not only broad, touching absolutely everything; it is also **very deep**, knowing all things about everything.

i. **Your thoughts are very deep**: "Verily, my brethren, there is no sea so deep as these thoughts of God, who maketh the wicked flourish, and the good suffer: nothing so profound, nothing so deep: therein every unbelieving soul is wrecked, in that depth, in that profundity. Dost thou wish to cross this depth? Remove not from the wood of Christ's cross; and thou shalt not sink: hold thyself fast to Christ." (Augustine, cited in Spurgeon)

c. **A senseless man does not know**: The **senseless** and the **fool** don't **understand** that God is infinitely smarter and greater than they are. It's very hard for some people to accept that God knows more than they do, and it can be even more difficult to really live as if that is true.

i. The **senseless man** doesn't understand the greatness of God as described in verse 5. Nor does he understand the coming judgment (despite present prosperity) described in verse 7.

ii. **A senseless man**: "*Ish baar*, the human hog – the stupid bear – the *boor*; the man who is all flesh; in whom *spirit* or *intellect* neither seems to work nor exist. The *brutish man*, who never attempts to see God in his works." (Clarke)

iii. "The word "senseless" (*ba'ar*, v. 6; cf. 49:10; 73:22; Prov 12:1; 30:2) is expressive of animal-like behavior. As an animal shows no perception or analytic ability, so the fool has no common sense (cf. Isa 1:2)." (VanGemeren)

iv. Boice suggested a connection to Psalm 8: "By calling him 'a little lower than the heavenly beings' rather than 'a little higher than the beasts,' it indicates that it is man's calling to look up to God and become like God, in whose image he is made. But if he will not look up, the only place he will be able to look is down, and he will begin to behave like an animal." (Boice)

2. (7-9) God judges His enemies.

When the wicked spring up like grass,
And when all the workers of iniquity flourish,
***It is* that they may be destroyed forever.**
But You, LORD, *are* on high forevermore.
For behold, Your enemies, O LORD,
For behold, Your enemies shall perish;
All the workers of iniquity shall be scattered.

a. **When the wicked spring up like grass**: The psalmist saw many times when **the wicked** seemed to prosper. They grew quickly **like grass** and seemed to **flourish**. Yet he also knew that their prosperity was only the prelude to their destruction (**it is that they may be destroyed forever**).

i. **Spring up...flourish**: "The apparent success of the wicked is as a pleasant slope that leads downward. The quicker the blossoming, the sooner the petals fall." (Maclaren)

ii. "The favour of God towards man is not to be known by outward prosperity; nor is his disapprobation to be known by the adverse circumstances in which any person may be found. When, however, we see the wicked flourish, we may take for granted that their *abuse* of God's mercies will cause him to cut them off as cumberers of the ground; and, dying in their sins, *they are destroyed for ever.*" (Clarke)

iii. **Destroyed forever**: "Destruction *'for ever'* is a portion far too terrible for the mind to realise. Eye hath not seen, nor ear heard, the full terror of the wrath to come!" (Spurgeon)

iv. "Little do they think that they are suffered to prosper that like *beasts* they may be fitter for slaughter. The fatter they are, the fitter for slaughter, and the sooner slain." (Bogan, cited in Spurgeon)

b. **But You, LORD, are on high forevermore**: In contrast to the wicked who have only temporary prosperity, God is set **on high forevermore**. His **enemies shall perish** and all the wicked **shall be scattered**.

c. **For behold, Your enemies, O LORD**: The phrase is repeated for emphasis. Those **enemies** of the LORD will be destroyed, and God's people are called upon to **behold** this as another of God's great works.

i. "The psalmist, by this demonstrative particle 'lo,' [**behold**] points to it as it were with the finger, as a thing most evident and undoubted." (Trapp)

ii. In the end, God is determined to destroy those who make themselves His **enemies**. "That is a weak and perilous tenderness which permits evil to continue its work of destruction. That is a strong and tender pity which without relenting, smites evil, and destroys it." (Morgan)

iii. Kidner on verse 9: "This verse, with its cumulative force, is noticeably similar to certain lines from Ugarit, written some centuries earlier. If these were well known, the present verse could be a pointed assertion that it is the Lord, not Baal, who will triumph, and that his victory will rid the world of evil, rather than relieve a mere nature-god of his rivals." (Kidner)

3. (10-11) The psalmist's experience of blessing and deliverance.

But my horn You have exalted like a wild ox;
I have been anointed with fresh oil.
My eye also has seen *my desire* on my enemies;

My ears hear *my desire* on the wicked
Who rise up against me.

> a. **My horn You have exalted like a wild ox**: The **horn** was a symbol of strength and might. The wicked are destroyed (verse 7), but the righteous have their strength **exalted**.

>> i. **A wild ox**: The power and ferocity of this animal was proverbial." (VanGemeren)

>> ii. "The imagery of 'horn' also evokes the metaphor of 'oil,' as oil was poured from a horn (cf. 1 Sam 16:13)." (VanGemeren)

> b. **I have been anointed with fresh oil**: The **anointing with fresh oil** brought refreshment and honor: the blessing and power and enabling of God poured out upon the one **anointed**.

>> i. **With fresh oil**: "Each morning bend your heads, ye priests of the Most High, for the fresh anointing for the new ministries that await you. The former grace and strength will not suffice; old texts must be rejuvenated and reminted; old vows must be re-spoken; the infilling of the Holy Spirit must be as vivid, and may be as definite, as at the first." (Meyer)

>> ii. "Sometimes, when we meet with believers who are full of grace, full of patience, full of courage, full of zeal, full of love, we say, 'I can never get where they are.' Yes, we can, for we shall be anointed with fresh oil, and if we obtain fresh grace there is no place of eminence we cannot reach." (Spurgeon)

>> iii. "*Fresh oil*, in such a context, speaks eloquently of a renewed anointing…or consecration, to serve God. There may be the additional thought of preparing a 'living sacrifice', since the verb is used elsewhere not for anointing but for moistening the meal-offering with oil before presenting it at the altar (Exod. 29:40)." (Kidner)

> c. **My eye has also seen my desire on my enemies**: The psalmist had the additional blessing of *seeing* his triumph over his enemies. Victory is assured for the people of God (Romans 8:37), but sometimes it is only understood by faith and not seen with the natural eye.

>> i. "It is intended to express an assurance of faith, a humble confidence in the promises of God, that our efforts shall at length be crowned with victory over every thing which reisteth and opposeth itself; and that the day is coming, when we shall view all the enemies of our salvation dead at our feet." (Horne)

4. (12-15) God makes the righteous flourish.

The righteous shall flourish like a palm tree,
He shall grow like a cedar in Lebanon.
Those who are planted in the house of the LORD
Shall flourish in the courts of our God.
They shall still bear fruit in old age;
They shall be fresh and flourishing,
To declare that the LORD is upright;
He is my rock, and *there is* no unrighteousness in Him.

a. **The righteous shall flourish**: The wicked have their season of flourishing (verse 7), but the righteous **shall flourish** like the ever-green **palm tree**. The wicked should understand that this world provides the best they will ever experience, and the righteous should know that this world provides the worst they will experience.

i. **Like a palm tree**: "When we see a noble palm standing erect, sending all its strength upward in one bold column, and growing amid the dearth and drought of the desert, we have a fine picture of the godly man, who in his uprightness aims alone at the glory of God; and, independent of outward circumstances, is made by divine grace to live and thrive where all things else perish." (Spurgeon)

b. **He shall grow like a cedar in Lebanon**: The cedar trees of Lebanon were known for their size, strength, durability, beauty, and usefulness. The blessings to come upon the righteous bring the same attributes.

i. "The *cedar* gives us the idea of *majesty, stability, durableness*, and *incorruptibility*." (Clarke)

c. **Those who are planted in the house of the LORD shall flourish in the courts of our God**: God's house, the place of His presence, is the place where believers are both **planted** and where they continually live and **flourish**. One might say that they are in the presence of the LORD from beginning to end, and they **still bear fruit in old age** – even as Moses did (Deuteronomy 34:7).

i. **Planted in the house of the LORD**: "It is questionable whether there are trees planted in the courts of the Temple; but the psalmist's thought is that the righteous will surely be found there, and that it is their native soil, in which rooted, they are permanent." (Maclaren)

ii. **Still bear fruit in old age**: "It is not the greenness of perpetual youth, but the freshness of age without sterility, like that of Moses whose 'eye was not dim, nor his natural force abated' (Deut. 34:7); whose wisdom was mature and his memory invaluably rich." (Trapp)

iii. As 2 Corinthians 4:16 indicates, it is possible to be outwardly wasting away, yet inwardly renewed day by day. "When their natural strength decayeth, it shall be renewed; their last days shall be their best days, wherein as they shall grow in grace, so they shall increase in comfort and blessedness." (Meyer)

iv. "I once heard a good Christian man say that he was confessing a fault. He said, 'I am afraid that the fruit of my old age is peevishness.' 'No,' I said, 'that is not a fruit of your old age; it is a fruit of your old nature.' But the fruit of old age, where there is grace in old age, should be patience." (Spurgeon)

d. **To declare that the LORD is upright**: This is why the people of God live in a blessed way that gives honor and attention to God (**bear fruit**). It isn't to draw attention to themselves as wonderful people, but to shout out **that the LORD is upright**.

i. "'That the Lord is upright.' Well, how does the fruit-bearing of an aged Christian show that? Why, it shows that God has kept his promise. He has promised that he will never leave them nor forsake them. There you see it. He has promised that when they are weak they shall be strong. There you see it. He has promised that if they seek him they shall not lack any good thing. There you see it." (Spurgeon)

e. **He is my rock, and there is no unrighteousness in Him**: This was the confident, proven experience of the psalmist. He knew from both understanding and life experience that God could be trusted and did all things in goodness.

Psalm 93 – The Lord Reigns

There is no title to this psalm in the Hebrew text. It is a short, bold declaration of God's might, power, and holiness. G. Campbell Morgan said of Psalm 93, "Interpretation is almost an impertinence. Let it be done reverently."

"Psalm 93 describes a theocracy, as do the seven psalms that follow it. The words Yahweh melek *('Jehovah reigns' or 'Jehovah is king') are the watchwords of these theocratic psalms." (James Montgomery Boice)*

A. The majesty of God.

1. (1) God's majesty expressed by His raiment.

The Lord reigns, He is clothed with majesty;
The Lord is clothed,
He has girded Himself with strength.
Surely the world is established, so that it cannot be moved.

a. **The Lord reigns**: Psalm 93 begins suddenly and wonderfully with the proclamation of Yahweh's rule. This lifts the covenant God of Israel over every idol and pretender of sovereignty.

 i. **The Lord reigns**: "The emphatic position of 'the Lord' in the Masoretic Text leaves no ambiguity in the affirmation that it is Yahweh, and no other deity, who reigns in glory." (VanGemeren)

 ii. "There is a decisiveness in the Hebrew for *The Lord reigns* which at least calls for an exclamation mark (as in Today's English Version, 'The Lord is king!'). It has the ring of a proclamation." (Kidner)

 iii. "What can give greater joy to a loyal subject than a sight of the king in his beauty? Let us repeat the proclamation, *'the* Lord reigneth,' whispering it in the ears of the desponding, and publishing it in the face of the foe." (Spurgeon)

 iv. "This psalm was written in all likelihood after some deliverance Jehovah wrought for His people, but through the open window

111

the singer, consciously or unconsciously, saw the far distant light of another day in which the Kingdom of God will be set up in His might, and the song of an established order shall be the anthem of His praise." (Morgan)

b. **He is clothed with majesty**: God is adorned with the garments fitting His sovereignty; He is clothed with **majesty** and **strength**. They surround and mark Him like clothing marks the man.

i. **Clothed with majesty**: "He hath now put off his arms [armor], and put on his robes, he will henceforth rule all wisely and righteously." (Trapp)

ii. **With majesty**: "Majesty is a hard idea to define, but it has to do with dignity, authority of sovereign power, stateliness, and grandeur. It is the proper characteristic of earthly monarchs, who have often gone to great lengths to enhance the impression of their majesty by multiplications of trappings of power. But it is supremely the attribute of him who is the Monarch over all and who does not need to multiply the trappings of his power." (Boice)

iii. "Every verse of this song, except the last, reverberates with doubled or even trebled expressions, a powerful feature which it shares with some of the earliest biblical and Canaanite poetry." (Kidner)

c. **Surely the world is established**: God's strength and majesty are not only displayed by His person, but also by what He *does*. In his **strength**, **majesty**, and genius, God has constructed a **world** that is firmly **established** and **cannot be moved** – unless *He* moves it.

2. (2) God's majesty expressed by His throne.

Your throne *is* established from of old;
You *are* from everlasting.

a. **Your throne is established from of old**: Not only is the world established, but so is the **throne** of God. His reign is without challenge. There are rebels against His reign, but they do not have the slightest chance of success.

i. "Earthly thrones are temporary; they are set up and cast down against, neither is any trust to be reposed in them. But the throne of Christ is eternal and unchangeable. Constituted before the foundation of the world, it is to endure when no traces of such a system having once existed shall any more be found." (Horne)

ii. "And this kingdom of thine is no new or upstart kingdom, as it may seem to the ignorant world, but the most ancient of all kingdoms, being from everlasting to everlasting, although it was not always equally manifested in the world." (Poole)

b. **You are from everlasting**: God's eternal authority extends to His very being. He is eternal in a sense none other is; His life is without a beginning and without an ending. In these and in other ways, God stands majestically above and beyond His creation.

i. "There never was a time in which God did not reign, in which he was not a supreme and absolute Monarch; for he is from *everlasting*. There never was a time in which he was not; there never can be a period in which he shall cease to exist." (Clarke)

B. The might of God.

1. (3-4) His might over creation.

The floods have lifted up, O LORD,
The floods have lifted up their voice;
The floods lift up their waves.
The LORD on high *is* mightier
Than the noise of many waters,
***Than* the mighty waves of the sea.**

a. **The floods have lifted up, O LORD**: There are strong things that seem to oppose God. A flood of water seems unstoppable and unsparing in its destruction. Like the mighty **waves** of the ocean, the **floods** rise up against God with their **voice**.

i. "The figure of the storm-tossed sea is made use of to indicate the strength of this opposition." (Morgan)

ii. "Observe that the Psalmist turns to the Lord when he sees the billows foam, and hears the breakers roar; he does not waste his breath by talking to the waves, or to violent men." (Spurgeon)

b. **The LORD on high is mightier than the noise of many waters**: As fearsome and powerful as the **mighty waves of the sea** are, they are not higher or stronger than God. He reigns over all that might challenge or oppose, and over the mightiest things of this earth.

i. "The sea with its mighty mass of waters, with the constant unrest of its waves, with its ceaseless pressing against the solid land and foaming against the rocks, is an emblem of the Gentile world alienated from and at enmity with God." (Delitzsch, cited in Boice)

ii. **Mightier than the noise of many waters**: "He defeats tyrants and persecutors, be they never so terrible for noise and number. If he but thunder they are hushed, and glad to wriggle, as worms, into their holes." (Trapp)

iii. "He sits as King, higher than the spray is tossed, deeper than the fathomless depths, mightier than the strongest billow. Let Him but say, 'Peace, be still!' and the greatest storm that ever swept the waves with wild fury sinks into the tranquil sleep of childhood." (Meyer)

iv. "The danger may exceed thy resistance, but not God's assistance; the enemies' power may surpass thy strength, their subtlety outwit thy prudence, but neither can excel the wisdom and might of God that is with thee." (Wright, cited in Spurgeon)

2. (5) The might of His holiness.

Your testimonies are very sure;
Holiness adorns Your house,
O LORD, forever.

a. **Your testimonies are very sure**: As in other psalms, **testimonies** is a poetic reference to God's word. The psalmist understood that the might, sovereignty, and strength of God was powerfully expressed in and through His word.

i. **Testimonies** is used more than 20 times in Psalm 119 in reference to God's word. These **testimonies** are connected to previous idea of God's reign in that, "His reign…is revealed in His testimonies – that is, His law, His word to men, is sure." (Morgan)

ii. "As in providence the throne of God is fixed beyond all risk, so in revelation his truth is beyond all question. Other teachings are uncertain, but the revelations of heaven are infallible." (Spurgeon)

b. **Holiness adorns Your house**: This mighty God is *holy*, different from any man or woman. His power is holy power and His sovereignty is a holy sovereignty. His **holiness** is connected to all He is and does, and could be said to adorn His very **house**. This is true both for the representation of His **house** on earth (the temple under the Old Covenant) and His ultimate **house** in heaven.

i. If taken as an exhortation to God's people to display holiness as His inheritance, His **house**, this idea has parallels in the New Testament:

- *If anyone defiles the temple of God, God will destroy him. For the temple of God is holy, which temple you are* (1 Corinthians 3:17).

- *But you are a chosen generation, a royal priesthood, a holy nation, His own special people, that you may proclaim the praises of Him who called you out of darkness into His marvelous light* (1 Peter 2:9).

ii. "If we are not holy, how can we adorn the house of God? We cannot! We do the very opposite. We dishonor it – and the God we profess to serve." (Boice)

iii. "Thy *nature* is holy, all thy *works* are holy, and thy *word* is holy; therefore, thy *house* – thy *Church*, should be holy. The *building* itself should be *sanctified* – should be so *consecrated* to thy worship alone, that it shall never be employed in any other service. The *ministers* of this Church should be holy, the *members* holy, the *ordinances* holy; its *faith*, its *discipline*, and its *practice* holy. And this at all times, and in all circumstances; for holiness becometh thine house – for ever." (Clarke)

c. **O LORD, forever**: God's great being and character – His might, sovereignty, strength, and holiness – are His eternally. He is *from everlasting* (Psalm 93:2) and unchanging; He is **forever**. He will not diminish or devalue with time.

i. **Forever**: "*For evermore* is literally 'to length of days', as in the final phrase of Psalm 23. Here, as there, the length is undefined, and it is left to the New Testament to explore it further and find it as eternal as God himself (Rev. 21:22-22:5)." (Kidner)

ii. "Is all this so? Does Jehovah reign? Then let us offer the sacrifices of praise and thanksgiving. He is worthy to receive; and in our giving, there is also the receiving of the benefits of His reign which enrich and glorify our lives." (Morgan)

Psalm 94 – The Lord, My Defense

"In this song we see how the very things which assault faith, and threaten to produce despair, may be made the opportunity for praise, in the place and act of worship." (G. Campbell Morgan)

A. The rebellious and wicked who must hear and obey God.

1. (1-3) Recognizing God as Judge of the earth.

O Lord God, to whom vengeance belongs—
O God, to whom vengeance belongs, shine forth!
Rise up, O Judge of the earth;
Render punishment to the proud.
Lord, how long will the wicked,
How long will the wicked triumph?

a. **O Lord God, to whom vengeance belongs**: The psalmist begins with the simple and profound recognition that **vengeance belongs** to God. He sees and judges righteously among mankind and will bring **vengeance** as appropriate.

- This means that vengeance does not belong to man.

- This means that vengeance belongs to One who sees more than we see and knows more than we know.

- This means it is appropriate to ask God to dispense vengeance and trust His superior knowledge, wisdom, and timing in doing so.

    i. In Jeremiah 51:56, God is given the title, *the God of recompense*, and we are assured, *He will surely repay*.

    ii. "God is the author of *retributive justice*, as well as of *mercy*. This retributive justice is what we often term *vengeance*, but perhaps improperly; for vengeance with us signifies an excitement of *angry passions*, in order to *gratify* a *vindictive spirit*, which supposes itself to have received some real injury; whereas what is here referred to is that simple act of justice which gives to all their due." (Clarke)

iii. "Dr. Samuel Johnson, the maker of the first great English dictionary, made the distinction well when he said, 'Revenge is an act of passion, vengeance of justice; injuries are revenged, crimes are avenged.'" (Boice)

b. **O God, to whom vengeance belongs, shine forth**: The repetition of the statement adds more than emphasis and intensity. It also connects God's **vengeance** with His glory, His *shining forth*. In the end, vengeance upon sin and sinners is part of God's own glory.

i. Maclaren spoke to the repetition of the request: "A man in straits continues to cry for help till it comes, or till he sees it coming."

ii. "The prayer for Yahweh to 'shine forth' is a prayer for a theophany, when the Lord appears in his royal splendor to bring justice into a world of anarchy." (VanGemeren)

c. **Rise up, O Judge of the earth**: The psalmist has committed the work of vengeance to God but will still pray that God fulfills His office and will **render punishment to the proud**.

i. Morgan described how, through the centuries, God's persecuted people have prayed like this: "In catacombs, in dungeons, in places of the uttermost desolation – when it has seemed to sense that the way of God was blocked, that His rule was overcome, that all evil things had gained the victory – these songs have arisen, proclaiming Him King, mocking all the vain and foolish thoughts of man, and declaring His ultimate victory."

ii. "They who have no profound loathing of sin, or who have never felt the crushing weight of legalised wickedness, may shrink from such aspirations as the psalmist's, and brand them as ferocious; but hearts longing for the triumph of righteousness will not take offence at them." (Maclaren)

iii. "If the execution of justice be a right thing – and who can deny the fact? – then it must be a very proper thing to desire it; not out of private revenge, in which case a man would hardly dare to appeal to God, but out of sympathy with right, and pity for those who are made wrongfully to suffer." (Spurgeon)

d. **Lord, how long?** This adds a note of urgency to the psalmist's prayer. With a combination of boldness and humility, he asks God to account for the time until this righteous vengeance will be accomplished. Like the souls under the altar, the psalmist cries out, **how long?** (Revelation 6:9-10)

i. "So the only question about the power of evil is *how long*? (94:3); there is no room for the crippling suspicion that God, perhaps, is blind (94:7) or has done a deal with darkness (94:20). Nothing has changed the Sun or corrupted the Judge: it is simply that the night is long (94:1b, 2a)." (Kidner)

ii. **How long?** "Many a time has this bitter complaint been heard in the dungeons of the Inquisition, at the whipping-posts of slavery, and in the prisons of oppression. In due time God will publish his reply, but the full end is not yet." (Spurgeon)

2. (4-7) Recognizing the rebellion of the wicked.

They utter speech, *and* speak insolent things;
All the workers of iniquity boast in themselves.
They break in pieces Your people, O LORD,
And afflict Your heritage.
They slay the widow and the stranger,
And murder the fatherless.
Yet they say, "The LORD does not see,
Nor does the God of Jacob understand."

a. **They utter speech, and speak insolent things**: The first thing noted about the wicked is their *words*. They speak defiant, **insolent things** and they **boast in themselves**. Conversely, a mark of the righteous is their humble, gracious speech.

i. "Words often wound more than swords, they are as hard to the heart as stones to the flesh; and these are poured forth by the ungodly in redundance." (Spurgeon)

b. **They break in pieces Your people, O LORD**: The next thing noted about the wicked is their actions against God's **people**, those who are His **heritage**. They destroy them (**break in pieces**) and **afflict** them. Conversely, a mark of the righteous is their love for God's people.

i. "These tyrants are not necessarily foreign; they may equally be home-born, like the apostate King Manasseh or the cynics of Isaiah 5:18ff." (Kidner)

c. **They slay the widow and the stranger**: The third thing noted about the wicked is their attack against the weak and disadvantaged, extending even to **murder**. Conversely, a mark of the righteous is their care for the weak and disadvantaged.

i. "Must not such inhuman conduct as this provoke the Lord? Shall the tears of widows, the groans of strangers, and the blood of orphans be poured forth in vain? As surely as there is a God in heaven, he will visit those who perpetrate such crimes; though he bear long with them, he will yet take vengeance, and that speedily." (Spurgeon)

d. **The LORD does not see**: The fourth thing about the wicked is their ignorance and arrogance toward God. They deny that He exists in the manner that He is revealed in the Bible. This ignorance of God leads to a deluded arrogance toward Him.

i. "They were blindly wicked because they dreamed of a blind God. When men believe that the eyes of God are dim, there is no reason to wonder that they give full license to their brutal passions." (Spurgeon)

ii. "There is no obligation to speak smooth words to rulers whose rule is injustice and their religion impiety. Ahab had his Elijah, and Herod his John Baptist. The succession has been continued through the ages." (Maclaren)

iii. **The God of Jacob**: "So they call him sarcastically; he who taketh that name to himself, but hath no regard to his people, but gives up his Jacob to the spoil, and to the rage of their enemies." (Poole)

3. (8-11) Rebuking the senseless rebels.

Understand, you senseless among the people;
And *you* fools, when will you be wise?
He who planted the ear, shall He not hear?
He who formed the eye, shall He not see?
He who instructs the nations, shall He not correct,
He who teaches man knowledge?
The LORD knows the thoughts of man,
That they *are* futile.

a. **Understand, you senseless among the people**: The psalmist attempted what some think is a useless mission – to help the **senseless** and **fools** with instruction and understanding. He specifically spoke to those mentioned in the previous verse, who believed God did not see or understand their wickedness.

i. The idea of **senseless** is the same as in Psalm 92:6 – a brutish man, as much animal as human. "You who, though you think yourselves the wisest of men, yet in truth are the most brutish of all people.... You that have only the shape, but not the understanding, of a man in you." (Poole)

b. **He who planted the ear, shall He not hear?** The logic is simple and solid. The God who created the **ear** can hear, and the God who created the **eye** can see. The God of all wisdom and knowledge will hold men and women to account for their lives.

i. "The logic is inescapable, once the premise is accepted that God is our Maker. What the psalm does not contemplate is the crowning absurdity, reserved for modern man, of rejecting even this." (Kidner)

ii. "The psalmist does not say, He that planted the ear, *hath he not an ear?* He that formed the eye, *hath he not eyes?* No; but, Shall he not *hear?* Shall he not *see!* And why does he say so? To prevent the error of humanizing God, of attributing members or corporeal parts to the infinite Spirit." (Clarke)

c. **The LORD knows the thoughts of man**: God's wisdom is so great that He even knows the **thoughts** of men and women. This great God must be appropriately feared, respected, and obeyed. This was important for the **senseless** and **fools** to hear and maybe even understand.

i. The Apostle Paul later quoted Psalm 94:11 in 1 Corinthians 3:20 speaking of God's triumph over the exaltation of defiant human wisdom and knowledge, and in Romans 1:21 speaking of the futility of man's intellect against God.

B. The people of God who must hear and obey His instruction.

1. (12-15) Consolation for God's people – they will never be cast off.

Blessed *is* the man whom You instruct, O LORD,
And teach out of Your law,
That You may give him rest from the days of adversity,
Until the pit is dug for the wicked.
For the LORD will not cast off His people,
Nor will He forsake His inheritance.
But judgment will return to righteousness,
And all the upright in heart will follow it.

a. **Blessed is the man whom You instruct**: Perhaps the senseless and fools will never listen to God, but His people must. He will **instruct** and **teach** them from His word (**out of Your law**).

i. "Here it is the pupil speaking, not the teacher, and the words are a triumph of faith: a positive reaction to present trouble." (Kidner)

ii. "All the chastening in the world, without divine teaching, will never make a man blessed; that man that finds correction attended with instruction, and lashing with lessoning, is a happy man." (Brooks, cited in Spurgeon)

b. **That You may give him rest from the days of adversity**: This is a wonderful promise to those who receive the teaching from God's Word. They have **rest** when the inevitable **days of adversity** come. This **rest** is theirs **until the pit is dug for the wicked,** until God sets all things right in His judgment.

i. "There is rest from evil even while in evil, if we understand the purpose of evil." (Maclaren)

ii. **Days of adversity**: "Remember the martyr-age, and the days of the Covenanters, who were hunted upon the mountains like the partridge. You must not wonder if the easy places of the earth are not yours, and if the sentinel's stern duties should fall to your lot. It is so, and so it must be, for God has so ordained it." (Spurgeon)

iii. **Until the pit is dug for the wicked**: "...until the cold grave hold his body, and hot hell hold his soul." (Trapp)

c. **For the LORD will not cast off His people**: This is beautiful and powerful assurance, given first to Israel under the Old Covenant but extending to the child of God under a better covenant. Some teach that God *did* **cast off** Israel, but this and many other passages contradict that idea. With repetition and emphasis, God insists: **Nor will He forsake His inheritance**.

i. "Even if Satan should come, and whisper to you, 'The Lord has cast thee off,' do not believe it; it cannot be. The devil has his cast-offs, but God has no cast-offs. Sometimes he takes the devil's castaways, and makes them to be the trophies of his mighty grace." (Spurgeon)

d. **Judgment will return to righteousness**: God promises to bring His righteous reign and judgment to all things, bringing satisfaction to **the upright in heart**.

i. "All shall be set to rights, and every one have his due, according to Romans 2:6-10, if not sooner, yet at the day of judgment without fail." (Trapp)

2. (16-19) Comfort for God's people – God will help them.

Who will rise up for me against the evildoers?
Who will stand up for me against the workers of iniquity?
Unless the LORD had been my help,
My soul would soon have settled in silence.
If I say, "My foot slips,"
Your mercy, O LORD, will hold me up.
In the multitude of my anxieties within me,
Your comforts delight my soul.

a. **Who will rise up for me against the evildoers?** The previous lines of this psalm expressed satisfaction in God's ultimate righteous judgment. Now the psalmist considers that this hoped-for day is not yet. He understands and expresses his own limitations in dealing with **evildoers** and **workers of iniquity**.

b. **Unless the LORD had been my help**: His rhetorical question was answered; the LORD **had been** and would be his help against the wicked.

i. "If we could find friends elsewhere, it may be our God would not be so dear to us; but when, after calling upon heaven and earth to help, we meet with no succour but such as comes from the eternal arm, we are led to prize our God, and rest upon him with undivided trust." (Spurgeon)

ii. **Settled in silence**: "The psalmist confesses that he is deeply troubled by the evildoers, even so that he nearly slipped away into the netherworld." (VanGemeren)

c. **Your mercy, O LORD, will hold me up**: God's mercy would sustain him in the difficult day; even when it seemed that his **foot** slipped, he would not fall.

i. **Will hold me up**: "It is a metaphor taken from anything *falling*, that is *propped, shored up*, or *buttressed*. How often does the *mercy* of God thus prevent the ruin of weak believers, and of those who have been unfaithful!" (Clarke)

d. **Your comforts delight my soul**: With enemies and difficulties about him, the psalmist needed help and comfort from God. The LORD answered with many **comforts** that brought **delight** to his **soul**. This rescued him from the **multitude of anxieties within**.

i. **Your comforts**: "How sweet are the comforts of the Spirit! Who can muse upon eternal love, immutable purposes, covenant promises, finished redemption, the risen Saviour, his union with his people, the coming glory, and such like themes, without feeling his heart leaping with joy?" (Spurgeon)

ii. **In the multitude of my anxieties within**: "…whilst my heart was filled with *various and perplexing thoughts*, as this Hebrew word signifies, and tormented with cares and fears about my future state." (Poole)

3. (20-23) Cover for God's people – God is their defense.

Shall the throne of iniquity, which devises evil by law,
Have fellowship with You?
They gather together against the life of the righteous,
And condemn innocent blood.

But the LORD has been my defense,
And my God the rock of my refuge.
He has brought on them their own iniquity,
And shall cut them off in their own wickedness;
The LORD our God shall cut them off.

a. **Shall the throne of iniquity, which devises evil by law, have fellowship with You?** The psalmist knew that wickedness is sometimes found in high places. Some thrones are marked by **iniquity** and some laws are devised by **evil**. Such will never fellowship with God.

i. This suggests the thought from 1 John 1:6: *If we say that we have fellowship with Him, and walk in darkness, we lie and do not practice the truth.*

ii. **Which devises evil by law**: "The height of crime is reached when rulers use the forms of justice as masks for injustice, and give legal sanction to 'mischief.' The ancient world groaned under such travesties of the sanctity of Law; and the modern world is not free from them." (Maclaren)

iii. **Which devises evil by law**: "They legalise robbery and violence, and then plead that it is the law of the land; and so indeed it may be, but it is a wickedness for all that." (Spurgeon)

b. **They gather together against the life of the righteous**: This kind of wickedness was described previously in verses 4-6, condemning **innocent blood**. John described the same wicked heart: *Do not marvel, my brethren, if the world hates you* (1 John 3:13).

i. **They gather together**: "In everything that is *evil*, they are in *unity*. The devil, his angels, and his children, all join and draw together when they have for their object the destruction of the works of the Lord." (Clarke)

c. **But the LORD has been my defense**: Though the wicked who were set against the psalmist were in high places, he had an even greater **defense**. God Himself was **the rock of my refuge**.

i. **My defense...my refuge**: "Having assured the righteous of things God will do for them, the writer now adds a word of personal testimony as if to say that what he has been promising to others he has proved true himself." (Boice)

ii. "In him, even in him alone, we find safety, let the world rage as it may; we ask not aid from man, but are content to flee into the bosom of omnipotence." (Spurgeon)

d. **He has brought on them their own iniquity**: The ultimate doom of the wicked is anticipated. His judgment would be righteous and fitting. Their doom would be connected to **their own iniquity** and **in their own wickedness**. The punishment would fit the crime and those who had cut off others would themselves be cut off. This was his confidence and defense.

i. **He has brought on them their own iniquity**: "That is the punishment of sin. It seems strange that it is so, but sin is the punishment of sin. When a man has once sinned, it is part of his punishment that he is inclined to sin again, and so on *ad infinitum*." (Spurgeon)

ii. The repetition of **cut them off** gives great emphasis to the idea. It also matches the repetition of "vengeance" in the first verse of this psalm. The psalm begins with trusting God to set things right and ends with the same confidence.

Psalm 95 – God Worthy of Our Humble and Obedient Worship

This wonderful psalm is quoted and analyzed in Hebrews 3:7-4:13. There (Hebrews 4:7) it is said to be "in David." This may indicate that David the Son of Jesse was the unattributed author, but it is also possible that the author of Hebrews simply referred to the Book of Psalms as "David's Book."

James Montgomery Boice observed regarding the commentary on Psalm 95 in Hebrews 3:7-4:13: "This is probably the most thorough citing of an Old Testament passage in the New Testament."

A. The how and Whom of worship.

1. (1-2) Worship in many forms.

Oh come, let us sing to the Lord!
Let us shout joyfully to the Rock of our salvation.
Let us come before His presence with thanksgiving;
Let us shout joyfully to Him with psalms.

> a. **Let us sing to the Lord:** The psalmist first mentions honoring God with *song* and doing so in *community*. Singing is not the only way to give honor and worship to God, but it is a chief and important way. Also, importantly, the exhortation is **let us sing** – that it should be done with the community of God's people.

> > i. "The invocation to praise in Psalm 95:1-2, gives a striking picture of the joyful tumult of the Temple worship. Shrill cries of gladness, loud shouts of praise, songs with musical accompaniments, rang simultaneously through the courts." (Maclaren)

> > ii. "Singing expresses human thought emotionally, and Christianity is a feeling religion. More particularly, singing expresses joy, and the Bible's religion at its heart is joyful." (Boice)

iii. Yet we are to **sing to the LORD**. "It is to be feared that very much even of religious singing is not unto the Lord, but unto the ear of the congregation. Above all things we must in our service of song take care that all we offer is with the heart's sincerest and most fervent intent directed towards the Lord himself." (Spurgeon)

b. **Let us shout joyfully**: God should be honored with a happy, enthusiastic heart. There is a place for a somber, reflective mood in worship, but it should not be the dominant tone. God's people have much to **shout joyfully** about.

i. "Before making ourselves small before him (as we must, Psalm 95:6f.), we greet him here with unashamed enthusiasm as our refuge and rescuer (Psalm 95:1)." (Kidner)

ii. "It is a part of Christian duty, and certainly of Christian wisdom, to try to catch that tone of joy in worship which rings in this psalm." (Maclaren)

c. **To the Rock of our salvation**: This is a title for God with both *experiential* and *theological* meaning. It points to a genuine *depth* of both thought and experience. Worship should not be simply saying things about God, but with thought and with a connection to what we have experienced or need to experience from Him.

d. **Let us come before His presence**: This means that worship should be done with a conscious sense of God's **presence**. God's people don't sing into empty space; He is in their **presence** and they are in **His presence**. There is – or should be – a true connection between God and His people in worship.

i. **His presence** doesn't mean God in the holy of holies, symbolized at the ark of the covenant. There could be no invitation to the community to **come before His presence** there. Even when they had the tabernacle and the temple, the Jewish people rightly understood the *spiritual* **presence** of God.

e. **With thanksgiving**: Our worship should express a heart of **thanksgiving** to our God, who has done so much for us.

i. "We are permitted to bring our petitions, and therefore we are in honour bound to bring our thanksgivings." (Spurgeon)

f. **Let us shout joyfully to Him with psalms**: This is what the psalmist himself intended with this psalm. We can also surmise that he turned the attention of God's people to the broader collection of psalms as a source of inspiration for their worship.

2. (3-5) The greatness of the God to be worshipped.

For the LORD is the great God,
And the great King above all gods.
In His hand *are* the deep places of the earth;
The heights of the hills *are* His also.
The sea *is* His, for He made it;
And His hands formed the dry *land.*

a. **For the LORD is the great God**: Understanding the greatness of God helps us to properly worship Him. Most everyone has some sense of awe or appreciation of greatness when in the presence of someone the culture regards as great. This is natural; it is even more natural and appropriate for us to deeply regard Yahweh as **the great God** and **the great King above all gods**.

i. "No doubt the surrounding nations imagined Jehovah to be a merely local deity, the god of a small nation, and therefore one of the inferior deities; the Psalmist utterly repudiates such an idea." (Spurgeon)

ii. Adam Clarke observed regarding verse 3: "The Supreme Being has *three* names here: EL, JEHOVAH, ELOHIM, and we should apply none of them to *false gods*. The *first* implies his *strength*; the *second* his *being* and *essence*; the *third*, his *covenant relation* to mankind."

b. **In His hand are the deep places of the earth**: One way God's greatness is illustrated is by His mastery over creation. From the lowest valley to the highest **hills**, from the **sea** to the **dry land**, God's **hands formed** them.

c. **The sea is His, for He made it**: The oceans and seas of this world belong to God. Whatever nation may make claim on the seas, or the concept of international waters may intend, the psalmist made a specific declaration that **the sea is** God's.

i. "To the heathen, incidentally, *the sea* might represent a power even older than the gods, not conquered without a bitter struggle. It is a far cry from this to the simplicity of *The sea is his, for he made it*." (Kidner)

ii. John Trapp thought of the contrast between the power of God and the old legend of King Canute of England, who commanded the tide of the sea to stop – but of course, it did not. "Canute confuted his flatterers (who told him that all things in his dominions were at his beck and check) by laying his command on the sea to come up no higher into his land, but it obeyed him not."

iii. "If God owns the sea because he made it, he owns you, because he made you too. You are his creature, and by all the rights of creatorship you belong to him. He claims you; will you dispute the claim?" (Spurgeon)

3. (6-7a) Invitation to humble worship.

Oh come, let us worship and bow down;
Let us kneel before the LORD our Maker.
For He *is* our God,
And we *are* the people of His pasture,
And the sheep of His hand.

a. **Oh come**: There is a sweet sense of emphasis in these words. There is a gentle plea here: exhorting the readers to do what is right before God – which is also good for them.

b. **Let us worship and bow down**: The ideas of community (**let us**) and **worship** are repeated from earlier in the psalm, with an added sense of humility (**bow down**). The idea behind the Hebrew word **worship** is essentially *to bow down*; the thought is emphasized and given more intensity through repetition.

i. "In His presence, man must bow down before Him, man must kneel in the attitude of complete submission and obeisance. This is a truth of which we need to remind ourselves." (Morgan)

ii. "It is not always easy to unite enthusiasm with reverence, and it is a frequent fault to destroy one of these qualities while straining after the other." (Spurgeon)

iii. **Worship and bow down**: "Not before a crucifix, not before a rotten image, not before a fair picture of a foul saint: these are not *our makers;* we made them, they made not us. Our God, unto whom we must sing, in whom we must rejoice, before whom we must worship, 'is *a great King above all gods':* he is no god of lead, no god of bread, no brazen god, no wooden god; we must not fall down and worship our *Lady,* but our *Lord;* not any *martyr,* but our *Maker;* not any *saint,* but our *Saviour.*" (Boils, cited in Spurgeon)

c. **Let us kneel before the LORD our Maker**: In the previous verses the psalmist spoke of God's mastery over all creation. Now he includes humanity itself among God's creation. We owe humble worship to God because He *made* us. Worship is an obligation that the creature owes to the Creator.

i. The three main verbs in verse 6 are all connected with the idea of getting low and being humble. "*Three* distinct words are used here to express *three different acts of adoration*: 1. *Let us worship, nishtachaveh,* let us *prostrate* ourselves; the highest act of adoration by which the *supremacy* of God is acknowledged. 2. *Let us bow down, nichraah,* let us *crouch* or *cower down, bending the legs under,* as a dog in the presence of his master, which solicitously waits to receive his commands. 3. *Let us kneel, nibrachah, let us put our knees to the ground,* and thus put ourselves in the *posture* of those who *supplicate.*" (Clarke)

ii. The redeemed have at least two great reasons to humbly worship God. He is both their Maker and their Redeemer. They belong to Him twice over, in both creation and redemption.

iii. "We have the right to come before God with great gladness, but never without a sense of His majesty, and what is due to it." (Morgan)

d. **For He is our God, and we are the people of His pasture**: Yahweh is also worthy of our humble worship because **He is our God**. The ancient Hebrew had something of a *choice* of gods, and it was a deliberate act of allegiance to say, "Yahweh is my God. I belong to Him and He belongs to me – I am like **the sheep of His hand**."

i. "**The sheep of his hand;** which are under his special care and conduct, or government; which is oft expressed by the hand, as Numbers 4:28, 31:49, Judges 9:29." (Poole)

ii. "The repeated reference to the 'hand' of Jehovah is striking. In it are held the deeps: it is…'forming' the land, as a potter fashioning his clay: it is a shepherd's hand, protecting and feeding his flock (Psalm 95:7)." (Maclaren)

iii. "The familiar metaphors of verse 7 express his commitment, which is constant (*our God*), and his care, which is all-sufficing (*his pasture*) and personal (*his hand*). He is no hireling." (Kidner)

B. Warning to those who reject worship.

1. (7b-9) Exhortation to the people of God.

Today, if you will hear His voice:
"Do not harden your hearts, as in the rebellion,
As *in* the day of trial in the wilderness,
When your fathers tested Me;
They tried Me, though they saw My work."

a. **Today, if you will hear His voice**: The psalmist once again exhorts us to act, to **hear** the **voice** of God in the midst of their worship. God *spoke* to His people and He gave them and gave us a word of warning.

i. "If you want to worship God, make sure you do not harden your heart against God's Word, or quarrel with him or test him, as the ancients did." (Boice)

ii. This word of warning is important enough to be referenced three times in the book of Hebrews (Hebrews 3:7, 3:15, and 4:7). In Hebrews 4:7 the emphasis is on the word **today**, indicating the urgency of listening to God with a soft heart *today*.

iii. "This is the uniform time and tense of the Holy Ghost's exhortations. He saith nothing about tomorrow, except to forbid our boasting of it, since we know not what a day shall bring forth. All his instructions are set to the time and tune of 'Today, today, today.'" (Spurgeon)

iv. When the writer to the Hebrews quoted this passage in Hebrews 3:7, he specifically attributed it to the Holy Spirit: *Therefore, as the Holy Spirit says*. He was certain that the words of Psalm 95 were inspired by the Holy Spirit and that the Holy Spirit was Yahweh.

b. **Do not harden your hearts, as in the rebellion**: The **rebellion** and the **day of trial** refer primarily to the trial at Meribah (Numbers 20:1-13). But more generally, they speak of Israel's refusal to trust and enter the Promised Land during the Exodus (Numbers 13:30-14:10). God did not accept their unbelief and condemned that generation of unbelief to die in the wilderness (Numbers 14:22-23 and 14:28-32).

i. The appeal **do not harden your hearts** means there is some aspect of the will involved when it comes to the hardness (or softness) of heart. Many regard a hard or soft heart as something that just *happens* to someone and is beyond his ability to control. Here the Holy Spirit indicates differently.

ii. The strong words in the second half of this psalm are connected to the sweet, stirring words of the first half. Humble worship of Yahweh and the recognition of Him as Creator and God should lead to a listening ear and a soft, surrendered heart toward Him. There is something wrong when the worshipper does not obey and trust God.

iii. Charles Spurgeon suggested several ways that we may **harden** our **hearts**.

• Some harden their hearts by resolving not to demonstrate emotion in regard to spiritual things.

• Some harden their hearts by delaying a real relationship with God.

• Some harden their hearts by pretending doubts and foolish criticism.

• Some harden their hearts by getting into evil company.

- Some harden their hearts by focusing on silly amusements "all intended to kill time and prevent thought upon divine things."

- Some harden their hearts by indulging in a favorite sin.

c. **When your fathers tested Me**: We test God by our unbelief. Israel **saw** the **work** of God, yet would not trust Him at Meribah or in the wilderness in general. We are warned not to do the same.

i. To reject God's invitation **today** surely means to test Him. "Is God to wait as a lackey upon you? You deserve his wrath, will you slight his love? He speaks in amazing tenderness, will you exhibit astounding hardness?" (Spurgeon)

ii. **Though they saw My work** means that God gives us *reason* to trust Him. To ignore those reasons is to provoke and to test God.

iii. "Every one comes in the Christian life, once at least, to Kadesh-barnea [Numbers 13:26]. On the one hand the land of rest and victory; on the other the desert wastes. The balance, quivering between the two, is turned this way by faith; that by unbelief. Trust God, and rest. Mistrust Him, and the door closes on rest, to open to wanderings, failure, and defeat." (Meyer)

2. (10-11) Warning the people of God.

"For forty years I was grieved with *that* generation,
And said, 'It *is* a people who go astray in their hearts,
And they do not know My ways.'
So I swore in My wrath,
'They shall not enter My rest.'"

a. **For forty years I was grieved**: God offered the generation that came out of Egypt the opportunity to take the Promised Land by faith. Their unbelieving rejection of God's offer **grieved** Him for **forty years**. It was evidence that they went **astray in their hearts**, away from humble confidence in Him as Creator and Redeemer.

i. "The desert wanderings were but a symbol, as they were a consequence, of their wanderings in heart. They did not know His ways; therefore they chose their own." (Maclaren)

ii. "O the desperate presumption of man, that he should offend his Maker 'forty years!' O the patience and long suffering of his Maker, that he should allow him forty years to offend in!" (Horne)

iii. **Astray in their hearts**: "Their heart was obstinately and constantly at fault; it was not their head which erred, but their very heart was perverse." (Spurgeon)

b. **They do not know My ways**: To know God is to trust Him. Unbelief is evidence of small or faulty knowledge of God.

i. "**My ways**; either, 1. My laws or statutes, which are frequently called God's ways. Or rather, 2. My works, as it is expressed, Psalm 95:9, which also are commonly so called. They did not know nor consider and remember those great things which I had wrought for them and among them." (Poole)

c. **So I swore in My wrath**: God did not honor the unbelief of His people. It was an insult to Him, and prompted a solemn, angry declaration from Him.

i. "Be not wilfully, wantonly, repeatedly, obstinately rebellious. Let the example of that unhappy generation serve as a beacon to you; do not repeat the offences which have already more than enough provoked the Lord." (Spurgeon)

d. **They shall not enter My rest**: God condemned Israel's generation of unbelievers to die in the wilderness, so that a generation of faithful believers could inherit the Promised Land, His appointed place of **rest** for His people.

i. "There can be no rest to an unbelieving heart. If manna and miracles could not satisfy Israel, neither would they have been content with the land which flowed with milk and honey." (Spurgeon)

ii. "By ending on this note the psalm sacrifices literary grace to moral urgency. If this is a psalm about worship, it could give no blunter indication that the heart of the matter is severely practical: nothing less than a bending of wills and a renewal of pilgrimage." (Kidner)

Psalm 96 – Declaring the Glory of God to the Entire World

There are widening circles in this wonderful psalm. It first speaks to the people of God, then to all the nations of the earth, and finally to creation itself.

There is no author attributed in the Hebrew text, but Psalm 96 contains the middle verses of the psalm David sang for the entrance of the ark of the covenant into Jerusalem (1 Chronicles 16:23-33), suggesting that David was the author.

A. A new song for all the earth to sing.

1. (1-3) Worshipping God with a new song.

Oh, sing to the LORD a new song!
Sing to the LORD, all the earth.
Sing to the LORD, bless His name;
Proclaim the good news of His salvation from day to day.
Declare His glory among the nations,
His wonders among all peoples.

a. **Sing to the LORD a new song**: God loves to receive the rejoicing and praise of His people expressed in **song**, especially the **new song**. A **new song** can come from old saints as they gain fresh awareness of God's love and grace.

i. "The song is to be new, because a new manifestation of Jehovah's Kinghood has wakened once more the long-silent harps." (Maclaren)

ii. **A new song**: "A song of peculiar excellence, for in this sense the term *new* is repeatedly taken in the Scriptures. He has done extraordinary things for us, and we should *excel* in praise and thanksgiving." (Clarke)

iii. "A new song, always new; keep up the freshness of your praise. Do not drivel down into dull routine.... We have new mercies to celebrate, therefore we must have new songs." (Spurgeon)

b. **Sing to the LORD, all the earth**: Praise is due to Yahweh from **all the earth**. He isn't a local deity, meant for only Israel. Under the inspiration of the Holy Spirit, the psalmist saw a day when **all the earth** would **sing** a **new song** to the LORD, described in its fulfillment in Revelation 5:9.

c. **Proclaim the good news of His salvation**: These songs to the Lord were not only celebrations; they were also proclamations. They proclaimed **His salvation** and declared **His glory** and **His wonders** to the entire world, to **the nations**.

> i. **From day to day**: "Other news delights us only at first hearing; but the good news of our redemption is sweet from day to day…saith Luther, Christ is now as fresh unto me as if he had shed his blood but this very hour." (Trapp)

> ii. **From day to day** means we should never *stop* proclaiming **the good news of His salvation**. "Every man should praise God every day – on each returning morning, and on every evening – for the assurance that there is a way of salvation provided for him, and that he may be happy for ever." (Barnes, cited in Spurgeon)

> iii. **Declare His glory**: "*Glory* is a difficult word to define. It refers to the majestic aura of the divine presence, which is why the stanza speaks of 'the splendor of his holiness.' But it is also more than that. *Kabod*, the Hebrew word, refers to something that is impressive or weighty." (Boice)

> iv. "You know men are very much attracted by aught of glory and renown. They will even rush to the cannon's mouth for so-called glory…. tell them about the glory thereof, what a glory it brings to Christ, and to what a glory it will bring every sinner by- and-by." (Spurgeon)

> v. "If the Lord Jesus has become King of your heart, and has brought blessing to you, do not hesitate to give voice to your allegiance. In private, sing unto Him a new song; in public, show forth His salvation, and declare His glory." (Meyer)

2. (4-6) Why God deserves praise.

For the LORD is great and greatly to be praised;
He *is* to be feared above all gods.
For all the gods of the peoples *are* idols,
But the LORD made the heavens.
Honor and majesty *are* before Him;
Strength and beauty *are* in His sanctuary.

a. **For the LORD is great and greatly to be praised**: The psalmist would not give God empty or unthinking praise. He first spoke regarding the greatness of God, and noted that His greatness made Him **greatly to be praised**.

i. **For the LORD is great**: "He is, in every possible sense, 'great;' great in dignity, in power, in mercy; and therefore 'greatly to be praised' by every creature." (Horne)

b. **He is to be feared above all gods**: Yahweh deserves worship from the entire earth because He isn't like the **gods** and **idols** of the pagans. He is the *Creator* who **made the heavens**.

i. "**Idols;** or, *nothings*, as they are called, 1 Corinthians 8:4, 10:19; or, *vain things*, as the word signifies, and is translated by others. The sense is, Though they have usurped the name and place of the Divine Majesty, yet they have nothing of his nature or power in them." (Poole)

ii. "The term *idols* is *elilim*, which the Old Testament treats as a mere parody of *elohim* (God). It is the word translated 'worthless' in Job 13:4 ('worthless physicians') and Jeremiah 14:14 ('worthless divination')." (Kidner)

iii. "Yahweh alone is God and all other deities are 'fakes.' They cannot be gods, because Yahweh alone has made heaven. The pagans may claim that their gods have power over the heavenly realms, but this is excluded by virtue of Yahweh's sole claim to having created 'the heavens.'" (VanGemeren)

iv. "The contemptuous name of the nation's gods as 'Nothings' is frequent in Isaiah." (Maclaren)

c. **Honor and majesty are before Him**: God's greatness and power give Him a regal, royal bearing. He is marked by **strength and beauty**.

i. **Strength and beauty**: "In him are combined all that is mighty and lovely, powerful and resplendent. We have seen rugged strength devoid of beauty, we have also seen elegance without strength; the union of the two is greatly to be admired." (Spurgeon)

ii. "Not in outward show or parade of costly robes does the glory of God consist; such things are tricks of state with which the ignorant are dazzled; holiness, justice, wisdom, grace, these are the splendours of Jehovah's courts, these the jewels and the gold, the regalia, and the pomp of the courts of heaven." (Spurgeon)

iii. **Strength and beauty are in His sanctuary**: "If we ask whether this *sanctuary* is earthly or heavenly, the probable answer is both. The

earthly one was a 'copy and shadow' of the heavenly (Heb. 8:5)."
(Kidner)

3. (7-9) Calling the entire world to glorify God.

Give to the Lord, O families of the peoples,
Give to the Lord glory and strength.
Give to the Lord the glory *due* His name;
Bring an offering, and come into His courts.
Oh, worship the Lord in the beauty of holiness!
Tremble before Him, all the earth.

a. **Give to the Lord the glory due His name**: The theme is repeated –
God is worthy of praise from the entire earth, from all **families of the
peoples**. In this context, **give** means to recognize and to declare the **glory
and strength** that belong to God in all His being.

i. When we **give unto the Lord** these things, we do not give or
attribute things to Him that He did not have before. We recognize
things as they really are, because God is full of **glory and strength**.

ii. "Neither men nor angels can confer anything upon Jehovah, but
they should recognise his glory and might, and ascribe it to him in
their songs and in their hearts." (Spurgeon)

iii. "The meaning of the Hebrew word for worship is to prostrate
oneself, not to praise God for his attributes, which is what the
English word *worship* means. But here we must note that although
the meaning of the Hebrew word differs from the English word, the
Hebrew understanding of worship nevertheless also involves giving
God praise for his attributes. That is what is being said here. Here the
nations of the world are told to give God glory." (Boice)

b. **O families of the peoples**: God promised Abraham, *in you all the
families of the earth shall be blessed* (Genesis 12:3), and that promise would
be fulfilled in Abraham's greatest descendant, Jesus the Messiah. The same
word for *families* found in Genesis 12:3 is used in verse 7: **Give to the
Lord, O families of the peoples, give to the Lord glory and strength**.
This verse may refer to the fulfillment of the promise of Genesis 12:3.

c. **Give to the Lord...Give to the Lord.... Give to the Lord**: We come
into God's presence to receive, but also to **give** unto Him. We give Him our
time, our attention, our worship, our surrender, our service, our resources,
and much more.

i. "In this stanza the worship of God is described as our bringing
something to God rather than our coming to God to get something
from him. We usually think of it the other way around. We think of

coming to church to receive either: (1) knowledge through the teaching or (2) specific gifts from God as his answers to our prayers. But here worship is chiefly our bringing praise and offerings to God." (Boice)

ii. **Give to the LORD the glory due His name**: "It is a debt; and a debt, in equity, must be paid. The honour due to his name is to acknowledge him to be holy, just, true, powerful." (Clarke, cited in Spurgeon)

iii. The triple repetition of this phrase impresses the urgency of the call, and is a subtle reference to the Triune nature of God.

d. **Bring an offering, and come into His courts**: *Sacrifice* is appropriate for the worshipper. True worship is often revealed by sacrifice in some way.

i. **Bring an offering**: "The word here rendered '*offering*' – *minkhah* – is that which is commonly used to denote a *bloodless* offering, a thank-offering." (Barnes, cited in Spurgeon)

e. **In the beauty of holiness**: The psalmist called the world to **worship** God in recognition of His **holiness**, and to see that there is a **beauty** connected to His **holiness**.

i. **Beauty** and **holiness** are not often connected ideas in our popular culture. Yet in reality, there is surpassing allure and attractiveness in true holiness. If a purported type of holiness has little beauty, it may not be true holiness.

ii. "Fear of God is the blush upon the face of holiness enhancing its beauty." (Spurgeon)

iii. God's **holiness** – His "set-apart-ness" – has a wonderful and distinct **beauty** about it. It is *beautiful* that God is God and not man, that He is more than the greatest man or a super-man. His holy love, grace, justice, and majesty are *beautiful*.

B. The declaration to the nations and to creation.

1. (10) What to say among the nations.

Say among the nations, "The LORD reigns;
The world also is firmly established,
It shall not be moved;
He shall judge the peoples righteously."

a. **Say among the nations**: The theme of speaking to the entire earth continues, calling the people of the world to worship and honor God as they should.

b. **The LORD reigns**: This is a fundamental and powerful message for God's people to proclaim to the world. Whether others recognize His reign or not, the LORD nevertheless **reigns**, and that reign will one day be openly and obviously imposed upon the whole world.

    i. **Say among the nations, "The LORD reigns"**: "*Justin Martyr*, in his dialogue with *Trypho* the Jew, quotes this passage thus: 'Say among the nations, the Lord ruleth *by the wood*,' meaning the *cross*; and accuses the Jews of having blotted this word out of their Bibles, because of the evidence it gave of the truth of Christianity. It appears that this reading did exist anciently in the *Septuagint*, or at least in some ancient copies of that work, for the reading has been quoted by *Tertullian, Lactantius, Arnobius, Augustine, Cassiodorus, Pope Leo, Gregory of Tours*, and others." (Clarke)

c. **The world also is firmly established**: God's people are also meant to tell the world that His work as Maker of the earth is good and lasting. He didn't make the world in a careless way; it is **firmly established**, so that **it shall not be moved**.

d. **He shall judge the peoples righteously**: The world also needs to hear that God is a righteous **judge**, before whom the whole world must give account. When the world hears and believes this, they will rightly prepare themselves for that judgment to come.

    i. **"He shall judge the people righteously**; he shall not abuse his invincible power and established dominion to the oppression of his people, as other princes frequently do, but shall govern them by the rules of justice and equity, which is the only foundation of a true and solid peace." (Poole)

2. (11-13) The message of joy to all creation.

Let the heavens rejoice, and let the earth be glad;
Let the sea roar, and all its fullness;
Let the field be joyful, and all that *is* in it.
Then all the trees of the woods will rejoice before the LORD.
For He is coming, for He is coming to judge the earth.
He shall judge the world with righteousness,
And the peoples with His truth.

a. **Let the heavens rejoice, and let the earth be glad**: The thought introduced in the previous line is used as reason for all creation to be glad. The fact that God is a righteous judge who will call things into account is good for creation – good for the **heavens**, the **earth**, the **sea**, the **field**, and **all the trees**.

    i. "Transported with a view of these grand events, and beholding in spirit the advent of King Messiah; the Psalmist exults in most jubilant and triumphant strains, calling the whole creation to break forth into joy, and to celebrate the glories of redemption." (Horne)

ii. Paul had this concept in mind in Romans 8:21: *because the creation itself also will be delivered from the bondage of corruption into the glorious liberty of the children of God.*

iii. "The thought that inanimate nature will share in the joy of renovated humanity inspires many glowing prophetic utterances, eminently those of Isaiah – as *e.g.,* Isaiah 35:1-10. The converse thought, that it shared in the consequences of man's sin, is deeply stamped on the Genesis narrative." (Maclaren)

iv. **All the trees of the woods**: According to VanGemeren, the idea here is more than just a forest, but of wilderness or even thick jungle. The sense is that all creation is excited that God **is coming to judge the earth**.

b. **For He is coming to judge the earth**: The psalm ends with the joyful confidence that God will **judge** and set things right. The goodness of this is apparent to those who love God, love His ways, and hurt over the injustices of the present age.

i. **He is coming to judge the earth**: "To rule it with discretion; not to tax it, and control it by force, as kings often do, but to preside as magistrates do whose business it is to see justice carried out between man and man." (Spurgeon)

ii. "As C. S. Lewis points out, the ancients lived in a world where judges usually needed to be bribed and right judgment was exceedingly hard to come by, especially for weak, poor, or disadvantaged persons. In such a climate, the disadvantaged did not fear judgment but rather longed for it, because it meant a day when evil would be punished and those who did the right things would be vindicated." (Boice)

iii. "The world of men may be glad also, because the reign of Jesus means equity for the oppressed, equal-handed justice for the poor, peace among the nations." (Meyer)

iv. "Honesty, veracity, integrity, will rule upon his judgment-seat. No nation shall be favoured there, and none be made to suffer through prejudice. The black man shall be tried by the same law as his white master, the aboriginal shall have justice executed for him against his civilised exterminator, the crushed and hunted Bushman shall have space to appeal against the Boer who slaughtered his tribe, and the South Sea Islander shall gain attention to his piteous plaint against the treacherous wretch who kidnapped him from his home. There shall be true judgment given without fear or favour. In all this let the nations be glad, and the universe rejoice." (Spurgeon)

v. "He smites with destruction. But the fierceness of His wrath, the weight of His stroke, are inspired by His love of man, and His determination to establish that order of life in which strength and beauty shall abound." (Morgan)

Psalm 97 – The Greatness and Wisdom of God

Psalm 97 continues in the theme and tone of the previous psalms. It uses phrases found in other psalms and other Old Testament passages. "The psalmist's mind is saturated with old sayings, which he finds flashed up into new meaning by recent experiences. He is not 'original,' and does not try to be so; but he has drunk in the spirit of his predecessors, and words which to others were antiquated and cold blaze with light for him, and seem made for his lips." (Alexander Maclaren)

"The psalm contains many allusions to other parts of the Old Testament, all of which have been shaped into a magnificent hymn." (Willem VanGemeren)

G. Campbell Morgan summarized this psalm: "The effects of His judgments are declared. His adversaries are destroyed, His glory is revealed, His people are filled with joy."

"Psalms 96, 97, and 98 each hail God's coming as the world's King. But Psalms 96 and 98 soar with delight at what is in store for the world when God returns, while in Psalm 97 the frightening, awesome side of God's kingly rule is emphasized." (James Montgomery Boice)

A. Rejoicing in the greatness of God.

1. (1) A summons to rejoice in God's reign.

The LORD reigns;
Let the earth rejoice;
Let the multitude of isles be glad!

    a. **The LORD reigns**: Like Psalm 93, this psalm begins suddenly and wonderfully with the proclamation of Yahweh's rule. He is not a useless idol or local deity. Yahweh is not passive, nor the "watchmaker" who created all things and then left it alone. He **reigns**; the God of Abraham, Isaac, and Jacob actively plans, acts, and rules over the universe.

        i. **The LORD reigns**: "Here is a simple proposition, which is a self-evident axiom, and requires no proof: JEHOVAH is *infinite* and *eternal*; is possessed of *unlimited power* and *unerring wisdom*; as he is the *Maker*, so he must be the *Governor*, of all things. His authority is absolute, and his government therefore universal. In all places, on all occasions, and in all times, Jehovah reigns." (Clarke)

b. **Let the earth rejoice**: Yahweh's reign brings joy to the earth. We could imagine an evil or dark deity whose reign would bring terror. We see such in a limited sense, where men and devils are given room to exercise their wicked will. Yet the more Yahweh's reign is obvious and observed, the more rejoicing there is, extending to **the multitude of the isles**, the most distant places.

i. **The multitude of isles**: "The Hebrews called by the name of 'isles,' not only countries surrounded by the sea, but all the countries which the sea divided from them; so that the term became synonymous with 'Gentiles.'" (Horne)

2. (2-6) The LORD's greatness over creation.

Clouds and darkness surround Him;
Righteousness and justice *are* the foundation of His throne.
A fire goes before Him,
And burns up His enemies round about.
His lightnings light the world;
The earth sees and trembles.
The mountains melt like wax at the presence of the LORD,
At the presence of the Lord of the whole earth.
The heavens declare His righteousness,
And all the peoples see His glory.

a. **Clouds and darkness surround Him**: The psalmist may have had in mind the appearance of God at Mount Sinai, which was marked by *a thick cloud on the mountain* and *the smoke of a furnace* (Exodus 19:16-20).

i. "*Clouds and thick darkness* warn of his unapproachable holiness and hiddenness to presumptuous man (yet the hiddenness owes nothing to caprice: 2b), while the *fire* and *lightnings* reveal a holiness that is also devouring and irresistible (cf. Heb. 12:29)." (Kidner)

ii. Adam Clarke had a curious thought regarding **a fire goes before Him**: "Literally, this and the following verse may refer to the electric fluid, or to manifestations of the Divine displeasure, in which, by means of *ethereal fire*, God consumed his enemies." (Clarke)

b. **Righteousness and justice are the foundation of His throne**: God's throne is not based on deception, bribery, the blood of conquest, or even hereditary right. **The foundation of His throne** is nothing else but

righteousness and justice. This is why the earth can rejoice at His reign (verse 1).

> i. "Jehovah is an autocrat, but not a despot. Absolute power is safe in the hands of him who cannot err, or act unrighteously." (Spurgeon)

> ii. "We know that in His government there can be no departure from righteousness, no deflection of justice. This is the secret of our confidence, and should be the inspiration of perpetual songs, of ceaseless worship." (Morgan)

c. **A fire goes before Him**: This is a poetic description of the same kind of phenomena that happened at Mount Sinai (Exodus 19:16-20). This phrase either refers to what God did then or uses the same ideas to describe a future display of God's sovereign presence, **the presence of the Lord of the whole earth**, when **all the people see His glory**.

> i. "The lightning flash is meant to set forth the sudden, swift forth-darting of God's delivering power, which awes a gazing world, while the hills melting like wax from before His face solemnly proclaim how terrible its radiance is, and how easily the mere showing of Himself annihilates all high things that oppose." (Maclaren)

> ii. "The parallelism of 'LORD' (*YHWH* [Yahweh]) and 'Lord' (Adonai) affirms that Yahweh is the Lord ('great King') of all the earth." (VanGemeren)

> ii. "'The Lord of the whole earth' is an unusual designation, first found in a significant connection in Joshua 3:11; Joshua 3:13, as emphasising His triumph over heathen gods, in leading the people into Canaan." (Maclaren)

> iv. **The mountains melt like wax**: "Men cannot move the hills, with difficulty do they climb them, with incredible toil do they pierce their way through their fastnesses, but it is not so with the Lord, his presence makes a clear pathway, obstacles disappear, a highway is made, and that not by his hand as though it cost him pains, but by his mere presence, for power goes forth from him with a word or a glance." (Spurgeon)

> v. **All the peoples see His glory**: "This will be more eminently the case at the second advent, when the trumpet of the archangel shall proclaim his approach in the clouds of heaven, and all the tribes of the earth shall see him coming in the glory of his Father, with the holy angels." (Horne)

B. Instructing the people.

1. (7-9) Instructing the nations about the LORD's greatness.

Let all be put to shame who serve carved images,
Who boast of idols.
Worship Him, all *you* gods.
Zion hears and is glad,
And the daughters of Judah rejoice
Because of Your judgments, O LORD.
For You, LORD, *are* most high above all the earth;
You are exalted far above all gods.

a. **Let all be put to shame who serve carved images**: Considering the greatness and power of Yahweh, those who **boast of idols** should be ashamed. Poetically speaking, even the **gods** of the heathen **worship Him**.

i. "So the gods themselves are summoned to fall down before this triumphant Jehovah, as Dagon did before the Ark." (Maclaren)

b. **Zion hears and is glad**: The whole earth benefits from the majestic and awesome revelation of God, but His people are especially **glad**. His righteous **judgments** make **the daughters of Judah rejoice**.

i. Charles Spurgeon thought that this was relevant to an ultimate restoration of the land of Israel: "The day shall come when the literal Zion, so long forsaken, shall joy in the common salvation."

ii. **The daughters of Judah rejoiced**: "David alludes to a custom familiar in Judea, of forming choral bands of maidens after a victory or some happy circumstance." (Le Blanc, cited in Spurgeon)

c. **You, LORD, are most high above all the earth**: Previously the psalmist spoke about God to the world. Here he addresses God directly, praising and extolling Him as **exalted far above all gods**.

i. John Trapp connected verse 9 with Ephesians 1:21: *far above all principality and power and might and dominion, and every name that is named, not only in this age but also in that which is to come.*

2. (10-12) Instructing the people of God about His righteous deliverance.

You who love the LORD, hate evil!
He preserves the souls of His saints;
He delivers them out of the hand of the wicked.
Light is sown for the righteous,
And gladness for the upright in heart.
Rejoice in the LORD, you righteous,
And give thanks at the remembrance of His holy name.

a. **You who love the LORD, hate evil**: Again, the psalmist addresses the people of Israel who love the LORD, and introduces a strong statement.

Despite the seemingly abrupt transition, the psalmist sensibly connected the appearance of the God whose very throne is founded on righteousness and justice with the heart for righteousness and justice that His people should also have.

i. It may be that this command is one of the most often broken among God's people. We find it easy to be *too* loving, or rather express a twisted love that pretends to both **love the LORD** and love or accept the things that He hates.

ii. It is possible for us to be *angry* at sin or evil, without truly hating it. We may be angry at the trouble sin causes, but not hate it enough to repent and forsake our sin.

b. **He preserves the souls of His saints**: The psalmist described many ways that God blesses and protects His people.

- He cares for their **souls**.
- He **delivers** them from the **wicked**.
- He sends **light** before their path.
- He gives **gladness** unto them.

i. "...*preserves* would be better rendered 'guards' or 'watches over'; and *lives* [**souls**] is a word that includes the whole person. It is a promise of God's defence and watchful care, not a guarantee against casualties." (Kidner)

ii. **Preserves the souls**: "He may leave the bodies of his persecuted saints in the hand of the wicked, but not their souls, these are very dear to him, and he preserves them safe in his bosom." (Spurgeon)

iii. **Light is sown**: "You do not realize it, but you are sowing light. Each act of self-denial, in which you cast yourself into the ground to die, is a seed-germ of the harvest of gladness." (Meyer)

iv. **Light is sown**: "Every grace of God is a *seed*, which he intends should produce a *thousand* fold in the hearts of genuine believers. We do not so much require *more* grace from God, as the *cultivation* of what we have received. God will not give more, unless we improve what we have got. Remember *the parable of the talents*. Let the *light* and *gladness* be faithfully cultivated, and they will multiply themselves till the whole body shall be full of light, and the whole soul full of happiness." (Clarke)

v. Kidner argued that **light is sown** was not the best translation. "Light *dawns*...is surely the right reading here, following one Hebrew manuscript and all the ancient versions." (Kidner)

c. **Rejoice in the LORD, you righteous**: Considering the greatness of God and His goodness to His people, it is proper for them to **rejoice** in *Him*. The rejoicing should not be primarily in what He has given, but in the LORD Himself – with plenty of thanksgiving at even **the remembrance of His holy name**.

> i. "Having sung the glory of the Redeemer, the Psalmist delineates the duty of the redeemed." (Horne)

> ii. "It began by calling upon the people of the whole earth to rejoice in God's rule (v. 1). It ends by calling upon us to lead the way in this worship." (Boice)

Psalm 98 – A New Song for His Marvelous Things

This psalm is simply titled **A Psalm***, and it is the only one given that simple title with no other explanation. Like Psalm 96, it speaks of praise to God for His work of salvation in widening circles – first Israel, then all the earth, and finally all creation.*

"A noble, spirit-stirring Psalm. It may have been written on the occasion of a great national triumph at the time; but may, perhaps, afterwards be taken up at the period of the great millennial restoration of all things." (Thomas Chalmers, cited in Charles Spurgeon)

A. Singing praise to the Savior.

"There are striking parallels between the first part of Psalm 98 and Mary's Magnificat (Luke 1:46–55), which may mean that the mother of Jesus had the psalm in mind as she composed her hymn and that she rightly saw that the promises of the psalm were to be fulfilled in the spiritual victories to be achieved by Jesus Christ." (Boice)

1. (1) Praising Yahweh with a new song.

Oh, sing to the LORD a new song!
For He has done marvelous things;
His right hand and His holy arm have gained Him the victory.

> a. **Sing to the LORD a new song**: The idea of a **new song** is found in many places in Scripture (Psalms 33:3, 40:3, 96:1, 144:9 and 149:1; Isaiah 42:10; and Revelation 5:9 and 14:3). The concept of the **new song** means there should be something fresh and dynamic about worship and the songs we sing to God.

> > i. Miriam didn't use an Egyptian song. Deborah didn't use Miriam's song. "There must be new songs on new occasions of triumph." (Spurgeon)

> > ii. **A new song**: "The song of redeeming grace can never grow old, even though the same words recur.... Are not His mercies new every morning, and His faithfulness every night? Is not His love always at work spreading thy table for new meals, making thy bed for new

slumber, contriving new alleviations and delights? Look out for these till meditation induces thanksgiving." (Meyer)

iii. "The *new song*, in the context of this hope of victory, evidently means a song to be composed for the occasion; other suggestions seem over-elaborate." (Kidner)

b. **For He has done marvelous things**: The **new song** has a reason – to extol the great works of God, His **marvelous** things. It isn't empty praise or singing for the sake of singing. The worship is connected to life experience of His **marvelous things**.

i. **Marvelous things**: "*Niphlaoth*, 'miracles,' the same word as in Psalm 96:3, where we translate it *wonders*." (Clarke)

c. **His right hand and His holy arm**: These are the instruments of God's **victory**, the expressions of His skill and strength. As in Isaiah 52:10, the idea of **His holy arm** is that God has rolled up His sleeve to do His mighty work. Together, His hand and arm **have gained Him the victory**.

i. **Right hand**: "So Christ fought our battle with his right hand; he did it with ease, with strength, and with infinite wisdom." (Spurgeon)

ii. "As the singer rejoices over the salvation of God manifested on behalf of Israel, he emphasises the fact that it has been wrought by Jehovah alone. 'His right hand, and His holy arm'; these were the only instruments available for, or capable of working deliverance." (Morgan)

2. (2-3) The revelation of Yahweh's victory.

The Lord has made known His salvation;
His righteousness He has revealed in the sight of the nations.
He has remembered His mercy and His faithfulness to the house of Israel;
All the ends of the earth have seen the salvation of our God.

a. **The Lord has made known His salvation**: The *marvelous things* of verse 1 have been published **in the sight of the nations**.

- This is evident because of the public nature of God's unfolding work of redemption.
- This is a prophecy of a coming day when all the earth will hear.
- This is an exhortation to God's people to proclaim the message of His **salvation** and **righteousness**.

i. **Salvation, righteousness**: "Through his power the Lord has obtained victory – 'salvation' and 'righteousness.' In Isaiah these two words are synonyms for the establishment of God's just order on earth in fulfillment of the prophetic word (cf. Isa 46:13; 51:5–6, 8)." (VanGemeren)

ii. **Made known**: "The Lord is to be praised not only for effecting human salvation, but also for making it known, for man would never have discovered it for himself." (Spurgeon)

iii. The New Testament shows that God **made known His salvation** in a way beyond the psalmist's expectation. The Person and Work of Jesus Christ and the worldwide spread of the Gospel are fulfillments of this.

iv. "The Hebrew singer celebrated a truth the full value of which he hardly recognized." (Morgan)

b. **He has remembered His mercy and His faithfulness to the house of Israel**: One of God's *marvelous things* is His unending **mercy and faithfulness** to the covenant people of Abraham, Isaac, and Jacob. It is strange to think that some believe God has *forgotten* **His mercy and His faithfulness to the house of Israel**.

c. **All the ends of the earth have seen the salvation of our God**: God's work was centered in **the house of Israel**, but the **ends of the earth** were never to be forgotten. From the very beginning of His covenant plan with Abraham, all the families of the earth were in view (Genesis 12:3).

i. **All the ends of the earth**: "All the inhabitants of the earth, from one end to another." (Poole)

B. Bringing praise with music.

1. (4) The music of joyful song.

Shout joyfully to the LORD, all the earth;
Break forth in song, rejoice, and sing praises.

a. **Shout joyfully to the LORD, all the earth**: Since the great news of God's *marvelous things* (verse 1) goes to the *ends of the earth* (verse 3), it is right for **all the earth** to praise Yahweh.

i. "The *joyful noise* of verses 4 and 6 meets us elsewhere as the spontaneous shout that might greet a king or a moment of victory. It is the word translated 'shout aloud' in Zechariah 9:9, the prophecy that was fulfilled on Palm Sunday." (Kidner)

ii. "'The noise of temple worship was legendary,' according to Marvin E. Tate. He points to the accounts of Israel's worship in 2 Chronicles 29:25–30 and Ezra 3:10–13, where in the second passage the sound of the instruments and the shouts of the people are said to have been "heard far away" (Ezra 3:13)." (Boice)

b. **Break forth in song, rejoice**: The praise is to be enthusiastic, varied, and in song. This is the opposite of the dreary singing of somber songs.

2. (5-6) The music of many instruments.

Sing to the LORD with the harp,
With the harp and the sound of a psalm,
With trumpets and the sound of a horn;
Shout joyfully before the LORD, the King.

a. **Sing to the LORD with the harp**: This can be understood in two senses. The first is that musical instruments should accompany the singing mentioned in verse 4. The second is that the instruments themselves **sing to the LORD** a song of praise.

b. **With the harp...trumpets...a horn**: A band of musicians added to the praise of the song, the psalm, and the joyful shout. The combination of instruments assumes some level of effort and skill among the musicians.

i. **The sound of a psalm**: "I think *zimrah*, which we translate *Psalm*, means either a *musical instrument*, or a *species of ode* modulated by different voices." (Clarke)

ii. "*The horn* [shofar] proclaimed such events as the year of jubilee, or the accession of a king: Leviticus 25:9ff.; 1 Kings 1:39." (Kidner)

C. Majestic praise from all creation.

1. (7-8) The praise from all creation.

Let the sea roar, and all its fullness,
The world and those who dwell in it;
Let the rivers clap *their* hands;
Let the hills be joyful together before the LORD,

a. **Let the sea roar, and all its fullness**: The musical instruments mentioned in the previous verses were not the only voices to give God the praise He deserves. Now the **sea** itself is called to add its **roar** to the sound of praise. The **rivers** and **hills** are brought into the worship team with their **joyful** sounds.

i. "These appeals to nature in her great departments – of the sea in its mighty amplitude, and the earth with its floods and hills – form, not a warrant, but a call on Christian ministers to recognise God more in their prayers and sermons as the God of Creation, instead of restricting themselves so exclusively to the peculiar doctrines of Christianity. Do the one, and not leave the other undone." (Chalmers, cited in Spurgeon)

b. **The world and those who dwell in it**: The poetic image of praise from inanimate creation is wonderful, but not enough. The praise should also come from **those who dwell in it** – perhaps a reference not only to people, but the animal world as well.

i. "The Psalmist, beholding in spirit the accomplishment of the promises, the advent of Christ, and the glory of his kingdom…bids the whole earth break forth into joy." (Horne)

2. (9) The reason for this mighty praise.

For He is coming to judge the earth.
With righteousness He shall judge the world,
And the peoples with equity.

a. **For He is coming to judge the earth**: The strong and deep praise described in this psalm is not only for the *marvelous things* God has done (verse 1). It is also for the work He is about to do – **with righteousness He shall judge the world**. His righteous rule and reign will be a welcome relief for all creation that has suffered under the sin and rebellion of mankind.

i. "It makes the point which Romans 8:19ff. expounds: that nature will not come into its own until man himself, its proper master, is ruled in *righteousness* and *equity*." (Kidner)

ii. "I think of the way C. S. Lewis developed this idea in *The Lion, the Witch, and the Wardrobe*. In the first section of that book, when Narnia was under the power of the wicked Witch of the North, the land was in a state of perpetual winter. Spring never came. But when Aslan rose from the dead the ice began to melt, flowers bloomed, and the trees turned green. It is poetical writing, but it describes something that will happen. The rivers will indeed clap their hands. The mountains will indeed sing. And we will all join in." (Boice)

b. **And the peoples with equity**: In the ancient world, justice was rare – and this is still true sometimes. Judges were bribed or turned by ideology and prejudice. The idea of coming judgment **with equity** was a great relief to those who were often oppressed and denied justice.

Psalm 99 – The Holy God, Present and Revealed

This psalm, without title in the Hebrew text, is a triple proclamation of God's holiness, as Isaiah would later do (Isaiah 6:3).

"Here, after the carefree delight of Psalm 98, we recollect how exalted and holy he is, and how profound is the reverence we owe him." (Derek Kidner)

A. The holy presence of God.

1. (1) God is present in His sanctuary.

The LORD reigns;
Let the peoples tremble!
He dwells *between* the cherubim;
Let the earth be moved!

> a. **The LORD reigns**: For the third time, a psalm begins with this phrase (see also Psalm 93:1 and 97:1). Psalm 99 speaks of God's presence (**He dwells between the cherubim**), but in His presence He **reigns**. God isn't simply *there*; He is a reigning king.

> b. **Let the people tremble**: In the presence of a sovereign God, it is appropriate to **tremble**. Even the **earth** can be **moved** at His presence – much more so should **the people** be moved.

>> i. "Saints quiver with devout emotion, and sinners quiver with terror when the rule of Jehovah is fully perceived and felt." (Spurgeon)

>> ii. "Men of the world ridiculed '*the* Quakers' for trembling when under the power of the Holy Spirit; had they been able to discern the majesty of the Eternal they would have quaked also." (Spurgeon)

> c. **He dwells between the cherubim**: God is enthroned in His sanctuary. It is difficult to say whether the psalmist had in mind the heavenly sanctuary of God or the earthly representation of it (the tabernacle or temple); both are true and either one fits.

i. "His living throne of *cherubim* – not the weaponless cupids of religious art but the mighty beings whose forms summed up for Ezekiel the whole kingdom of earthly creatures – this living throne is a flying chariot, fiery with judgment and salvation." (Kidner)

2. (2-3) God is present in Zion.

The LORD is great in Zion,
And He *is* high above all the peoples.
Let them praise Your great and awesome name—
He *is* holy.

a. **The LORD is great in Zion**: God is present in heaven and in all the earth, but He has special regard for **Zion**, the city of Jerusalem. In that city set in the hills, He is **high above the peoples**.

i. **The LORD is great in Zion:** "In the Hebrew text the words lie in this order, *The Lord in Zion...*is great." (Poole)

b. **Let them praise Your great and awesome name**: God rightfully receives praise because of His greatness and because **He is holy**.

i. **He is holy**: Holiness, at its root, has the idea of *apartness*. It describes someone, or something, which is *set apart* from other people or things. An object can be holy if it is set apart for sacred service. A person is holy if he is are set apart for God's will and purpose.

ii. "*Holy* is a word to emphasize the distance between God and man: not only morally, as between the pure and the polluted, but in the realm of being, between the eternal and the creaturely." (Kidner)

iii. God Himself is set apart in many senses. He is set apart from creation, in that the Lord God is not a creature, and He exists outside of all creation. If all creation were to dissolve, the Lord God would remain. He is set apart from *humanity*, in that His nature or essence is *Divine*, not *human*. God is not a *super-man* or the *ultimate* man. God is not merely *smarter* than any man, *stronger* than any man, *older* than any man, or *better* than any man. You can't measure God on man's chart at all. He is *Divine*, and we are *human*.

iv. God's holiness is a part of everything He is and does. God's power is a *holy power*. God's love is a *holy love*. God's wisdom is a *holy wisdom*. Holiness is not an aspect of God's personality; it is the essence of His entire Being.

v. "While the word itself signifies simply separateness, and was used with reference to other gods by other peoples, it acquired a new significance in this Divine revelation.... God was revealed as separated from everything unjust, untrue, evil, in His character, and therefore in all His dealings with men, whether in the giving of law, or in the activities of government." (Morgan)

vi. **He is holy**: "As this not only ends this verse but the *fifth* also, and in effect the *ninth*, it seems to be a [kind] of *chorus* which was sung in a very solemn manner at the conclusion of each of these parts. His *holiness* – the immaculate purity of his nature, was the reason why he should be exalted, praised, and worshipped." (Clarke)

B. The holy strength of God.

1. (4) The strong righteousness of God.

The King's strength also loves justice;
You have established equity;
You have executed justice and righteousness in Jacob.

a. **The King's strength also loves justice**: God's great strength and sovereignty could, in theory, be used for evil. Yet Yahweh the King **loves justice** and has **established equity**.

i. "He is no arbitrary ruler. His reign is for the furtherance of justice." (Maclaren)

ii. "God abuseth not his kingly power to tyranny, but joineth it with his justice and uprightness. Regiment without righteousness is but robbery with authority." (Trapp)

b. **You have executed justice**: With God, **justice** and **equity** are not mere slogans or promises. He has **executed justice** among His people and in the world and will continue to do so.

i. "Most kingdoms have an establishment of some kind, and generally it is inequitable; here we have an establishment which is equity itself. The Lord our God demolishes every system of injustice, and right alone is made to stand." (Spurgeon)

ii. "That king-craft which delights in cunning, favouritism, and brute force is as opposite to the divine kingship as darkness to light. The palace of Jehovah is no robber's fortress nor despot's castle, built on dungeons, with stones carved by slaves, and cemented with the blood of toiling serfs." (Spurgeon)

2. (5) The proper response to His holy strength.

Exalt the LORD our God,
And worship at His footstool—
He *is* holy.

a. **Exalt the LORD our God**: Understanding the power, holiness, and goodness of God should lead us to **exalt** Him and to humbly **worship** Him.

b. **Worship at His footstool**: Most commentators regard this as the ark of the covenant, connected to their understanding of *between the cherubim* in verse 1. The ark of the covenant is called His footstool (1 Chronicles 28:2), but so are Jerusalem (Lamentations 2:1) and the earth as a whole (Isaiah 66:1, Matthew 5:35, Acts 7:49).

i. "The object of the exaltation and 'worship at his footstool' is to submit oneself to his sovereignty and to respond properly to his holy presence." (VanGemeren)

c. **He is holy**: The statement from verse 3 is repeated for emphasis. God **is holy** in all He is and all He does.

i. "The Bible calls God holy more than anything else, more than sovereign, more than just, more than merciful or loving. In fact 'holy' is the only epithet of God that is repeated three times for emphasis, like this: 'Holy, holy, holy' (Isa. 6:3; Rev. 4:8)." (Boice)

ii. "Holiness is the harmony of all the virtues. The Lord has not one glorious attribute alone, or in excess, but all glories are in him as a whole; this is the crown of his honour and the honour of his crown. His power is not his choicest jewel, nor his sovereignty, but his holiness." (Spurgeon)

C. The holy revelation of God.

1. (6-7) God revealed to His priests.

Moses and Aaron were among His priests,
And Samuel was among those who called upon His name;
They called upon the LORD, and He answered them.
He spoke to them in the cloudy pillar;
They kept His testimonies and the ordinance He gave them.

a. **Moses and Aaron were among His priests**: The psalmist listed three notable priests in the history of Israel – **Moses**, **Aaron**, and **Samuel**. These were ones who prayed (**called upon His name**) and God revealed Himself (**He answered them**).

i. "To encourage the faithful in the worship of God, the examples of Moses, Aaron, and Samuel are [cited as evidence], men of like infirmities with ourselves, whose prayers were heard, both for themselves and others." (Horne)

ii. "Priestly functions were exercised by Moses, as in sprinkling the blood of the covenant, [Exodus 24:1-18] and in the ceremonial connected with the consecration of Aaron and his sons, [Leviticus 8:1-36] as well as at the first celebration of worship in the Tabernacle [Exodus 40:18-33]." (Maclaren)

iii. **Priests**: "The noun is a participial form from the verb 'serve' and is here loosely used for 'servants' or 'intercessors.' Moses, Aaron, and Samuel interceded on Israel's behalf." (VanGemeren)

iv. **Among those who called upon His name**: "Evidently those that call upon the name of God compose a separate class.... It is a high honor to be included among them that call upon His name. If you cannot find your place in any other class, perhaps it is here." (Meyer)

b. **He spoke to them in the cloudy pillar**: The pillar of cloud was the physical representation of God's presence with Israel in the wilderness. God spoke to Moses from that **cloudy pillar** (Exodus 33:9).

c. **They kept His testimonies**: The psalmist noted the general obedience of **Moses**, **Aaron**, and **Samuel**.

2. (8-9) God revealed in forgiveness and holiness.

You answered them, O LORD our God;
You were to them God-Who-Forgives,
Though You took vengeance on their deeds.
Exalt the LORD our God,
And worship at His holy hill;
For the LORD our God *is* holy.

a. **You were to them God-Who-Forgives**: God **answered** these men (and others) who sought Him. He revealed Himself to them as the **God-Who-Forgives**. Significantly, even these men of whom it was said, *they kept His testimonies* (verse 7) need this revelation of the **God-Who-Forgives**.

b. **Though You took vengeance on their deeds**: It isn't clear if the ones referred to here are the *priests* mentioned in verse 6 (Moses, Aaron, and Samuel) or if it is referring to the people they prayed for (Israel as a whole). Most commentators regard **their deeds** as referring to Israel's deeds, but it is also true that Moses, Aaron, and Samuel were each disciplined by God in some way.

i. "God spared them, but showed his displeasure at their misdoings. He chastised, but did not consume them. This is amply proved in the history of this people." (Clarke)

ii. "Through all the history of His people He has been faithful, both in forgiveness and in vengeance, and that because He is holy. Therein is the reason for worship. Herein also is the reason for trembling." (Morgan)

c. **Exalt the** LORD **our God**: Once more the reader is compelled to **exalt** God, to **worship** Him, and to recognize God's holiness.

d. **For the** LORD **our God is holy**: For the emphatic third time, God's holiness is proclaimed. Later, in heavenly visions, the Prophet Isaiah (Isaiah 6:3) and the Apostle John (Revelation 4:8) would hear this three-time declaration of holiness combined into a single sentence.

i. "This is the supreme reason for confidence in Him, and so the supreme inspiration of worship." (Morgan)

Psalm 100 – A Psalm of Thanksgiving for All Lands

This psalm is simply titled **A Psalm of Thanksgiving,** *and it is the only psalm in the collection to bear this title. It speaks of an invitation to the whole earth to know and to worship God. "It is jubilant with confidence for the whole earth, as it contemplates the glory of that earth, when all its people are submitted to the reign of Jehovah." (G. Campbell Morgan)*

A. The what and why of giving praise.

1. (1-2) What to do: Praise God.

Make a joyful shout to the Lord, all you lands!
Serve the Lord with gladness;
Come before His presence with singing.

a. **Make a joyful shout to the Lord:** Unlike the several previous psalms, Psalm 100 does not begin with a declaration of God's sovereignty or character. It begins with the simple and direct exhortation to **all you lands** to praise God with **a joyful shout**. This is a call to the nations, extending far beyond Israel's borders.

i. **A joyful shout:** "The original word signifies a glad shout, such as loyal subjects give when their king appears among them. Our happy God should be worshipped by a happy people; a cheerful spirit is in keeping with his nature, his acts, and the gratitude which we should cherish for his mercies." (Spurgeon)

ii. "The *joyful noise* is…the equivalent in worship to the homage-shout or fanfare to a king." (Kidner)

iii. **All you lands:** "The nations must recognize who the Lord is. He is Yahweh, by whose grace and blessings his people exist. The nations too are invited to sing hymns to the Lord and to worship him." (VanGemeren)

b. **Serve the Lord with gladness:** The whole earth is invited to **serve the Lord**. The psalmist likely had in mind the service of worship or temple rituals, but the principle applies to *any* service directed to God. Those who **serve the LORD** should do it **with gladness**.

> i. **Serve the LORD with gladness**: "It is your privilege and duty to be happy in your religious worship. The religion of the true God is intended to remove human misery, and to make mankind happy. He whom the religion of Christ has not made happy does not understand that religion, or does not make a proper use of it." (Clarke)

> ii. "As for the true believer in Jesus, he serves his God because he loves to serve him; he assembles with the great congregation because it is his delight to worship the Most High." (Spurgeon)

c. **Come before His presence with singing**: As in many places in the psalms, praise is expressed in song. **Singing** is not the only way to praise God, but it is the chief way to praise Him.

2. (3) Why to do it: He is our Creator and Shepherd.

Know that the LORD, He *is* God;
It is He *who* has made us, and not we ourselves;
We are His people and the sheep of His pasture.

a. **Know that the LORD, He is God**: The praise that comes to God from His people and all **lands** should be mindful. We have many reasons to worship Yahweh, the covenant God of Israel, and the reasons begin with the recognition that **He is God**.

> i. "To *know* is to have firm ground underfoot, the prerequisite of praise (cf. 40:2f.), and this knowledge is ours by gift; indeed by command." (Kidner)

> ii. **Know that the LORD, He is God**: "Be convinced of it, ye heathens, whose fantasies have forged false gods." (Trapp)

b. **It is He who has made us**: The next reason to worship God is in appropriate recognition of His work as *creator*. The idea that we could make **ourselves** is absurd, and we should worship the One **who has made us**.

> i. "The sense of God's proprietorship is the true basis of our consecration. We must realize His rights over us before we can freely give Him His due. Those rights are manifold in their sweet reasonableness; but amongst them all, this of creation is one of the chief. God has a right to us because He has made us." (Meyer)

> ii. "Of course, if we do not need God as our Creator, then we do not need to be thankful. Why should we? We got here by ourselves, thank you. We have no one but ourselves to thank." (Boice)

iii. Under the New Covenant, the believer has a second and greater reason for praise: he or she is a *new* creation in Jesus Christ (2 Corinthians 5:17).

iv. **And not we ourselves:** "Therefore we owe him homage and service, and him only, and not other gods, who made us not." (Poole)

v. "For our part, we find it far more easy to believe that the Lord made us than that we were developed by a long chain of natural selections from floating atoms which fashioned themselves." (Spurgeon)

vi. "Some men live as if they made themselves; they call themselves '*self-made* men,' and they adore their supposed creators." (Spurgeon)

c. **We are His people and the sheep of His pasture:** The third reason to worship God is because He has chosen a **people** (orginally the Jewish people, then added the followers of Jesus Christ), and He cares for us as **the sheep of His pasture.**

B. The what and why of giving thanks.

1. (4) What to do: Come to His house with thanks and praise.

Enter into His gates with thanksgiving,
***And* into His courts with praise.**
Be thankful to Him, *and* bless His name.

a. **Enter into His gates with thanksgiving:** Now the psalmist pictures the people of God from *all you lands* (verse 1) entering through the **gates** and into the **courts** of the temple. As God's people approach, we should do so **with thanksgiving**, recognizing how much God has done for us.

i. **Enter into His gates with thanksgiving:** "Publicly worship God; and when ye come to the house of prayer, be thankful that you have such a privilege; and when you *enter his courts*, praise him for the permission." (Clarke)

ii. "It teaches that there is a special aspect of thanksgiving that involves the whole people of God together and not just the private prayers of individuals." (Boice)

b. **Into His courts with praise:** Thanks and **praise** merge together, as God's people are **thankful** and **bless His name.**

i. "It is as though the gates of the City, the courts of the Sanctuary, were suddenly thrown open, and all lands are called to *serve* Jehovah, to *know* that He is God, to *enter* into relationship with Him." (Morgan)

ii. Under the New Covenant, not only are the **gates** and **courts** open, but even the way to the Holy of Holies is thrown open (Hebrews 10:19).

2. (5) Why to do it: God is good and merciful.

For the Lord is good;
His mercy *is* everlasting,
And His truth *endures* to all generations.

a. **For the Lord is good**: Thanks and praise are right in recognition of God's *goodness*. He is good in His plans, good in His grace, good in His forgiveness, good in His covenant, and good in every aspect of His being.

i. **For the Lord is good**: "The gods of the heathen were not good. They were selfish and capricious. You could never know when they might turn against you and do you harm. Not so our God. The God of the Bible is and has always been good." (Boice)

b. **His mercy is everlasting**: The brief psalm ends with God's unending **mercy** and **truth**. These are **everlasting** reasons to give thanks and praise to God.

i. "So long as we are receivers of mercy we must be givers of thanks." (Spurgeon)

ii. "How glorious will be that day which shall behold the everlasting gates of heaven lifting up their heads, and disclosing to view those courts above, into which the children of the resurrection are to enter, there, with angels and archangels, to dwell and sing forevermore!" (Horne)

Psalm 101 – A King's Determination to Rule Righteously

This psalm is titled **A Psalm of David***. Alexander Maclaren described a likely background for this psalm: "He had but recently ascended the throne. The abuses and confusions of Saul's last troubled years had to be reformed. The new king felt that he was God's viceroy; and here declares what he will strive to make his monarchy – a copy of God's."*

David was anointed king three times. Samuel anointed David in his youth, really as a prophecy of his calling and destiny (1 Samuel 16:13). After Saul's death he was anointed king over the tribe of Judah at Hebron (2 Samuel 2:4). Seven years later he was anointed king over all the tribes of Israel (2 Samuel 5:3). Before he took the throne over all Israel, he had a lot of time to think about what kind of king he should be.

"In Europe the psalm came to be known as the 'prince's psalm,' owing to the concern for the proper conduct of a Christian magistrate, prince, or king." (Willem VanGemeren)

"I was startled to find that Martin Luther had done an exposition of the psalm that ran to eighty pages. The reason, I discovered, is that he was deeply concerned about civil government and wanted to expound the psalm as a listing of qualities toward which every Christian prince or magistrate should strive." (James Montgomery Boice)

"Eyring, in his 'Life of Ernest the Pious' (Duke of Saxe-Gotha), relates that he sent an unfaithful minister a copy of the 101st Psalm, and that it became a proverb in the country when an official had done anything wrong, he would certainly soon receive the prince's Psalm to read." (Franz Delitzsch, cited in Charles Spurgeon)

A. Determined in his personal conduct.

1. (1) The song to sing.

I will sing of mercy and justice;
To You, O LORD, I will sing praises.

a. **I will sing of mercy and justice**: David sang this song exalting the **mercy and justice** of God. The two go together; **mercy** can only be properly understood in light of **justice**. When **justice** pronounces its righteous penalty, **mercy** may grant relief.

i. As king, David was concerned with **mercy and justice**. He knew these principles were not rooted in man, but in God. Before he could exercise **mercy and justice** in His kingdom, he had to understand and extol the **mercy and justice** of God.

ii. "Mercy and judgment would temper the administration of David, because he had adoringly perceived them in the dispensations of his God." (Spurgeon)

iii. "His mercy encourageth the greatest of sinners to hope; his judgments forbid the best of men to presume." (Horne)

b. **To You, O Lord, I will sing praises**: David could only sing of **mercy and justice** in reference to songs of praise to Yahweh. David knew that the Lord was the source of all **mercy and justice**.

2. (2) A righteous life and the presence of God.

I will behave wisely in a perfect way.
Oh, when will You come to me?
I will walk within my house with a perfect heart.

a. **I will behave wisely in a perfect way**: David's longing for the Lord was connected to his desire to live a wise and holy life (**perfect way**). He determined that his reign would be marked by integrity and godliness.

i. As David came into a position of greater power, it was all the more important that he focus on personal godliness and **behave wisely in a perfect way**. Power often exposes the flaws of character, if it does not actually help create them.

ii. "He begins with himself. He will bring his own character and conduct into conformity with the way and will of Jehovah to Whom he offers his praise. Then he will govern according to the same standards." (Morgan)

iii. When David came to royal power, he didn't say:

- "Now I can live the good life." He said, **I will behave wisely**.
- "I'll have the biggest party ever." He said, **I will behave wisely**.
- "I'll show them all how important I am." He said, **I will behave wisely**.

- "I'll punish my enemies and show my power." He said, **I will behave wisely**.

b. **When will You come to me?** David understood that under the Old Covenant blessing, including the experience of God's presence, was connected to obedience (Deuteronomy 28).

   i. "He feels the need not merely of divine help, but also of the divine presence, that so he may be instructed, and sanctified, and made fit for the discharge of his high vocation. David longed for a more special and effectual visitation from the *Lord* before he began his reign." (Spurgeon)

   ii. David understood the principle later stated in 1 John 1:6-7 in connection with the New Covenant: *If we say that we have fellowship with Him, and walk in darkness, we lie and do not practice the truth. But if we walk in the light as He is in the light, we have fellowship with one another, and the blood of Jesus Christ His Son cleanses us from all sin.*

c. **I will walk within my house with a perfect heart**: David's righteous life had to be real in his conduct **within** his own **house** before it could be lived in the courts of his kingdom This was a standard that David only imperfectly lived, much to his own hurt.

   i. **Within my house**: "I will begin the intended reformation at myself, and then set things to rights in my family." (Trapp)

   ii. "No man is able to make the city in which he dwells anything like the city of God who does not know how to behave himself in his own house.... The first thing for every public man to do who would serve his city for God, is to see to it that his private life is ordered aright before Him." (Morgan)

   iii. "Reader, how fares it with your family? Do you sing in the choir and sin in the chamber? Are you a saint abroad and a devil at home? For shame! What we are at home, that we are indeed." (Spurgeon)

   iv. "This is the hardest place to walk in perfectly. It seems easier to walk perfectly among strangers than in one's own house. But you may rest assured that a man is really no better than he is to his own. You must not gauge your worth by what the outside world thinks and says." (Meyer)

   v. "It is easier for most men to walk with a perfect heart in the *Church*, or even in the *world*, than in their *own families*. How many are as meek as lambs among *others*, when at *home* they are *wasps* or *tigers*!" (Clarke)

vi. "Understand that in the home-life God is educating and training you for the greatest victories. There you are learning the deepest lessons in sanctification. You need not run to conventions, sermons, and holiness meetings; if you would resolve to walk in your house with a perfect heart, you would discover how far from perfect you are, and how you are the least of His saints." (Meyer)

3. (3-4) Describing the righteous life.

I will set nothing wicked before my eyes;
I hate the work of those who fall away;
It shall not cling to me.
A perverse heart shall depart from me;
I will not know wickedness.

a. **I will set nothing wicked before my eyes**: David knew that one measure of his righteous life was what he chose to set **before** his **eyes**. There are many **wicked** things to **set** the **eyes** upon, and the *lust of the eyes* is a significant aspect of the lure of this world (1 John 2:16).

i. David's words remind us of Job 31:1: *I have made a covenant with my eyes; why then should I look upon a young woman?* Like Job, David regarded discipline over the eyes as a primary measure of godliness.

ii. "The recesses of an Eastern palace were often foul with lust, and hid extravagances of caprice and self-indulgence; but this ruler will behave there as one who has Jehovah for a guest." (Maclaren)

iii. We wish that David had lived this principle more consistently. Instead, David took multiple wives (2 Samuel 3:2-5 and 5:13) in a seeming inability to restrain his sexual desires, and was led astray by the lust of his eyes (2 Samuel 11:2).

iv. Yet, we shouldn't think David was a hypocrite because he failed in completely living up to these high standards. It isn't hypocrisy to have a standard that you can't completely meet. Hypocrisy is when you have one standard for yourself and a higher standard for others.

b. **I hate the work of those who fall away**: David knew that if he wanted to live a godly life, it would be wise to keep some distance from those with **a perverse heart**. He knew what would be later stated in 1 Corinthians 15:33: *Evil company corrupts good habits.*

i. Boice explained the idea behind **those who fall away**: "It is the exact opposite of the 'covenant love' (*hesed*) idea introduced in verse 1."

ii. **It shall not cling to me**: "Sin, like pitch, is very apt to stick." (Spurgeon)

c. **I will not know wickedness**: David knew that a righteous life must have some sense of *determination* about it. Though he did not perfectly fulfill this determination, his life was undeniably more godly *with* this determination than *without* it.

i. **A perverse heart**: "The *perverseness* of verse 4 is more deliberate: a twisted mind and will which hate the plain truth and the straight path." (Kidner)

ii. "It is used of an unruly horse, that champs upon the bit through his fiery impatience; and when applied to a bad man, denotes one impatient of all restraint, of unbridled passions, and that is headstrong and ungovernable in the gratification of them, trampling on all the obligations of religion and virtue." (Chandler, cited in Spurgeon)

B. Determined in those he would appoint.

1. (5) Opposing the workers of wickedness.

Whoever secretly slanders his neighbor,
Him I will destroy;
The one who has a haughty look and a proud heart,
Him I will not endure.

a. **Whoever secretly slanders his neighbor**: It is a significant and grievous sin to lie or speak in an evil way against another. The worst of this slander is done **secretly**, and David was determined to oppose all who did so (**Him I will destroy**).

i. The one who **secretly slanders his neighbor** seek "to advance themselves by the ruin of others; which are the common pests of courts and kingdoms." (Poole)

ii. **Slanders his neighbor**: Clarke noted a Chaldean translation of this and its meaning: "'He who speaks with the *triple tongue* against his neighbour.' That is, the tongue by which he slays *three* persons, viz., 1. The *man* whom he slanders; 2. *Him* to whom he *communicates* the slander; and, 3. *Himself*, the slanderer. Every slanderer has his *triple tongue*, and by every *slander* inflicts those *three* deadly wounds."

b. **The one who has a haughty look and a proud heart**: David listed two additional related sins: the communication of arrogance by the facial expression (the **haughty look**) and the **proud heart** behind the expression. To all such who thought themselves better than their neighbors, David said "**Him I will not endure.**"

i. **A haughty look**: "Pride will sit and show itself in the eyes as soon as anywhere." (Trapp)

2. (6-8) The men David would choose to serve with him.

My eyes *shall be* on the faithful of the land,
That they may dwell with me;
He who walks in a perfect way,
He shall serve me.
He who works deceit shall not dwell within my house;
He who tells lies shall not continue in my presence.
Early I will destroy all the wicked of the land,
That I may cut off all the evildoers from the city of the LORD.

a. **My eyes shall be on the faithful of the land**: David refused to look to or at those who thought themselves better than others. Instead he looked at **the faithful**, deciding that they would **dwell** with him.

i. When David looked for leaders, he looked for **the faithful of the land**. "We need people who can get the job done, but we need 'the faithful of the land' to do it. It is a wise leader who seeks out such people and then puts authority into their hands" (Boice)

ii. "Is it not true that Jesus, like David, has his eyes alert for the faithful in the land, for those who will serve now and also dwell with him in glory at the end of time?" (Boice)

b. **He shall serve me**: Perhaps David spoke this as he came to the throne, vowing to find the right people to appoint to his government. He would reject one **who works deceit** and **he who tells lies**. He would look for the humble, not the proud – knowing they were much better to trust with authority and responsibility.

c. **Early I will destroy all the wicked of the land**: David's determination to rule in such a way that favored the godly and opposed the wicked was so fixed that he was determined to do it **early**. As he ruled in **the city of the LORD**, the wicked would not prosper.

i. "The commitment to excellence implies a difference in administration from the manner in which kings ruled in the ancient Near East. The godly king affirms that his loyalty is to Yahweh and not to the ways of this world." (VanGemeren)

ii. **From the city of the LORD**: "His ambition is to have Jehovah's city worthy of its true King, when He shall deign to come and dwell in it." (Maclaren)

iii. "The psalm is doubly moving: both for the ideals it discloses and for the shadow of failure which history throws across it. Happily the last word is not with David nor with his faithful historians, but with his Son. There, there is no shadow." (Kidner)

Psalm 102 – Afflicted, But Full of Trust

The title of this psalm is **A Prayer of the afflicted, when he is overwhelmed and pours out his complaint before the LORD.** *This afflicted one borrowed his tone and some of his phrasing from Job, who is the Old Testament's greatest example of affliction. Many phrases also match others in the psalms.*

This psalm describes Jerusalem (Zion) in a state of ruin. If this is taken as literal ruin, the psalm may have been written by those in exile who mourned over both their personal and national affliction. Adam Clarke followed this thinking and suggested the author could be Daniel, Jeremiah, or Nehemiah. However, it may be that the ruin of Zion described is more poetic in nature and the psalm is pre-exilic.

In traditional Christian liturgy, this has been regarded as one of the seven penitential psalms (along with Psalms 6, 32, 38, 51, 130, and 143).

A. A cry from the crisis.

1. (1-2) A plea for the presence of God.

Hear my prayer, O LORD,
And let my cry come to You.
Do not hide Your face from me in the day of my trouble;
Incline Your ear to me;
In the day that I call, answer me speedily.

a. **Hear my prayer, O LORD:** According to its title, this psalm comes from an anonymous afflicted one. The psalmist begs for God to **hear** his prayer, knowing that a good and compassionate God could not **hear** but still ignore his plea.

i. The first two verses of this psalm are filled with phrases that allude to other psalms (VanGemeren cites seven such phrases). "But the psalmist is not a cold-blooded compiler, weaving a web from old threads, but a suffering man…securing a certain solace by reiterating familiar petitions." (Maclaren)

168

b. **Do not hide Your face**: The affliction itself was bad enough, but it was made worse beyond measure by the sense that God did not see or care. When he had the sense that God's favor and face were evident, the affliction could be endured.

2. (3-7) The agony of being afflicted in health.

For my days are consumed like smoke,
And my bones are burned like a hearth.
My heart is stricken and withered like grass,
So that I forget to eat my bread.
Because of the sound of my groaning
My bones cling to my skin.
I am like a pelican of the wilderness;
I am like an owl of the desert.
I lie awake,
And am like a sparrow alone on the housetop.

a. **For my days are consumed like smoke**: In a style similar to Job, the psalmist described his agony. His days passed like meaningless **smoke**. Pain from deep inside his body made his **bones** feel as if they were burning. His **heart** ached and he had no appetite.

i. "**Like smoke;** which passeth away in obscurity, and swiftly, and irrecoverably." (Poole)

ii. "The effects of extreme grief on the human frame are compared to those which fire produceth upon fuel. It exhausts the radical moisture, and, by so doing, soon consumes the substance." (Horne)

iii. **I forget to eat my bread**: "Ahab, smitten with one kind of grief, David with another, and Daniel with a third, all 'forgot,' or 'refused to eat their bread:' 1 Kings 21:4, 2 Samuel 12:16; Daniel 10:3. Such natural companions are 'mourning and fasting.'" (Horne)

b. **My bones cling to my skin**: As in Job 19:20, he was so weak and thin that there seemed to be nothing between his **bones** and his **skin**. He felt like a lonely and restless bird (**pelican, owl,** or **sparrow**).

i. "**Pelican;** or, *bittern*, as the same word is translated, Isaiah 34:11, Zephaniah 2:14. It is a solitary and mournful bird, as also the owl here following is." (Poole)

ii. **Pelican, owl**: "The Psalmist likens himself to two birds which were commonly used as emblems of gloom and wretchedness." (Spurgeon)

iii. **Sparrow**: "But this Hebrew word doth not only signify a sparrow, but in general *any bird*, as Leviticus 14:4, Deuteronomy 14:11, Daniel

4:12,14,21. And so it may here design any one or more sort of birds which used to sit alone, watching and mourning upon house-tops." (Poole)

3. (8-11) The agony of being afflicted by enemies.

My enemies reproach me all day long;
Those who deride me swear an oath against me.
For I have eaten ashes like bread,
And mingled my drink with weeping,
Because of Your indignation and Your wrath;
For You have lifted me up and cast me away.
My days *are* like a shadow that lengthens,
And I wither away like grass.

a. **My enemies reproach me all day long**: The psalmist's affliction came from more than poor health; he had **enemies** set against him. They opposed him with constant disapproval and rejection. They added a tone of mocking and cursing (**who deride me and swear an oath against me**).

i. "The scoffs and reproaches of men are generally added to the chastisements of God; or rather, perhaps are a part, and sometimes the bitterest part of them." (Horne)

ii. **Swear an oath against me**: "Have sworn my death, or do swear and curse by me." (Trapp)

b. **I have eaten ashes like bread**: The life of the psalmist seemed to be constant mourning. The marks of mourning – **ashes** and **weeping** were as familiar to him as food and drink.

c. **Because of Your indignation and Your wrath**: The mourning was all the more bitter because of the sense that this affliction came as some kind of punishment from God.

i. **You have lifted me up and cast me away**: "He felt that God was treating him as wrestlers treat one another, when a man deliberately lifts up his opponent in order that he may give him the worse fall." (Spurgeon)

d. **I wither away like grass**: Overwhelmed with a sense of divine rejection (**You have lifted me up and cast me away**), he felt that his life was short and had little meaning.

i. **A shadow that lengthens**: "A 'shadow' never continueth in one stay, but is still gliding imperceptibly on, lengthening as it goes, and at last vanishing into darkness." (Horne)

ii. "Here, to the twelfth verse, is a most lively picture of a dejected person, such as can hardly be paralleled." (Trapp)

B. Praising the LORD who builds up Zion.

1. (12) Recognizing the everlasting God.

But You, O LORD, shall endure forever,
And the remembrance of Your name to all generations.

a. **But You, O LORD, shall endure forever**: The previous lines spoke of the psalmist's frailty and the fleeting nature of life. The present line gives a sharp and wonderful contrast. Man may have days like shadows or *wither away like grass*, but Yahweh **shall endure forever**. The psalmist can therefore reject all self-reliance and hold on to a true reliance upon God.

i. We note the contrast between the first 11 verses, which were filled with personal references (I, me, and my) and verses 12 and following. With the words, **but You**, the focus changes and is set on God.

ii. "This, then, is the light which banishes darkness – the sense of the eternity of God. Then all life is seen as being under His control, and therefore conditioned in the wisdom and intention which include far more than the passing moment, taking into account all the ages." (Morgan)

b. **The remembrance of Your name to all generations**: Not only would the Lord Himself endure, but His influence and greatness would be declared **to all generations**, never passing away.

2. (13-14) Recognizing the favor of God to Jerusalem.

You will arise *and* have mercy on Zion;
For the time to favor her,
Yes, the set time, has come.
For Your servants take pleasure in her stones,
And show favor to her dust.

a. **You will arise and have mercy on Zion**: Though in deep affliction, the psalmist had steadfast confidence that God *would* act and show **mercy** to Jerusalem once again.

b. **Yes, the set time, has come**: At God's appointed time, Jerusalem would be the object of God's **favor**. He had a **set time** for their restoration and would not forever leave them in ruin.

i. If this psalm describes the time in exile, **the set time** points to the 70 years set by God for Israel's captivity (Jeremiah 25:11-13 and 29:10).

ii. "There was an appointed time for the Jews in Babylon, and when the weeks were fulfilled, no bolts nor bars could longer imprison the ransomed of the Lord." (Spurgeon)

c. **Your servants take pleasure in her stones**: It is in our nature to reject that which is broken or torn down, but God's **servants** have a love that goes beyond human nature. They see the ruined city, **take pleasure in her stones** and **show favor to her dust**.

i. The psalmist was overwhelmed by a sense of his *own* ruin and need (Psalm 102:1-11). Yet he did not allow that to turn him completely inward; he also cared for his community.

ii. "When the people of God cease thinking about themselves so much and begin thinking about the state of things around them, particularly our cities and those who are suffering in them, then God may indeed hear our prayers and send a revival." (Boice)

iii. If every stone of God's city was precious to His **servants**, then by analogy, so is every stone representing the people of God in His great building (1 Peter 2:5). "The poorest church member, the most grievous backslider, the most ignorant convert, should be precious in our sight, because [they form]…a part, although possibly a very feeble part, of the new Jerusalem." (Spurgeon)

3. (15-17) Recognizing God's exaltation among the nations.

So the nations shall fear the name of the LORD,
And all the kings of the earth Your glory.
For the LORD shall build up Zion;
He shall appear in His glory.
He shall regard the prayer of the destitute,
And shall not despise their prayer.

a. **So the nations shall fear the name of the LORD**: The restoration of mercy to Jerusalem is only the first part of a much larger work among **the nations**. God would so reveal Himself that **all the kings of the earth** would honor His name and glory.

b. **He shall appear in His glory**: The kings and kingdoms of the world honor Yahweh because He reveals Himself in His work towards Zion. His blessing and mercy to Jerusalem are a foretaste of His goodness to all the earth, when **He shall regard the prayer of the destitute**.

i. "A wondering world will adore her delivering God." (Maclaren)

ii. **The prayer of the destitute**: "Only the poorest of the people were left to sigh and cry among the ruins of the beloved city; as for the rest, they were strangers in a strange land, and far away from the holy place, yet the prayers of the captives and the forlorn offscourings of the land would be heard of the Lord." (Spurgeon)

4. (18-22) Recognizing the great deliverance God brings.

This will be written for the generation to come,
That a people yet to be created may praise the LORD.
For He looked down from the height of His sanctuary;
From heaven the LORD viewed the earth,
To hear the groaning of the prisoner,
To release those appointed to death,
To declare the name of the LORD in Zion,
And His praise in Jerusalem,
When the peoples are gathered together,
And the kingdoms, to serve the LORD.

a. **This will be written for the generation to come**: God's goodness to Zion and the whole earth is a testimony for the future, so that **a people yet to be created may praise the LORD.**

i. **This will be written**: "This wonderful deliverance shall not be lost nor forgotten, but carefully recorded by thy people." (Poole)

ii. "Registers of divine kindness ought to be made and preserved: we write down in history the calamities of nations – wars, famines, pestilences, and earthquakes are recorded; how much rather then should we set up memorials of the Lord's lovingkindnesses!" (Spurgeon)

iii. "Nothing is more tenacious than man's memory when he suffers an injury; nothing more lax if a benefit is conferred. For this reason God desires lest his gifts should fall out of mind, to have them committed to writing." (Le Blanc, cited in Spurgeon)

iv. The idea that God considers and plans for those **yet to be created** is an interesting revelation. We don't first enter into the consciousness of God when we are conceived in our mother's womb, but when we are conceived in His heart and mind.

b. **He looked down from the height of His sanctuary**: The psalmist pictured God bending down low from heaven:

- To see (**viewed the earth**).
- To hear (**the groaning of the prisoner**).
- To act (**to release those appointed to death**).
- To proclaim (**the name of the LORD in Zion**).

- To gather (**when the peoples are gathered together**).

- To receive service (**peoples are gathered...to serve the LORD**).

    i. Horne took these words and made them into a fit prayer for the afflicted believer today: "Look down, O Lord Jesu, yet once again upon thy servants, still under the dominion of death, and the bondage of corruption; loose these chains, even these also, O Lord, and bring us forth into the glorious liberty of thy children."

C. The weakness of man and the strength of God.

1. (23) A confession of weakness and its cause.

He weakened my strength in the way;
He shortened my days.

a. **He weakened my strength in the way**: The psalmist began this song by recognizing his own weakness (verses 1-11). Then he praised God for His deliverance and ultimate victory (verses 12-22). Now in the last section of this psalm, he confessed once again his weakness and frailty (**shortened my days**).

b. **He weakened...He shortened**: In addition, the psalmist recognized that it was *God* who either caused or allowed his weakness and frailty. Here the psalmist wrote with a point much like that of the much later Apostle Paul, who saw God's plan and even glory in his present weakness (2 Corinthians 12:9-10).

2. (24-28) A prayer from the afflicted psalmist.

I said, "O my God,
Do not take me away in the midst of my days;
Your years *are* throughout all generations.
Of old You laid the foundation of the earth,
And the heavens *are* the work of Your hands.
They will perish, but You will endure;
Yes, they will all grow old like a garment;
Like a cloak You will change them,
And they will be changed.
But You *are* the same,
And Your years will have no end.
The children of Your servants will continue,
And their descendants will be established before You."

a. **O my God, do not take me away**: Overwhelmed by both his sense of great weakness in affliction, and by the awareness of God's greatness and ultimate victory, the psalmist did the right thing. He cried out in prayer, pleading for God's merciful help.

b. **Of old You laid the foundation of the earth**: Verses 25-27 are quoted in Hebrews 1:10-12 as the words of God the Father unto God the Son, the Messiah.

i. In the Hebrew text of verses 25-27, the psalmist says this to Yahweh, but the idea that God Himself speaks these words is more clear in the Greek translation of the Hebrew (the Septuagint), which the author of Hebrews quoted.

ii. "The epistle opens our eyes to what would otherwise be brought out only by the LXX [Septuagint] of verses 23f....namely that the Father is here replying to the Son, 'through whom all things were made'." (Kidner)

iii. "The writer of the Epistle is not asserting that the psalmist consciously spoke of the Messiah, but he is declaring that his words, read in the light of history, point to Jesus as the crowning manifestation of the redeeming, and therefore necessarily of the creating, God." (Maclaren)

iv. "When the psalmist wrote these words he was thinking of God the Father, as he has been throughout the psalm. There is very little intimation of the Trinity or the person of the Son of God in the Old Testament. Still, the author of Hebrews is right when he views these words as spoken by the Father to Jesus Christ." (Boice)

c. **They will perish, but You will endure**: The contrast was clear to the psalmist. The mighty God is eternal (**throughout all generations**) and can do all things (**You laid the foundation of the earth**). The things God creates may **perish**, but He Himself **will endure**.

i. "Did He make all things? Then He can unmake them, and be Himself evermore the same." (Meyer)

ii. "There is nothing more calculated to strengthen the heart in suffering, or inspire the spirit with the courage in days of danger and difficulty, than the sense of the eternity of God.... Let us set our limitations always in the light of His limitlessness." (Morgan)

d. **You will change them**: God has complete power over creation, including the power to **change** the heavens as He pleases. Yet He Himself is unchanging (**You are the same**) and eternal (**Your years will have no end**).

i. "Amidst the changes and chances of this mortal life, one topic of consolation will ever remain, namely, the eternity and immutability of God our Saviour, of him who was, and is, and is to come." (Horne)

e. **The children of Your servants will continue**: The psalmist ended his prayer and this psalm with a note of confidence, even triumph. His affliction seems to have remained, and he does not proclaim hope for his present trouble. At the same time, he is utterly confident of God's goodness and ultimate victory for His people (**Your servants**). If the psalmist did not see it in his own day, his **children** surely would, **and their descendants will be established** by God's goodness and strength.

i. This is a remarkable declaration of trust in God's promise to make all things right and good, if not in the present day, then in days to come. It shows a wonderful progression in this psalm.

- He began with an honest declaration of his own misery.
- Then he looked outside himself to his community.
- Then he looked outside his community to the world.
- Then he looked outside his time to future generations.

ii. "It is remarkable that the psalmist does not draw the conclusion that he himself shall receive an answer to his prayer, but that 'the children of Thy servants shall dwell' *i.e.,* in the land, and that there will always be an Israel 'established before Thee.'" (Maclaren)

iii. "Whatever be the fate of the present generation, whether they may live to see the accomplishment of all that has been foretold or not, yet the word of God standeth sure; there shall be always a church, and a holy seed, to whom the promises shall be made good." (Horne)

Psalm 103 – Bless the Lord, O My Soul

This psalm is simply titled **A Psalm of David***. We don't know the circumstances in which it was written, but since David was a man who knew the grace and deliverance of God many times, it could have been written at many different times of his life.*

However, Charles Spurgeon thought, "We should attribute it to his later years when he had a higher sense of the preciousness of pardon, because a keener sense of sin, than in his younger days. His clear sense of the frailty of life indicates his weaker years, as also does the very fulness of his praiseful gratitude." (Charles Spurgeon)

"It is perhaps the most perfect song of pure praise to be found in the Bible.... Through centuries it has been sung by glad hearts, and today is as fresh and full of beauty as ever." (G. Campbell Morgan)

A. Reasons to bless and honor God.

1. (1-2) Blessing God for all His benefits.

Bless the Lord, O my soul;
And all that is within me, *bless* His holy name!
Bless the Lord, O my soul,
And forget not all His benefits:

> a. **Bless the Lord:** David did not mean this in the sense that a greater person bestows a blessing on a lesser person. God is infinitely greater than man, and in this sense man could never give a blessing to God. David meant this in the sense that it blesses and honors God when His creatures praise Him and thank Him appropriately.

> b. **Bless the Lord, O my soul:** David called upon his **soul** to bless Yahweh. It was as if David looked at his soul and understood that it was not praising God enough. He called upon his **soul** to do more.

>> i. David understood that true worship was something deeply inward, of the **soul**. It is not just about outward forms or expressions, but also

about something real from the **soul**. "Soul music is the very soul of music." (Spurgeon)

ii. "Let others murmur, but do thou *bless*. Let others bless themselves and their idols, but do thou bless *the Lord*. Let others use only their tongues, but as for me I will cry, 'Bless the Lord, O my *soul*.'" (Spurgeon)

c. **All that is within me, bless His holy name**: David also understood that worship had to be more than superficial; it had to be offered as completely as possible. He wanted *everything* **within** to praise God. He set his heart in tune as well as setting his instruments in tune.

i. We often praise and thank God halfheatedly – or less! David called for *everything* within him (**all that is within me**) to give honor and praise to God.

ii. **All that is within me**: "What a rebuke to much of what passes for praise in our assemblies. We come to church, but we leave our minds at home. We hear of God's grace, but our hearts have been hardened by a critical and carping spirit." (Boice)

iii. "The singer addresses himself. He realizes that he has power over himself, that he is able to give or to withhold that which is due to God." (Morgan)

iv. "The one value of these opening words is that they show us that worship is not involuntary, automatic. It calls for the coordination of all our powers.... The sanctuary is not a lounge, a place of relaxation. We should enter it with all the powers of personality arrested, arranged, dedicated. Then we may render a service of praise that is worthy and acceptable." (Morgan)

v. **Bless His holy name**: "Only a holy man can delight in holy things. Holiness is the terror of unholy men; they love sin and count it liberty, but holiness is to them a slavery. If we be saints we shall bless God for his holiness." (Spurgeon)

d. **Bless the LORD, O my soul, and forget not all His benefits**: In the pattern of Hebrew poetry, David used repetition for emphasis. He then added an important idea – that this praise and honor to God should be given unto Him for *rational reasons*, not on the basis of mere emotion or excitement. True **benefits** are given by God unto His people, and we must not **forget** them. Instead, we should use the remembrance of those things as reasons to praise.

i. 2 Chronicles 32:25 describes a king who *did* forget God's benefits, at least for a time: *But Hezekiah did not repay according to the favor shown him, for his heart was lifted up; therefore wrath was looming over him and over Judah and Jerusalem.*

ii. "Thanksgiving cannot be sincere and hearty, unless a man bear impressed upon his mind, at the time, a quick sense of 'benefits' received." (Horne)

iii. "Praise is the response of awe for God, while reflecting on what the Lord has done for the people of God throughout the history of redemption, for creation at large, for the community, and for oneself." (VanGemeren)

2. (3-5) Blessing God who redeems.

Who forgives all your iniquities,
Who heals all your diseases,
Who redeems your life from destruction,
Who crowns you with lovingkindness and tender mercies,
Who satisfies your mouth with good *things,*
***So that* your youth is renewed like the eagle's.**

a. **Who forgives all your iniquities**: One of the great *benefits* mentioned in verse 3 is the forgiveness of **all** our sins. When the magnitude of our sin and the righteousness of God are understood, this forgiveness is a staggering reason for praising and honoring God.

i. This begins a series of great benefits God brings to His believing people. "He selects a few of the choicest pearls from the casket of divine love, threads them on the string of memory, and hangs them about the neck of gratitude." (Spurgeon)

ii. Significantly, this is the benefit listed *first*. In David's mind, the most important thing was to have sins forgiven, even more important than physical healing.

iii. "The profound consciousness of sin, which it was one aim of the Law to evoke, underlies the psalmist's praise." (Maclaren)

b. **Who heals all your diseases**: Another great benefit is God's care for our bodies. He brings healing to us in this life through both natural and miraculous ways. He promises ultimate healing for all His people in the age to come.

i. Many commentators understand these **diseases** as spiritual in nature. Horne described this thinking: "What is pride, but lunacy? What is lust, but a leprosy? What is sloth, but a dead palsy? Perhaps there are spiritual maladies similar to all [bodily] ones." While it is true that sin leads to spiritual illness, here David seems to refer to physical **diseases**.

ii. "Some suggest that David is speaking about spiritual illness, such as the burdens of sin. But that is not it. I think he really is speaking of diseases. He is saying that when we are healed, as we often are, it is God who has done it. He is the healer of the body as well as of the soul. Therefore, such health as we have been given is a sure gift from God. God should be praised for it." (Boice)

c. **Who redeems your life from destruction**: Many know the powerful blessing of God's rescue from sure **destruction**. Many calamities are spared the child of God, whether he knows it or not.

i. **Who redeems**: "Preservation from destruction, *haggoel*, properly, *redemption of life by the kinsman*; possibly looking forward, in the spirit of prophecy, to him who became partaker of our flesh and blood, that he might have the right to redeem our souls from death by dying in our stead." (Clarke)

d. **Who crowns you with lovingkindness and tender mercies**: God's greatness extends beyond sparing us from sin, disease, or trouble. Through God's blessing, we are crowned with His great love and mercy.

e. **Who satisfies your mouth with good things**: The result of God's work, both in what He saves us from and what He saves us unto, is to bring true *satisfaction* to our lives. This is different from mere pleasure or entertainment; God wants to bring true satisfaction to our lives from **good things**. This satisfaction becomes a source of strength and energy to His people (**your youth is renewed like the eagle's**).

i. "It is God who gives us the 'good things' of this world, and who giveth us likewise an appetite and a taste to enjoy them." (Horne)

ii. **Who satisfies**: "No man is ever filled to satisfaction but a believer, and only God himself can satisfy even him. Many a worldling is satiated, but not one is satisfied." (Spurgeon)

iii. **Your youth is renewed like the eagle's**: "The second line is not implying…that eagles have the power of self-renewal; only that God renews us to…the very picture of buoyant, tireless strength which Isaiah 40:30f. takes up." (Kidner)

3. (6-7) Blessing God who is righteous.

The Lord executes righteousness
And justice for all who are oppressed.
He made known His ways to Moses,
His acts to the children of Israel.

a. **The Lord executes righteousness and justice**: In the previous section, David described the greatness of God in His work to the individual. Yet God also shows His greatness in bringing **righteousness and justice** to societies.

    i. "Our own personal obligations must not absorb our song; we must also magnify the Lord for his goodness to others." (Spurgeon)

b. **He made known His ways**: Another aspect of God's greatness is His self-revelation. God could be content to hide Himself, but instead He wanted to make **known His way** and **His acts**.

4. (8-10) Blessing God who is gracious.

The Lord is merciful and gracious,
Slow to anger, and abounding in mercy.
He will not always strive *with us,*
Nor will He keep *His anger* forever.
He has not dealt with us according to our sins,
Nor punished us according to our iniquities.

a. **The Lord is merciful and gracious**: In the previous lines, David described the righteousness and justice of God. Those aspects of God's character are true, but so also are His mercy and graciousness. His **anger** comes, but slowly and after much **mercy** has been shown.

    i. "All the world tastes of his sparing mercy, those who hear the gospel partake of his inviting mercy, the saints live by his saving mercy, are preserved by his upholding mercy, are cheered by his consoling mercy, and will enter heaven through his infinite and everlasting mercy." (Spurgeon)

b. **Abounding in mercy**: David's statements remind us of God's revelation of Himself to Moses in Exodus 34: *The Lord, the Lord God, merciful and gracious, longsuffering, and abounding in goodness and truth* (Exodus 34:6).

    i. **He will not always strive with us**: "These very human terms point the contrast between God's generosity and the heavy-handed wrath of man, who loves to keep his quarrels going (*chide* [**strive**] translates a term much used for disputes, especially at law) and to nurse his grievances." (Kidner)

c. **He has not dealt with us according to our sins**: David knew the slow anger and abounding mercy of God *personally*. He knew that his sins (and the sins of his people) deserved much greater judgment or discipline than they had received.

i. "We ought to praise the Lord for what he has not done as well as for what he has wrought for us; even the negative side deserves our adoring gratitude." (Spurgeon)

ii. "Why is it that God hath not dealt with us after our sins? Is it not because he hath dealt with another after our sins? Another who took our sins upon him." (Baker, cited in Spurgeon)

5. (11-12) The greatness of God's gracious forgiveness.

For as the heavens are high above the earth,
***So* great is His mercy toward those who fear Him;**
As far as the east is from the west,
***So* far has He removed our transgressions from us.**

a. **For as the heavens are high above the earth**: This is a description of the *abounding* mercy of God mentioned in verse 8. The distance from the earth to the heavens measures the greatness of His mercy **toward those who fear Him**. By instinct, we often think of God's mercy as *less* than it really is.

i. There were three concepts of heaven in the ancient Biblical world. The first heaven is the blue sky, the atmosphere with its sun. The second heaven is the night sky, the stars and constellations. The third heaven is the place where God dwells and is enthroned. It's interesting to wonder which of the three concepts of heaven David had in mind with this wonderful statement.

b. **As far as the east is from the west**: This is a description of the great forgiveness of God mentioned in verse 10. We have no idea if David knew the shape of the earth, but the Holy Spirit who inspired David to write this did, and the nature of the earth and our way of describing directions makes this statement particularly inspiring.

i. **As far as the east is from the west** is much greater than saying *as far as the north is from the south,* **so far has He removed our transgressions from us**. If you travel north on a globe, you begin to travel south as soon as you go over the North Pole. But if you travel east, you will continue east forever. Given the true shape of the earth, **east** and **west** never meet – and this is how far God has removed our sins from us!

ii. "As the east and the west can never meet in one point, but be for ever at the same distance from each other, so our sins and their decreed punishment are removed to an eternal distance by his mercy." (Clarke)

iii. "God loves us, and he will love us for ever. He loves us infinitely, and he could not love us more than that if we had never fallen." (Spurgeon)

6. (13-14) Blessing God who shows great sympathy.

As a father pities *his* children,
So the LORD pities those who fear Him.
For He knows our frame;
He remembers that we *are* dust.

a. **The LORD pities those who fear Him**: David continues to describe the abounding mercy and goodness of God. The way that a good father cares for and even **pities his children** in their frailty and weakness, so the **LORD pities those who fear Him**.

i. We think of a loving father dealing with his tired children. He does not demand more of them than they can perform, but with care takes into account their weaknesses. He comforts them and measures his expectations according to his wisdom and compassion.

ii. Spurgeon considered the many ways God may pity His children:

- He pities our childish ignorance.
- He pities our childish weakness.
- He pities our childish foolishness.
- He pities our childish naughtiness.
- He pities our childish stumbles and falls.
- He pities the pain of His children.
- He pities the child when another has wronged him.
- He pities the fears of His children.

iii. "It is in the present tense, and carries the idea of continuity: at this very moment he is now pitying them that fear him. Though he knows your trials will work for your good, yet he pities you. Though he knows that there is sin in you, which, perhaps, may require this rough discipline ere you be sanctified, yet he pities you. Though he can hear the music of heaven, the songs and glees that will ultimately come of your present sighs and griefs, yet still he pities those groans and wails of yours." (Spurgeon)

iv. "We may lose ourselves amid the amplitudes of the lofty, wide-stretching sky, but this emblem of paternal love goes straight to our hearts. A pitying God! What can be added to that?" (Maclaren)

v. The wise reaction to this is, **fear** *the* LORD! How much better to be on the side of His pity and compassion than to be on the side of His anger or righteous judgment!

b. **For He knows our frame**: The pity and compassion of God towards those who fear Him are rooted in His knowledge and understanding of our inherent weakness and impermanence, our transience.

i. "The word rendered 'frame' is literally, 'formation' or 'fashioning,' and comes from the same root as the verb employed in Genesis 2:7 to describe man's creation. 'The Lord God formed man of the dust of the ground.' It is also used for the potter's action in moulding earthen vessels. (Isaiah 29:16, etc.) So, in the next clause, 'dust' carries on the allusion to Genesis, and the general idea conveyed is that of frailty." (Maclaren)

ii. "In all his conduct towards us he considers the frailty of our nature, the untowardness of our circumstances, the strength and subtlety of temptation, and the sure party (till the heart is renewed) that the tempter has within us." (Clarke)

iii. This **pity** and remembrance were turned to empathy at the incarnation. God Himself added humanity to His deity and experienced **our frame** and our **dust**-like weakness. What before He knew by observation, He submitted to know by *experience*.

B. Contrasts that display the greatness of God.

1. (15-18) The contrast between man's moment and God's permanence.

As for man, his days *are* like grass;
As a flower of the field, so he flourishes.
For the wind passes over it, and it is gone,
And its place remembers it no more.
But the mercy of the LORD is from everlasting to everlasting
On those who fear Him,
And His righteousness to children's children,
To such as keep His covenant,
And to those who remember His commandments to do them.

a. **As for man, his days are like grass**: David expanded the thought of man's weak frame and dust-like nature. Humanity is so transient that **his days are like grass** and like a **flower of the field** that blooms one day and withers the next. When the flower is gone, virtually nothing remains – **its place remembers it no more**.

i. "**A flower of the field;** which is more exposed to winds and other violences than the flowers of the garden, which are secured by the art and care of the gardener." (Poole)

ii. "The flower which faded in Adam, blooms anew in Christ, never to fade again." (Horne)

b. **But the mercy of the** L<small>ORD</small> **is from everlasting to everlasting**: This is true of God's mercy and of God Himself, the source of mercy. His *hesed* – covenant love, loyal kindness – endures from all ages to all ages. **Those who fear Him** receive the benefit of this everlasting mercy, as do their **children's children**.

i. "God's love does not alter with our alterings, or change with our changes. Does the mother's love fluctuate with the moods of her sick babe?" (Meyer)

ii. "There never was a time when He did not love you. His mercy is from everlasting; nor a time when He will love you less – it is to everlasting." (Meyer)

c. **To such as keep His covenant**: These promises of everlasting love and mercy are given with conditions. The promises are made to **those who fear Him**, to those who **keep His covenant**, and those who **remember His commandments to do them**.

2. (19) The contrast between Yahweh and all creation.

The L<small>ORD</small> has established His throne in heaven,
And His kingdom rules over all.

a. **The L<small>ORD</small> has established His throne in heaven**: David celebrated God's secure reign from heaven. God is enthroned **in heaven**, beyond the troubles and corruptions of earth. It is **established**, and will never be moved.

b. **And His kingdom rules over all**: An eternal contrast is made between the Ruler and the ruled. There is no aspect of the universe that is not under His reign.

i. "When Melancthon was extremely solicitous [worried] about the affairs of the church in his days, Luther would have him admonished in these terms, *Monendus est Philippzzs ut desinat esse rector mundi,* Let not Philip make himself any longer governor of the world." (Clarkson, cited in Spurgeon)

3. (20-22) The contrast between God and His angels.

Bless the L<small>ORD</small>, you His angels,
Who excel in strength, who do His word,
Heeding the voice of His word.
Bless the L<small>ORD</small>, all *you* His hosts,
***You* ministers of His, who do His pleasure.**
Bless the L<small>ORD</small>, all His works,

In all places of His dominion.
Bless the LORD, O my soul!

a. **Bless the LORD, you His angels**: David began the psalm by telling his own soul to bless the Lord, but he knew the praise and honor to God should go beyond what he could give. It should extend all the way to the angels, and David boldly told them to also **bless the LORD**.

b. **Who excel in strength, who do His word**: The angels are strong and obedient, but even they should **bless the LORD**, giving Him praise and honor.

c. **Bless the LORD, all you His hosts**: The angels also make up God's **hosts**: His heavenly army under His command **who do His pleasure**. As God's soldiers, they should give Him the honor and praise due to Him.

d. **Bless the LORD, all His works**: David extended the call to honor and praise God further than the angels to **all** of God's **works**, in **all places of His dominion**.

i. **All His works**: "His song is no solo, for all creation is singing – or will sing – with him; but his voice, like every other, has its own part to add, its own 'benefits' (2ff.) to celebrate, and its own access (cf. Ps. 5:3) to the attentive ear of God." (Kidner)

ii. "Man is but little, yet, placing his hands upon the keys of the great organ of the universe, he wakes it to thunders of adoration! Redeemed man is the voice of nature, the priest in the temple of creation, the precentor in the worship of the universe." (Spurgeon)

iii. "The 'my' of personal experience merges into the 'our' of social fellowship, thus culminates in the 'all' of universal consciousness." (Morgan)

e. **Bless the LORD, O my soul**: David ended the psalm as he began it, with a call to his own **soul** to bless God, giving Him the honor and praise due to Him. After the many reasons given in Psalm 103, David had *more* reasons to **bless the LORD** at the end of the psalm.

Psalm 104 – LORD of All Creation

"This Psalm has no title either in the Hebrew or Chaldee; but it is attributed to David by the Vulgate, Septuagint, Ethiopic, Arabic, and Syriac." (Adam Clarke)

"The Psalm gives an interpretation to the many voices of nature, and sings sweetly both of creation and providence. The poem contains a complete cosmos: sea and land, cloud and sunlight, plant and animal, light and darkness, life and death, are all proved to be expressive of the presence of the Lord." (Charles Spurgeon)

A. The glory of God's creation in light, angels, earth, and waters.

1. (1-2) Praising the God of honor, majesty, and might.

Bless the LORD, O my soul!
O LORD my God, You are very great:
You are clothed with honor and majesty,
Who cover *Yourself* with light as *with* a garment,
Who stretch out the heavens like a curtain.

a. **Bless the LORD, O my soul**: Repeated three times in the previous psalm, this phrase is a call to worship God in spirit and in truth, and to do so from one's inmost being.

b. **You are very great**: The psalmist worshipped Yahweh as his **God**, and as the **great** One who is **clothed with honor and majesty**. The idol gods of the nations were often described as crude and shameful in their conduct, but Yahweh, the covenant God of Israel, is known for His **honor and majesty**.

i. "The verse sums up the whole of the creative act in one grand thought. In that act the invisible God has arrayed Himself in splendour and glory, making visible these inherent attributes. That is the deepest meaning of Creation. The Universe is the garment of God." (Maclaren)

c. **Who cover Yourself with light as with a garment**: God's **honor and majesty** are as apparent as a person's clothing, and so is the **light**-like

187

purity of His being. Just as the creation in Genesis begins with describing the creation of light, so the psalmist first mentions light.

i. "The patterns are close enough to show that the psalmist had Genesis in mind as he worked on his composition. We will not be far wrong if we think of Psalm 104 as a poetic reflection on the more factual account in Genesis." (Boice)

ii. "The structure of the psalm is modelled fairly closely on that of Genesis 1, taking the stages of creation as starting-points for praise." (Kidner)

iii. In a small way, we can understand this idea of **light as a garment** by consider the appearance of Jesus at His transfiguration: *His face shone like the sun, and His clothes became as white as the light* (Matthew 17:2).

iv. 1 Timothy 6:16 says God dwells *in unapproachable light.* Perhaps this is another description or allusion to **light as a garment**. "If light itself is but his garment and veil, what must be the blazing splendour of his own essential being! We are lost in astonishment, and dare not pry into the mystery lest we be blinded by its insufferable glory." (Spurgeon)

d. **Who stretch out the heavens like a curtain**: God's power is also apparent as the One who created the vast heavens. Since the Creator is greater than His creation, the God who created the **heavens** is impressive, indeed.

2. (3-4) The supreme might of God seen in creation.

He lays the beams of His upper chambers in the waters,
Who makes the clouds His chariot,
Who walks on the wings of the wind,
Who makes His angels spirits,
His ministers a flame of fire.

a. **He lays the beams of His upper chambers in the waters**: The God of all creation can build and do what no one else can. He does not share the limitations of the creation; He makes **the clouds His chariot** and He **walks on the wings of the wind**.

i. The picture described is full of activity and excitement. "The metaphor of his taking up its parts and powers as his robe, tent, palace and chariot invites us to see the world as something he delights in, which is charged with his energy and alive with his presence." (Kidner)

ii. "The Lord is surrounded by his servants, whether they be created like the angels or be powers inherent in his created order (winds, lightning). The Creator-King is, as it were, driving his chariot, symbolic of his governance of his creation." (VanGemeren)

iii. **Upper chambers**: "The 'chambers,' built above the first story of a house for the purpose of privacy and seclusion (cf. 1 Kings 17:19; 2 Kings 4:10), represent God's involvement with and separation from his world (Amos 9:6)." (VanGemeren)

b. **Who makes His angels spirits, His ministers a flame of fire**: God also rules over the angels, equipping and commissioning them as it pleases Him.

i. Later, the writer of Hebrews quoted Psalm verse 4 and revealed that the **His** in that verse refers to the Messiah, Jesus Christ (Hebrews 1:7). This confirms the deity of Jesus the Messiah, because the angels belong to *Him* – they are **His angels** and **His ministers**.

3. (5-9) The power of God evident at the flood and its aftermath.

You who **laid the foundations of the earth,**
So *that* **it should not be moved forever,**
You covered it with the deep as *with* **a garment;**
The waters stood above the mountains.
At Your rebuke they fled;
At the voice of Your thunder they hastened away.
They went up over the mountains;
They went down into the valleys,
To the place which You founded for them.
You have set a boundary that they may not pass over,
That they may not return to cover the earth.

a. **You who laid the foundations of the earth**: The psalmist understood that *God* was the Creator of all things, and that it was He who **laid the foundations of the earth**. It did not happen by chance or random events. There is a Creator behind all things.

i. In some ways, the modern age is significantly defined by man's rejection of God as Creator. Having abandoned this fundamental truth, humanity drifts without a proper sense of responsibility or accountability toward its Creator.

b. **So that it should not be moved forever**: What God built, He built well. The earth's **foundations** are solid and will **not be moved** until God Himself moves them.

i. **The foundations of the earth**: "Upon itself, or its own weight, whereby it stands as fast and unmovable, as if it were built upon the strongest foundations imaginable; which is a stupendous work of Divine power and wisdom." (Poole)

c. **You covered it with the deep**: The psalmist had in mind two events. The separation of the waters at creation (Genesis 1:9-10) and the global flood described in Genesis 7. From reading Genesis 7:19-20, the psalmist understood that **the waters stood above the mountains** (*And the waters prevailed exceedingly on the earth, and all the high hills under the whole heaven were covered. The waters prevailed fifteen cubits upward, and the mountains were covered*).

i. "Indeed, the process at the creation was so exactly similar to that at the deluge, with regards to the circumstances here mentioned, that it matters not to which we apply the beautiful and truly poetical passage before us." (Horne)

d. **At Your rebuke they fled**: When the waters had covered the earth long enough, God made them recede (Genesis 8:3), and the psalmist poetically described it as God's **rebuke** of the waters. God's **voice** is poetically described as **thunder**.

i. Centuries later, God the Son would rebuke waters and calm them (Matthew 8:26).

e. **To the place which You founded for them**: The waters receded to the place God had appointed for them, and He **set a boundary** for the waters so they could never again **cover the earth**, as He promised (Genesis 8:11-17).

i. "The waters of the sea are not only prevented from destroying the earth, but, by a wonderful machinery, are rendered the means of preserving every living thing which moveth thereon." (Horne)

4. (10-13) What God did with the waters of the earth.

He sends the springs into the valleys;
They flow among the hills.
They give drink to every beast of the field;
The wild donkeys quench their thirst.
By them the birds of the heavens have their home;
They sing among the branches.
He waters the hills from His upper chambers;
The earth is satisfied with the fruit of Your works.

a. **He sends the springs into the valleys**: In the previous section, the psalmist referred to what God did with the waters of the earth after the flood in Noah's day. Now he considers how God distributed waters across the land, sending **springs into the valleys** to **give drink to every beast of the field**.

b. **The earth is satisfied with the fruit of Your works**: The psalmist considered how the water, plants, and animals of the earth each find their place in God's plan and order. The **wild donkeys** drink their water, the **birds** have a home so they may **sing among the branches**. He saw a good, harmonious world in nature and knew Yahweh was responsible for it.

i. **Wild donkeys**: "Which he mentions, partly because they are dry and thirsty creatures; and partly because they live in dry and desolate wildernesses, and are neither ruled nor regarded by men, and are most stupid creatures, and yet are plentifully provided for by the care and bounty of Divine Providence." (Poole)

ii. **They sing among the branches**: "If these little choristers of the air, when refreshed by the streams near which they dwell, express their gratitude by chanting, in their way, the praises of their Maker and Preserver, how ought Christians to blush, who, besides the comforts and conveniences of this world, are so indulged with copious draughts of the water of eternal life, if, for so great blessings, they pay not their tribute of thanksgiving, and sing not unto the Lord the songs of Sion!" (Horne)

B. The glory of God's creation in living things, plants and animals.

1. (14-18) God's wonderful world of nature.

He causes the grass to grow for the cattle,
And vegetation for the service of man,
That he may bring forth food from the earth,
And wine *that* **makes glad the heart of man,**
Oil to make *his* **face shine,**
And bread *which* **strengthens man's heart.**
The trees of the LORD are full *of sap,*
The cedars of Lebanon which He planted,
Where the birds make their nests;
The stork has her home in the fir trees.
The high hills *are* **for the wild goats;**
The cliffs are a refuge for the rock badgers.

a. **He causes grass to grow for the cattle**: The psalmist continued his thoughts on nature, seeing how God provides **grass** for animals and **vegetation for the service of man**.

i. "Divine power is as truly and as worthily put forth in the feeding of beasts as in the nurturing of man; watch but a blade of grass with a devout eye and you may see God at work within it." (Spurgeon)

b. **That he may bring forth food from the earth**: God designed the ecology of the world so that with work, man may **bring forth food**. Under God's blessing and man's work, the food brought forth is wonderful. God's earth gives us **wine**, **oil**, and **bread** – each with their own blessing and goodness.

i. **Wine that makes glad the heart of man**: "*Wine*, in moderate quantity, has a wondrous tendency to revive and invigorate the human being. *Ardent spirits* exhilarate, but they *exhaust* the strength; and every dose leaves man the worse. Unadulterated wine, on the contrary, *exhilarates* and *invigorates*: it makes him cheerful, and provides for the continuance of that cheerfulness by *strengthening* the *muscles*, and *bracing* the *nerves*. This is its *use*. Those who continue drinking till wine inflames them, *abuse* this mercy of God." (Clarke)

c. **The trees of the LORD are full of sap**: The psalmist had a vision of how *healthy* and vigorous nature is. He thought of the mighty **cedars of Lebanon** and how, in their **sap**-filled health, they give a place **where the birds make their nests**.

i. They are **the trees of the LORD** in the sense that no human hand planted them; **He planted** these mighty trees. "Who ever planted the seeds of the cedars of Lebanon, or of the thousands of woods and forests on the globe? God himself sowed those seeds, and they have sprung up and flourished without the care of man." (Clarke)

ii. "What would our Psalmist have said to some of the trees in the Yosemite Valley? Truly these are worthy to be called the trees of the Lord, for towering stature and enormous girth. Thus is the care of God seen to be effectual and all-sufficient. If trees uncared for by man are yet so full of sap, we may rest assured that the people of God who by faith live upon the Lord alone shall be equally well sustained." (Spurgeon)

iii. "You will observe that the word 'sap,' is inserted in italics; it is not there in the Hebrew. 'The trees of the Lord are full,' or rather, which gives the meaning clearly, 'The trees of the Lord are satiated – are satisfied – the cedars of Lebanon, which he hath planted.'" (Spurgeon)

iv. "A traveler tells us that in the wood bark, and even the cones of the cedar there is an abundance of resin. They are saturated with it so that he says he can scarcely touch one of the cedars of Lebanon without having the turpentine or resin of them upon his hands. That is always the way with a truly healthy Christian, his grace is externally manifested." (Spurgeon)

d. **The stork has her home**: The birds have their nests, but the other animals have their homes also, including the **stork**, the **wild goats**, and the **rock badgers**. A wise and loving God provides for them all.

i. "The *badger* is a misnomer for the hyrax, a small and shy rock-dweller (cf. Prov. 30:26)." (Kidner)

2. (19-23) The sun and moon bless the world God created.

He appointed the moon for seasons;
The sun knows its going down.
You make darkness, and it is night,
In which all the beasts of the forest creep about.
The young lions roar after their prey,
And seek their food from God.
When the sun rises, they gather together
And lie down in their dens.
Man goes out to his work
And to his labor until the evening.

a. **He appointed the moon for seasons**: The psalmist turned his attention to the **moon** and the **sun**. They operate according to God's plan, providing **darkness** so that **all the beasts of the forest creep about**.

i. "The moon is named first, because the Hebrew day began with the evening." (Maclaren)

ii. "Canaanites attributed rain, sunlight, and the lunar cycle to specific deities. For Israel the Lord sovereignly rules over all creation and establishes order by his wise administration." (VanGemeren)

b. **When the sun rises**: Just as God provided for the night, He also provided for the day, when **lions** and other nocturnal animals **lie down in their dens**. When the lions sleep, **man goes out to his work** until **the evening**. All operate according to God's wise plan for creation.

i. "God feeds not only sheep and lambs, but wolves and lions. It is a strange expression that young lions when they roar after their prey, should be said to *seek their meat of God;* implying that neither their own strength nor craft could feed them without help from God. The strongest creatures left to themselves cannot help themselves." (Caryl, cited in Spurgeon)

ii. "And as it would not be convenient for man and the wild beasts of the forest to collect their food *at the same time*, he has given the *night* to them as the proper time to procure their prey, and the *day* to rest in. When *MAN labours, THEY rest; when MAN rests, THEY labour.*" (Clarke)

3. (24-26) The wonder of the sea God created.

O Lord, how manifold are Your works!
In wisdom You have made them all.
The earth is full of Your possessions—
This great and wide sea,
In which *are* innumerable teeming things,
Living things both small and great.
There the ships sail about;
***There is* that Leviathan**
Which You have made to play there.

a. **O Lord, how manifold are Your works**: The psalmist continues in amazement as he looks at nature and creation. He sees it all not as the result of random and purposeless events, but as the wise **works** of a great God who has right of ownership over all of it (**Your possessions**).

i. **Your works.... Your possessions**: "They are all God's *property*, and should be used only in reference to the end for which they were created. All *abuse* and *waste* of God's creatures are spoil and robbery on the property of the Creator." (Clarke)

b. **This great and wide sea**: The psalmist thought of the greatness of the oceans (in his case, the Mediterranean Sea). The vast waters contain **innumerable teeming things**, including great and mysterious things such as **Leviathan** which is also described in Job 41.

i. "There is not in all nature a more august and striking object than the ocean." (Horne)

ii. **Leviathan**: "This may mean the *whale*, or any of the large marine animals. The *Septuagint* and *Vulgate* call it *dragon*. Sometimes the *crocodile* is intended by the original word." (Clarke)

iii. "As for *Leviathan*, a name which can have a sinister ring (see on 74:13-15), he makes his appearance simply as some large and sportive creature, whose very existence glorifies and delights its Maker." (Kidner)

C. God and the world He created.

1. (27-30) Creation's dependence upon God.

These all wait for You,
That You may give *them* their food in due season.

What You give them they gather in;
You open Your hand, they are filled with good.
You hide Your face, they are troubled;
You take away their breath, they die and return to their dust.
You send forth Your Spirit, they are created;
And You renew the face of the earth.

a. **These all wait for You, that You may give them their food**: The psalmist considered all kinds of created things from the land, sea, and air. He recognized that they **all** depended upon God, who provided for them **in due season**.

i. **In due season**: "God has a timing for all things, and does not feed his creatures by fits and starts; he gives them daily bread, and a quantity proportioned to their needs. This is all that any of us should expect; if even the brute creatures are content with a sufficiency we ought not to be more greedy than they." (Spurgeon)

b. **What You give them they gather in**: God feeds the animals, but does not from heaven pour food into their mouths. He provides, but they must **gather in**.

i. "When we see the chickens picking up the corn which the housewife scatters from her lap we have an apt illustration of the manner in which the Lord supplies the needs of all living things – he gives and they gather." (Spurgeon)

ii. "The verb rendered '*gather*' means to pick up or collect from the ground. It is used in the history of the manna (Exodus 16:1, 5, 16), to which there is obvious allusion. The act of gathering from the ground seems to presuppose a previous throwing down from heaven." (Alexander, cited in Spurgeon)

iii. This is a wonderful way for God's people to think of His provision. God provides, but we must gather in. His provision is all around us, and we simply need the wisdom and effort to gather it in.

iv. This principle also has application to evangelism: "God will give us souls if we pray for them, but we must seek after them. When the Lord calls a man to speak in his name, he intends to give him some success, but he must be on the watch to gather it." (Spurgeon)

c. **You hide Your face, they are troubled**: Creation is so dependent upon God that if He were to **hide** His presence or **take away their breath**, they would soon perish. There is a real sense in which creation is much more responsive and surrendered to God than humanity.

d. **You send forth Your Spirit, they are created**: The withdrawal of God's presence or favor means ruin for all creation, but the outpouring of His **Spirit** means life and renewal.

  i. **You send forth Your Spirit, they are created**: "The Spirit of God creates every day: what is it that continueth things in their created being, but providence? That is a true axiom in divinity, *Providence is creation continued.*" (Caryl, cited in Spurgeon)

2. (31-32) Blessing the God of all creation.

May the glory of the Lord endure forever;
May the Lord rejoice in His works.
He looks on the earth, and it trembles;
He touches the hills, and they smoke.

  a. **May the glory of the Lord endure forever**: As the psalmist considered the power and wisdom of God in all creation, it made him long for His **glory** to **endure forever**.

  i. "His works may pass away, but not his glory. Were it only for what he has already done, the Lord deserves to be praised without ceasing." (Spurgeon)

  b. **May the Lord rejoice in His works**: The psalmist also wanted God to find pleasure in what He had created. This implies that His creatures that are gifted with rational choice (such as humanity) should deliberately choose to give God reasons to **rejoice in His works**.

  i. "This is perhaps the highest and most daring note in all this wonderful song of praise. So impressed with the glory and wonder and beauty of creation was the singer, that he positively called upon God to rejoice in what He had wrought." (Morgan)

  ii. "As he did at the creation, when he saw all to be good, and very good; so still, it doth God good, as it were, to see the poor creatures feed, and men to give him the honour of all." (Trapp)

  iii. "There is nothing irreverent in this. It is rather an expression of the soul's profound understanding of what God actually feels in view of His own mighty and marvelous works." (Morgan)

  c. **He looks on the earth, and it trembles**: The shaking earth and smoking hills may be a reference to God's manifested presence at Mount Sinai (Exodus 19). These are reminders of the overwhelming power and might of God.

3. (33-35) A determination to praise God in song and in meditation.

I will sing to the LORD as long as I live;
I will sing praise to my God while I have my being.
May my meditation be sweet to Him;
I will be glad in the LORD.
May sinners be consumed from the earth,
And the wicked be no more.
Bless the LORD, O my soul!
Praise the LORD!

a. **I will sing to the LORD as long as I live**: This remarkable psalm has little or no focus on God as redeemer and savior. Its focus is on the greatness and goodness of God as displayed in creation. Yet that was enough to make the psalmist determined to say **I will sing to the LORD as long as I live**. The God of all creation is worthy of our life-long praise.

> i. "As far as he was concerned, an entire lifetime of praise would be insufficient to honor God properly." (Boice)

> ii. This again shows the importance of *knowing God as creator*. The rejection of God as creator has had deep and terrible effects upon the hearts and minds of the modern world.

b. **May my meditation be sweet to Him**: The psalmist understood that God is also worshipped by our *thoughts*. What we choose to set our mind on is a measure of what we truly value. Knowing the greatness and goodness of God as revealed in creation, the psalmist wanted his thoughts to be pleasing to God.

> i. Creation is a wonderful subject for sweet meditation, but we have even greater subjects. "Redemption is a choicer theme for meditation than creation is, for its wonders are far greater." (Spurgeon)

> ii. "The last words ever written by Henry Martyn, dying among Mohammedans in Persia, was: I sat in the orchard and thought with sweet comfort and peace of my God, in solitude my company, my Friend and Comforter." (Spurgeon)

c. **I will be glad in the LORD**: We again sense a note of determination. He *chose* to be **glad in the LORD**, making a rational choice in light of God's revelation of Himself through creation.

d. **May sinners be consumed from the earth**: This seems a strange and solemn declaration in this psalm. Yet it is the logical consequence for those who *reject* God as creator. Paul later developed this thought in Romans 1, speaking of the guilt and consequences due to those who reject God as creator and worship the creature rather than the creator.

i. "The psalmist is not vindictive in his prayer against the wicked but longs for a world fully established and maintained by the Lord, without outside interference." (VanGemeren)

e. **Bless the Lord, O my soul**: The psalmist was compelled to consider the dark consequences due to those who rejected the creator God, but he could not end this remarkable psalm on a dark note. He ends with another rousing call to His own soul to **bless the Lord**, and to **praise the Lord**. This is the fitting response of the creature to the Creator.

i. **Praise the Lord**: "This is the first psalm which closes with Hallelujah (Praise Jehovah)." (Maclaren)

ii. "This is the first occurrence of *hallelujah* in the Psalter, and it is significant that it is joined to a prayer for the destruction of the wicked, just as it is in Revelation 19." (Boice)

Psalm 105 – The LORD's Blessings on His Covenant People

Whoever arranged and ordered the psalms placed Psalm 105 and Psalm 106 together purposefully. "This and the following psalm are companions. They reveal the two sides of the relation between God and His people during a long period. This one sings the song of His faithfulness and power; while the next tells the sad story of repeated failure and rebellion on the part of His people." (G. Campbell Morgan)

The first 15 verses of Psalm 105 are also found in 1 Chronicles 16:8-22 and presented there as a composition of David, written and sung for the bringing of the ark of the covenant into Jerusalem. We can therefore conclude that though this psalm is not here specifically attributed to King David, he is the author of it.

A. A call to the people of God.

1. (1-3) A call to worship the LORD.

Oh, give thanks to the LORD!
Call upon His name;
Make known His deeds among the peoples!
Sing to Him, sing psalms to Him;
Talk of all His wondrous works!
Glory in His holy name;
Let the hearts of those rejoice who seek the LORD!

a. **Oh, give thanks to the LORD:** Previous psalms focused on stirring one's soul to bless the LORD. Now David encouraged himself and others to **give thanks to the LORD**, and Psalm 105 will give many reasons for this thanksgiving. This is the first of several quickly stated encouragements to honor and worship God.

i. These first six verses of Psalm 105 "...are full of exultation, and, in their reiterated short clauses, are like the joyful cries of a herald bringing good tidings to Zion." (Maclaren)

199

b. **Call upon His name**: This probably has the idea of calling upon Yahweh and *not* upon the idols of the nations. He alone deserves to be called upon to praise and to rely on.

c. **Make known His deeds among the peoples**: David will recount the amazing **deeds** God has done in the sight of all **peoples**, and he encouraged all who heard him to do the same. God's people should **talk of all His wondrous works!**

d. **Sing to Him**: As in many other places in the psalms, God's people are told the importance of praising Him in song. The songs should be sung **to Him**, and not to an audience or merely for one's own pleasure.

e. **Glory in His holy name**: We can glory in many things. Some glory in wealth or status, while others glory in pleasure or entertainment. God's people rightly find their greatest **glory in His holy name**.

i. VanGemeren suggested three goals accomplished with praise in the context of this psalm.

- Praise magnifies the LORD, attributing power, holiness, and glory to Him.
- Praise intensifies an appreciation of the history of redemption.
- Praise witnesses to those outside the covenant community.

2. (4-6) A call to seek the LORD and remember His great works.

Seek the LORD and His strength;
Seek His face evermore!
Remember His marvelous works which He has done,
His wonders, and the judgments of His mouth,
O seed of Abraham His servant,
You children of Jacob, His chosen ones!

a. **Seek the LORD and His strength**: God's people are invited to not only **seek** God Himself, but also His **strength**. This strength is given to God's people as they seek Him, as Paul would later write: *Be strong in the Lord and in the power of His might* (Ephesians 6:10).

i. "Seek, seek, seek, we have the word three times, and though the words differ in the Hebrew, the sense is the same. It must be a blessed thing to *seek,* or we should not be thus stirred up to do so." (Spurgeon)

b. **Remember His marvelous works which He has done**: There is the constant danger that God's people would *forget* **His marvelous works**. It dishonors God when we forget His great works, and we will always drift to forgetfulness if we do not actively **remember**.

i. "Alas, we are far more ready to recollect foolish and evil things than to retain in our minds the glorious deeds of Jehovah. If we would keep these in remembrance our faith would be stronger, our gratitude warmer, our devotion more fervent, and our love more intense." (Spurgeon)

c. **O seed of Abraham His servant**: This psalm is especially directed towards God's covenant people, the descendants of Abraham, Isaac, and **Jacob**. These were **His chosen ones** in His covenant plan.

i. "Abraham is here called 'his servant' (v. 6; cf. v. 42), a term of closeness and of special appointment." (VanGemeren)

B. God's care for Israel under the patriarchs.

1. (7-12) God's marvelous covenant with the patriarchs.

He *is* the LORD our God;
His judgments *are* in all the earth.
He remembers His covenant forever,
The word *which* He commanded, for a thousand generations,
The covenant which He made with Abraham,
And His oath to Isaac,
And confirmed it to Jacob for a statute,
To Israel *as* an everlasting covenant,
Saying, "To you I will give the land of Canaan
As the allotment of your inheritance,"
When they were few in number,
Indeed very few, and strangers in it.

a. **His judgments are in all the earth**: Before focusing on the works and promises God made unto the people of Israel, David reminds us that God is over **all the earth**. His covenant focus on Israel does not take away from His interest and lordship over the whole earth.

i. **He is the LORD our God**: "He is *Jehovah*, the self-existent and eternal God. He is *our God*, he is our portion; has taken us for his people, and makes us happy in his love." (Clarke)

b. **He remembers His covenant forever**: God made a significant covenant with Abraham, Isaac, and Jacob that was passed to the nation of Israel. It is an **everlasting covenant**, and Israel's role as God's covenant people remains until the end of the age.

i. **The word which He commanded**: "Notice the expression, *the word that he commanded*, as a parallel term to *his covenant*. It puts the stress on God's initiative and authority in the covenant-making, which means that this bond with men is by grace, not mutual bargaining, and serves the interests of God's kingdom, not the selfish ends of men." (Kidner)

ii. Already in Psalm 105 we have repetition of the word **He**. "The master word in the psalm is the pronoun 'He.' In constant repetition it shows the one thought uppermost in the mind of the singer. It is that of perpetual activity of God in all those experiences through which His people have passed." (Morgan)

iii. Zacharias, the father of John the Baptist, seems to have paraphrased verses 8-11 as recorded in Luke 1:72-75. "Zacharias, under the immediate influence and direction of the Holy Spirit, transfers the language of the old dispensation to the affairs of the new one; he celebrates the redemption of the world, by Christ, from sin and death, in words which literally describe the redemption of Israel from Egypt by Moses." (Horne)

c. **I will give the land of Canaan**: One aspect of this **everlasting covenant** is the land God appointed for Israel. It is **the allotment of** their **inheritance**, given to them when they were **few in number**. God promised the land to Abraham when he and his family were only a small group of people in the land of Canaan.

2. (13-15) God's protection of the patriarchs.

When they went from one nation to another,
From *one* kingdom to another people,
He permitted no one to do them wrong;
Yes, He rebuked kings for their sakes,
***Saying*, "Do not touch My anointed ones,**
And do My prophets no harm."

a. **When they went from one nation to another**: The patriarchs had their seasons of wandering. Abraham came from Ur of the Chaldeans (Genesis 11:31-12:4) and journeyed to Egypt (Genesis 12:10-20). Jacob also lived for many years with Laban in *the land of the people of the East* (Genesis 29:1).

b. **He permitted no one to do them wrong**: In all their wanderings among the nations, God protected them. He even **rebuked kings for their sakes** (for example, Genesis 12:17-20 and Genesis 26).

i. "Destitute as they were of earthly help, the mightiest kings could not hurt them." (Horne)

c. **Do not touch My anointed ones**: God protected Abraham and Sarah before the king Abimelech, and did not let Abimelech **touch** her (Genesis 20:6). God protected Abraham, Isaac, and Jacob as His **prophets**.

i. **Do not touch My anointed ones**: "The words here mentioned may not have been actually spoken, but the impression of awe which fell upon the nations is thus poetically described." (Spurgeon)

ii. "This God speaketh not of kings, but to kings, concerning his people who have an unction from the Father, being sanctified and set apart for his peculiar purposes. To touch these is to touch the apple of God's eye, Zechariah 2:8; they are sacred persons." (Trapp)

iii. "It is supposed that the *patriarchs* are here intended; but the whole people of Israel may be meant. They were a kingdom of *priests* and *kings* unto God; and *prophets, priests*, and *kings* were always *anointed*." (Clarke)

iv. **Do My prophets no harm**: "The patriarch had deceived Abimelech by saying that Sarah was his sister rather than his wife, and Abimelech had almost taken her before God intervened to warn him that she was married to Abraham. It was then that God referred to Abraham as 'a prophet' (Gen. 20:7). Yet a 'lying' prophet! Obviously the emphasis here is upon God's faithfulness, not man's." (Boice)

3. (16-22) God's care for the patriarchs in the days of Joseph.

Moreover He called for a famine in the land;
He destroyed all the provision of bread.
He sent a man before them—
Joseph—*who* was sold as a slave.
They hurt his feet with fetters,
He was laid in irons.
Until the time that his word came to pass,
The word of the LORD tested him.
The king sent and released him,
The ruler of the people let him go free.
He made him lord of his house,
And ruler of all his possessions,
To bind his princes at his pleasure,
And teach his elders wisdom.

a. **He called for a famine in the land**: The great famine that came upon the greater region in the days of Joseph (Genesis 41:53-57) was no accident. God **called** the famine, and **destroyed all the provision of bread**.

b. **He sent a man before them**: David understood that the injustice and misfortune which came upon Joseph was ordained by God, so that in His plan he could be **sent** ahead to Egypt to save the patriarchs (and the whole region) from famine.

c. **They hurt his feet with fetters**: Joseph's pain in his slavery was real, yet it did not cancel the plan of God. His season of affliction was a time when **the word of the LORD tested him**.

> i. **He was laid in irons**: "Heb. His soul came into iron; or, the iron entered into his soul; but sin entered not into his conscience. See a like phrase Luke 2:35." (Trapp)

> ii. "May we not yet again turn the sentence round, and say that the iron entered into his soul? When we first meet him, Joseph is a tender, yielding lad, with dreams of rule, but no conspicuous power. Yet he emerges from his captivity well qualified to take the helm of Egypt." (Meyer)

> iii. "The iron fetters were preparing him to wear chains of gold, and making his feet ready to stand on high places. It is even so with all the Lord's afflicted ones, they too shall one day step from their prisons to their thrones." (Spurgeon)

d. **He made him lord of his house**: Joseph was brought low, but in God's timing he was lifted up. He was given authority over all the **possessions** of the house, and authority over **princes** and **elders**.

4. (23-25) God's preservation of Israel in Egypt.

Israel also came into Egypt,
And Jacob dwelt in the land of Ham.
He increased His people greatly,
And made them stronger than their enemies.
He turned their heart to hate His people,
To deal craftily with His servants.

a. **Israel also came into Egypt**: After God sent Joseph ahead, He took the people of Israel into the land of Egypt for their own provision and protection as a people.

> i. **Into Egypt**: "Whither he feared to go, till God promised him his presence and protection, Genesis 46:3-4. God saith the same in effect to us, when to descend into the grave, Fear not to go down, I will go down with thee, and be better to thee than thy fears." (Trapp)

b. **He increased His people greatly**: In Egypt, God's covenant people multiplied with very little intermarriage with the Egyptians. They were able to grow **greatly** (Exodus 1:7), and eventually they became **stronger than their enemies**.

c. **He turned their heart to hate His people**: The people of Israel were welcomed into the land of Egypt in the days of Joseph, but in later generations they were hated and made into slaves for the Egyptians (Exodus 1:8-12).

> i. "God cannot in any sense be the author of sin so far as to be morally responsible for its existence, but it often happens through the evil which is inherent in human nature that the acts of the Lord arouse the ill-feelings of ungodly men." (Spurgeon)

C. God's care for the Israelites as they came into the Promised Land.

1. (26-36) The deliverance from Egypt.

He sent Moses His servant,
And Aaron whom He had chosen.
They performed His signs among them,
And wonders in the land of Ham.
He sent darkness, and made *it* dark;
And they did not rebel against His word.
He turned their waters into blood,
And killed their fish.
Their land abounded with frogs,
Even in the chambers of their kings.
He spoke, and there came swarms of flies,
And lice in all their territory.
He gave them hail for rain,
And flaming fire in their land.
He struck their vines also, and their fig trees,
And splintered the trees of their territory.
He spoke, and locusts came,
Young locusts without number,
And ate up all the vegetation in their land,
And devoured the fruit of their ground.
He also destroyed all the firstborn in their land,
The first of all their strength.

> a. **He sent Moses His servant**: With Israel under slavery and bondage in Egypt, God raised up deliverers for His people at the appointed time: **Moses** (given the wonderful title **His servant**) and his brother **Aaron**. God gave these men the ability to perform **His signs** to authenticate their work.

> b. **He sent darkness, and made it dark**: David clearly regarded the record in Exodus as historically true. He recounted the plagues God sent upon Egypt, all according to the **word** God gave to Moses and Aaron (**they did not rebel against His word**).

i. "In order to understand these plagues we need to understand that they were directed against the gods and goddesses of Egypt and were intended to show the superiority of the God of Israel to the Egyptian gods." (Boice)

- When God **sent darkness**, He showed Himself greater than *Ra* (the sun God) and *Nut* (the sky goddess).

- When God **turned their waters into blood**, He showed Himself greater than *Osiris* (god of the Nile) and *Khnum* (the guardian of the Nile).

- When God made their **land** abound **with frogs**, He showed Himself greater than the goddess *Hekt* (the frog-goddess of fertility).

- When God sent **swarms of flies** and **lice**, He showed Himself greater than the fly-god *Uatchit*.

- When God sent **hail for rain**, He showed Himself greater than *Geb*, the god of the earth; *Nepri*, the goddess of grain; and *Anuibis*, the guardian of the fields.

- When God sent **locusts without number**, He showed Himself greater than *Shu*, the god of the atmosphere, and *Min*, the deity of the harvest.

ii. David listed eight of the ten plagues described in Exodus 7-12, but not in the same order as in the Exodus account. Psalm 78 also has a partial listing of the plagues.

iii. "The plagues are presented here not to trace the progress of Pharaoh's hardening – he is not mentioned – but to praise the decisive and versatile power of God." (Kidner)

iv. **He struck their vines also, and their fig trees**: "This is not mentioned in Exodus; but we have had it before, Psalm 78:47." (Clarke)

c. **He also destroyed all the firstborn in their land**: The final and greatest plague against the Egyptians was the terrible death of the firstborn in every household which was not protected by the blood of the Passover lamb.

2. (37-41) The deliverance from Egypt into the wilderness.

He also brought them out with silver and gold,
And *there was* none feeble among His tribes.
Egypt was glad when they departed,
For the fear of them had fallen upon them.
He spread a cloud for a covering,

And fire to give light in the night.
The people asked, and He brought quail,
And satisfied them with the bread of heaven.
He opened the rock, and water gushed out;
It ran in the dry places *like* a river.

a. **He also brought them out with silver and gold**: When Israel came out of Egypt, the Egyptians gave them great riches (Exodus 12:35-36). The Egyptians were so crushed by the many plagues that **Egypt was glad when they departed**.

i. **There was none feeble among His tribes**: "Diseased or unable for his journey; which in so vast a body, and in a time of such mortality as it had been in Egypt, and in a people which had been so long and so dreadfully oppressed as the Israelites were, was wonderful; but they all journeyed on foot, Exodus 12:37." (Poole)

ii. "See the contrast between Egypt and Israel – in Egypt one dead in every house, and among the Israelites not one so much as limping." (Spurgeon)

b. **He spread a cloud for a covering**: As they journeyed through the wilderness, God gave Israel the protection of a **cloud** by day. He also provided **fire to give them light in the night**. These remarkable emblems of God's presence and care led Israel through the wilderness.

c. **The people asked, and He brought quail**: God miraculously supplied nourishment for Israel in the wilderness, providing **quail** and manna (**the bread of heaven**), and **water** that gushed forth from rocks.

i. David gave a distinctly *positive* remembrance of Israel in the wilderness, not mentioning their many sins, rebellions, and examples of unbelief. His purpose here is to remember the great works of God, and not to focus on the failings of man.

ii. This is stated "…without one disturbing reference to the sins and failures which darkened the forty years. These are spread out at length, without flattery or minimising, in the next psalm; but here the theme is God's wonders." (Maclaren)

iii. Adam Clarke had a curious comment on verse 41, **He opened the rock**: "I can now add, that a piece of this rock, broken off by the hand of my nephew, E. S. A. Clarke, in the course of the present year [1822,] now lies before me. It is fine *granite*; and so well distinguished as a granite, that the *feldt-spar*, the *mica*, and the *quartz*, of which granite is composed, appear very distinctly."

3. (42-45) God graciously brought Israel into the land of Canaan.

For He remembered His holy promise,
***And* Abraham His servant.**
He brought out His people with joy,
His chosen ones with gladness.
He gave them the lands of the Gentiles,
And they inherited the labor of the nations,
That they might observe His statutes
And keep His laws.
Praise the Lord!

a. **He remembered His holy promise**: God's faithfulness to Israel in taking them out of Egypt, through the wilderness, and into Canaan was all based on a fulfillment of **His holy promise**. God binds Himself by His promises, and regards them as **holy**.

b. **He brought out His people with joy**: We could say that this joy both belonged to the Israelites and to Yahweh, their covenant God. It pleased both God and His people to rescue the Israelites from their bondage and to bring them into their inheritance (**the lands of the Gentiles**).

i. **They inherited the labor of the nations**: "By right of conquest they freely inherited from the Canaanites cities, vineyards, orchards, cisterns, and all kinds of material benefits." (VanGemeren)

c. **That they might observe His statutes**: At the conclusion of the psalm, David brought home a point of moral obligation. God rescued the Israelites and brought them into the land, setting them free not for the ultimate purpose of personal indulgence, but so they could **observe His statutes** and **keep His laws**.

i. "The emphasis throughout the psalm lies on God's goodness: his promise, protection, providence, and presence. He is true to his word. And as an afterthought, the author reminds God's people of their responsibility. Keeping the precepts of the Lord is, therefore, an expression of joyous gratitude for all the benefits the Lord has provided for his people." (VanGemeren)

ii. "The final verse shows why grace abounded; not that sin might also abound, but (to quote a New Testament equivalent of verse 45), 'that the righteousness of the law might be fulfilled in us, who walk not after the flesh, but after the Spirit' (Rom. 8:4)." (Kidner)

d. **Praise the Lord**: Psalm 105 ends just as the previous psalm, with the Hebrew word *Hallelujah*. It is right and worthy for God's people to remember His marvelous works and to praise Him for all He has done.

Psalm 106 – The LORD's Mercy to His Covenant People

"This psalm is the dark counterpart of its predecessor, a shadow cast by human self-will in its long struggle against the light." (Derek Kidner)

Alexander Maclaren observed, "The keynote of Psalm 105 is, 'Remember His mighty deeds,' that of Psalm 106 is, 'They forgot His mighty deeds.'"

"Israel's history is here written with the view of showing human sin, even as the preceding Psalm was composed to magnify divine goodness. It is, in fact, A NATIONAL CONFESSION." (Charles Spurgeon)

A. Praise and prayer.

1. (1) Praising God for His enduring mercy.

Praise the LORD!
Oh, give thanks to the LORD, for *He is* good!
For His mercy *endures* forever.

a. **Praise the LORD**: This psalm begins the way the previous psalm ended, saying *hallelujah!* Psalm 105 gave praise because of God's many gifts and blessings to Israel. This psalm gives praise because of God's great mercy to an often rebellious and ungrateful Israel.

b. **Oh, give thanks to the LORD**: There is a sense of *pleading* in this phrase, as if the psalmist was desperate to draw greater gratitude from himself and God's people, especially in light of His goodness.

i. **For He is good**: "Surely the thought of God's unspeakable goodness most appropriately precedes the psalmist's confession, for nothing so melts a heart in penitence as the remembrance of God's love, and nothing so heightens the evil of sin as the consideration of the patient goodness which it has long flouted." (Maclaren)

c. **His mercy endures forever**: The rest of this long psalm will describe God's great **mercy** (*hesed*, God's loyal covenant love) to a disobedient Israel.

> i. "Since man ceases not to be sinful, it is a great blessing that Jehovah ceases not to be merciful." (Spurgeon)

> ii. "For all its exposure of man's ingratitude, this is a psalm of praise, for it is God's extraordinary longsuffering that emerges as the real theme." (Kidner)

2. (2-3) Praising God for His mighty acts.

Who can utter the mighty acts of the LORD?
Who can declare all His praise?
Blessed *are* those who keep justice,
***And* he who does righteousness at all times!**

a. **Who can utter the mighty acts of the LORD?** In the midst of his praise, the psalmist recognized that his praise wasn't enough. God's **mighty acts** are so many that they are beyond description. Because of this, we cannot fully **declare all His praise**.

> i. "Who is sufficient for a work that demandeth the tongues and harps of angels?" (Horne)

b. **Blessed are those who keep justice**: Those who walk in obedience to God (**keep justice...does righteousness**) do their part in declaring God's **praise**.

> i. **Blessed are those** "…that are of right principles and upright practices; this is real and substantial praising of God. Thanks doing is the proof of thanksgiving; and the good life of the thankful is the life of thankfulness." (Trapp)

3. (4-5) Praying to be visited by God's salvation.

Remember me, O LORD, with the favor *You have toward* Your people.
Oh, visit me with Your salvation,
That I may see the benefit of Your chosen ones,
That I may rejoice in the gladness of Your nation,
That I may glory with Your inheritance.

a. **Remember me, O LORD**: With a preface and foundation of praise, the psalmist felt the door was open to ask God for help. He knew that for God to **remember** was to stir His compassionate action. For God to **visit** meant He would come with His **salvation**, bringing deliverance from the present trouble.

i. Horne called the prayer of verses 4-5 "The most spiritual and heavenly petition that the devoutest Christian can [bring] to the throne of grace."

b. **Oh, visit me with Your salvation**: The plea is made as if the psalmist were too sick to go to the doctor for necessary care, and must have the doctor **visit** him.

i. "There is no salvation apart from the Lord, and he must visit us with it or we shall never obtain it. We are too sick to visit our Great Physician, and therefore he visits us." (Spurgeon)

c. **That I may see the benefit of Your chosen ones**: Three reasons for the request are given, each one concerned with the honor and fame of God.

- **That I may see the benefit**: "LORD, I want to see Your people blessed by Your mighty works toward them."

- **That I may rejoice**: "LORD, I want to share in the joy with your blessed and redeemed people."

- **That I may glory**: "LORD, I want to be part of Your victory and the victory of Your people."

B. Confessing Israel's sin and need for God's mercy.

1. (6-7) Israel's guilt in the past and present.

We have sinned with our fathers,
We have committed iniquity,
We have done wickedly.
Our fathers in Egypt did not understand Your wonders;
They did not remember the multitude of Your mercies,
But rebelled by the sea—the Red Sea.

a. **We have sinned with our fathers**: This psalm mainly focuses on the repeated failure of Israel through her history. Yet the singer of this psalm did not see failure as something only of Israel's past. He identified his present generation with Israel of old, connected in their sin, their iniquity, and their wicked deeds.

i. This is a remarkably humble and straightforward confession of sin. "Such a prayer stands in the closest relation to the theme of the psalm, which draws out the dark record of national sin, in order to lead to that national repentance.... Precisely because the hope of restoration is strong, the delineation of sin is unsparing." (Maclaren)

ii. **We have sinned with our fathers**: "The fathers' sins are often reflected in their children; and each new reflection, instead of being weaker, is stronger than the foregoing." (Horne)

iii. "Men may be said to have sinned with their fathers when they imitate them, when they follow the same objects, and make their own lives to be mere continuations of the follies of their sires." (Spurgeon)

b. **Our fathers in Egypt did not understand Your wonders**: Based on the lines from verse 6, we understand this to suggest, "Our **fathers** sinned and **rebelled**, and so have we." He recounted Israel's sin at Marah, shortly after coming from the **Red Sea** (Exodus 15:22-27).

i. **They did not remember the multitude of Your mercies**: "The contrast between the loving acts (v. 7, pl. of *hesed*; NIV, 'kindnesses') of the Lord and Israel's lack of responsiveness dramatizes the greatness of God's love and salvation. He delivered a people who did not respond to his love!" (VanGemeren)

2. (8-12) The mercy of God's salvation to rebellious Israel.

Nevertheless He saved them for His name's sake,
That He might make His mighty power known.
He rebuked the Red Sea also, and it dried up;
So He led them through the depths,
As through the wilderness.
He saved them from the hand of him who hated *them*,
And redeemed them from the hand of the enemy.
The waters covered their enemies;
There was not one of them left.
Then they believed His words;
They sang His praise.

a. **Nevertheless He saved them for His name's sake**: The Israelites responded to God's great deliverance with ingratitude and rebellion. Despite all that (**nevertheless**), God answered with rescue, but not only for Israel's sake. **He saved them** so that **He might make His mighty power known**.

i. "Thus Israel's history is as much the story of God's mercy, faithfulness, and long-suffering as it is the story of Israel's faithlessness and unbelief. In fact, it is against the background of their sin that God's patience is most fully illuminated." (Boice)

ii. **His name's sake**: "The Lord very jealously guards his own name and honour. It shall never be said of him that he cannot or will not save his people, or that he cannot abate the haughtiness of his defiant foes. This respect unto his own honour ever leads him to deeds of mercy, and hence we may well rejoice that he is a jealous God." (Spurgeon)

b. **He rebuked the Red Sea**: The great works of God are remembered, from the dividing of the Red Sea to the destruction of the Egyptian army (**waters covered their enemies**).

c. **They believed His words; they sang His praise**: Israel's reaction to God's saving works was not *all* rebellion and disobedience. There were times they trusted God's **words** and praised Him in song (for example, Exodus 15).

> i. Spurgeon detected a fault even in this belief and praise: "That is to say, they believed the promise when they saw it fulfilled, but not till then."

3. (13-15) Because of their sin, God gave them leanness of soul.

They soon forgot His works;
They did not wait for His counsel,
But lusted exceedingly in the wilderness,
And tested God in the desert.
And He gave them their request,
But sent leanness into their soul.

a. **They soon forgot His works**: Israel moved quickly from faith and celebration of God's works (verse 12) to ingratitude and disobedience. Their lust after physical, material things (**lusted exceedingly**) was an important factor in this (Numbers 11).

> i. **Soon forgot His works**: "In the hour of deliverance faith aided by sight is strong, and it is easy to sing. But directly strain and stress return, the past of God's might is forgotten, and His counsel is not sought." (Morgan)

> ii. "Is it that way with you? You see God's miracles, but at the first sign of any new opposition you forget what God has done and are soon rebelling against what you suppose to be your hard and painful life? Then, when God saves you again, you sing his praises but soon forget even that deliverance? That is exactly what you and I are like." (Boice)

> iii. **Lusted exceedingly**: The Hebrew for this phrase is simply a repetition of the word *lust* – as in, *they lusted a lust*.

b. **Tested God in the desert**: The psalmist repeated the idea from Psalm 78:18, which spoke of the Israelites testing God with their unbelief regarding His ability to provide for their needs in the wilderness.

c. **He gave them their request, but sent leanness into their soul**: God gave the Israelites the meat they craved (Numbers 11). Yet the meat was also sent with an associated curse, and what they wanted became something bad. The prodigal son and Lot are two other examples of those who received what they wanted, but came to ruin because of it.

i. When we allow ungodly cravings to rule our lives, God may send what we crave – and **leanness into** our **soul** as well. Better to deny one's self those cravings, yet enjoy a "fat" and healthy soul. "They had their desire, but their souls were starved." (Meyer)

ii. "For whoever sets his hot desires in self-willed fashion on material good, and succeeds in securing their gratification, gains…the loss of a shrivelled spiritual nature. Full-fed flesh makes starved souls." (Maclaren)

iii. **He gave them their request**: "Oh, do not seek to impose your will on God; do not insist on anything with too great vehemence; let God choose. Whenever you make request for things, which are not definitely promised, ask God not to grant them, except it be for the very best." (Meyer)

iv. The judgment mentioned here (and in Numbers 11) was strict, but it was a *help* to the Israelites because it taught them not to be ruled by their cravings and lusts. They came to call this place *Kibroth Hattaavah* – meaning, "Graves of Craving" (Numbers 11:34). Many since have allowed their cravings to become their graves.

4. (16-18) Because of their sin, God sent fire and judgment.

When they envied Moses in the camp,
***And* Aaron the saint of the LORD,**
The earth opened up and swallowed Dathan,
And covered the faction of Abiram.
A fire was kindled in their company;
The flame burned up the wicked.

a. **When they envied Moses in the camp**: This refers to the rebellion led by Korah, recorded in Numbers 16. Korah believed that Moses and Aaron were arrogant and proud, accusing them: *You take too much upon yourselves, for all the congregation is holy, every one of them, and the LORD is among them. Why then do you exalt yourselves above the assembly of the LORD?* (Numbers 16:3).

i. "The self-righteous attacks on Moses' spiritual and temporal leadership in Numbers 16:3 and 16:13 are unmasked in the simple words, *men… were jealous*. Such directness is as characteristic of Scripture as are the elaborate self-justifications of men." (Kidner)

ii. "Who can hope to escape envy when the meekest of men was subject to it? How unreasonable was this envy, for Moses was the one man in all the camp who laboured hardest and had most to bear. They should have sympathised with him; to envy him was ridiculous." (Spurgeon)

b. **Aaron the saint of the LORD**: This was the psalmist's generosity towards an often-erring servant (as in Exodus 32, the golden calf incident). Whatever faults Aaron had, he was God's appointed priest and Korah directed his rebellion against *both* Moses and Aaron.

c. **The earth opened up and swallowed Dathan**: Korah had two leading conspirators, **Dathan** and **Abiram**. Dramatically, God **opened up** the earth and they were **swallowed** in the giant crevice (Numbers 16:31-33).

d. **The flame burned up the wicked**: Numbers 16:35 describes the fire that consumed 250 men who also conspired with Korah.

5. (19-23) Because of their sin, God set Himself against Israel.

They made a calf in Horeb,
And worshiped the molded image.
Thus they changed their glory
Into the image of an ox that eats grass.
They forgot God their Savior,
Who had done great things in Egypt,
Wondrous works in the land of Ham,
Awesome things by the Red Sea.
Therefore He said that He would destroy them,
Had not Moses His chosen one stood before Him in the breach,
To turn away His wrath, lest He destroy *them.*

a. **They made a calf in Horeb**: The writer of this psalm didn't present the Exodus account in chronological order. Here he remembered Israel's sin with the golden **calf**, which happened well before the rebellion of Korah.

b. **Worshipped the molded image**: This sin of ingratitude, unbelief, idolatry, and immorality is recorded in Exodus 32. The graciousness of the psalmist toward Aaron continues in that Aaron's role in Israel's transgression is not mentioned.

c. **Thus they changed their glory into the image of an ox**: Israel's idolatry with the golden calf did not actually debase *God*; it debased *them.* They lowered themselves to be the creatures and servants of a man-made beast.

i. "The strange perverseness which turned away from such a radiance of glory to bow down before an idol is strikingly set forth by the figure of bartering it for an image and that of an ox that ate grass." (Maclaren)

ii. Paul quoted from the Septuagint translation of this phrase from Psalm 106:20 in Romans 1:23, using it as a strong accusation against idolaters of all kinds. As Paul's application of this in Romans 1:23 demonstrates, "It is not Israel alone that has been guilty of the sin of idolatry. This is humanity's sin in general. We too are idolaters when we put anything but God in God's place." (Boice)

d. **They forgot God their Savior**: Their sin was not only of idolatry and immorality, but also of plain *ingratitude*. The God who did **great things**, **wondrous works** and **awesome things** in bringing them out of Egypt was ignored in their praise of the golden calf.

e. **Therefore He said that He would destroy them**: Exodus 32:9-10 records the remarkable words of God to Moses, explaining that He would **destroy** the rebellious people of Israel and build the nation again through Moses.

> i. God told Moses, "*Let Me alone, that My wrath may burn hot against them*" (Exodus 32:10). God did not ask for the opinion or participation of Moses in this matter. He simply told Moses, "*Let Me alone* so I can do this." The clear impression was that if Moses did *nothing*, the plan would go ahead.

f. **Moses His chosen one stood before Him in the breach**: Moses did something, not nothing. He did not fatalistically say, "Well, whatever God will do, God will do." Moses pleaded with the LORD, asking Him to **turn away His wrath**, because in a larger sense he believed this to be God's heart (Exodus 32:11-13). God answered the prayer of Moses, and Israel was spared.

> i. **In the breach**: "The metaphor 'stood in the breach' derives from military language, signifying the bravery of a soldier who stands in the breach of the wall, willing to give his life in warding off the enemy (cf. Ezekiel 22:30). So Moses stood bravely in the presence of Almighty God on behalf of Israel." (VanGemeren)

> ii. "Like a bold warrior who defends the wall when there is an opening for the adversary and destruction is rushing in upon the city, Moses stopped the way of avenging justice with his prayers." (Spurgeon)

> iii. "God had made a hedge or wall about them; but they had made a gap or breach in it by their sins, at which the Lord, who was now justly become their enemy, might enter to destroy them; which he had certainly done, if Moses by his prevailing intercession had not hindered him." (Poole)

> iv. **To turn away His wrath**: "Mighty as was the sin of Israel to provoke vengeance, prayer was mightier in turning it away. How diligently

ought we to plead with the Lord for this guilty world, and especially for his own backsliding people!" (Spurgeon)

6. (24-27) Because of their sin, God overthrew them in the wilderness.

Then they despised the pleasant land;
They did not believe His word,
But complained in their tents,
***And* did not heed the voice of the LORD.**
Therefore He raised up His hand *in an oath* against them,
To overthrow them in the wilderness,
To overthrow their descendants among the nations,
And to scatter them in the lands.

a. **They despised the pleasant land; they did not believe His word**: This refers to the Israelites' sinful unbelief at Kadesh Barnea (Numbers 14:1-4). They did not believe the promise of God or the report of Joshua and Caleb, the two faithful spies (Numbers 13:30).

i. **Complained in their tents**: "Murmuring is a great sin and not a mere weakness; it contains within itself unbelief, pride, rebellion, and a whole host of sins. It is a home sin, and is generally practised by complainers 'in their tents,' but it is just as evil there as in the streets, and will be quite as grievous to the Lord." (Spurgeon)

b. **Did not heed the voice of the LORD**: God *promised* them the land of Canaan, no matter what the opposition. It was plain unbelief, masked by a supposed concern for their wives and children (Numbers 14:3).

c. **He raised up His hand in an oath against them**: God promised that the generation of unbelief in the wilderness would not inherit the land of Canaan (Numbers 14:22-25). That generation would die in the wilderness and the new generation would have their opportunity to take the land by faith.

i. **He raised up His hand**: "He sware, as this phrase is commonly used, as Genesis 14:22, Deuteronomy 32:40, Nehemiah 9:15, Revelation 10:5,6: of this dreadful and irrevocable sentence and oath of God," (Poole)

7. (28-31) Because of their sin, God sent a plague.

They joined themselves also to Baal of Peor,
And ate sacrifices made to the dead.
Thus they provoked *Him* to anger with their deeds,
And the plague broke out among them.
Then Phinehas stood up and intervened,
And the plague was stopped.

And that was accounted to him for righteousness
To all generations forevermore.

a. **They joined themselves also to Baal of Peor**: Numbers 25 tells the story of how the young women of Moab enticed the men of Israel to idolatry and immorality at **Baal of Peor**. In their idolatry they **ate sacrifices made to the dead**.

b. **Plague broke out among them**: God sent a **plague** as a judgment against the Israelites, and the plague was only stopped when righteous **Phinehas** brought God's judgment against an Israelite man and Moabite woman apparently in the midst of immorality at or near the tabernacle itself (Numbers 25:6-9). This act of righteousness **stopped** the plague.

i. "This brave and decided deed was so acceptable to God as a proof that there were some sincere souls in Israel that the deadly visitation went no further." (Spurgeon)

ii. John Trapp emphasized the truth that no one should used Phinehas as an example of taking violence against sinners: "By a secret, heroical, and extraordinary motion of God's Spirit, such as may not be drawn into example. All things reported and commended in Scripture may not be imitated."

c. **That was accounted to him for righteousness**: In recognition of his righteous act, God made a covenant regarding the priesthood with Phinehas and his descendants (Numbers 25:10-13).

8. (32-33) Because of their sin, God disciplined Moses.

They angered *Him* also at the waters of strife,
So that it went ill with Moses on account of them;
Because they rebelled against His Spirit,
So that he spoke rashly with his lips.

a. **They angered Him also at the waters of strife**: Numbers 20:9-11 explains how the Israelites **angered** Moses at Meribah by their complaining and contention. Nevertheless, God commanded Moses to speak to the rock (Numbers 20:7-8), and God promised to miraculously provide water from the rock.

b. **It went ill with Moses on account of them**: Moses did not *speak* to the rock as God commanded. In anger he *struck* the rock (Numbers 20:9-11). God provided the water, but Moses misrepresented God and was therefore denied entrance into the Promised Land (Numbers 20:12-13).

c. **Because they rebelled against His Spirit**: The author of this psalm put the emphasis on how the Israelites provoked Moses by their rebellion, which him angry. Moses was truly provoked, but God still held him responsible for *his* reaction to the provocation.

i. Spurgeon noted that sometimes congregations provoke their ministers or pastors as Israel provoked Moses. "We ought also to be very careful how we treat the ministers of the gospel, lest by provoking their spirit we should drive them into any unseemly behaviour which should bring upon them the chastisement of the Lord. Little do a murmuring, quarrelsome people dream of the perils in which they involve their pastors by their untoward behaviour."

ii. **He spoke rashly with His lips**: "For this *sentence* we have only these *two words* in the Hebrew, *vayebatte bisephathaiv, he stuttered* or *stammered with his lips*, indicating that he was transported with anger." (Clarke)

9. (34-39) Because of their sin, the land was polluted.

They did not destroy the peoples,
Concerning whom the LORD had commanded them,
But they mingled with the Gentiles
And learned their works;
They served their idols,
Which became a snare to them.
They even sacrificed their sons
And their daughters to demons,
And shed innocent blood,
The blood of their sons and daughters,
Whom they sacrificed to the idols of Canaan;
And the land was polluted with blood.
Thus they were defiled by their own works,
And played the harlot by their own deeds.

a. **They did not destroy the peoples, concerning whom the LORD had commanded them**: When the Israelites came into the Promised Land, God **commanded them** to **destroy** the Canaanite nations living in the land.

i. This was a unique war of judgment that God commanded Israel to perform against depraved cultures, ripe and even overdue for judgment.

b. **They mingled with the Gentiles and learned their works**: God wanted the Israelites to make war against the Canaanites to serve His purpose of judgment. But God also wanted the Canaanites removed so they would not be an evil influence upon the Israelites, leading them into the worship of their idols and their evil ways. Israel's failure to do as God commanded meant this evil influence corrupted God's people.

> i. "They found evil company, and delighted in it. Those whom they should have destroyed they made their friends. Having enough faults of their own, they were yet ready to go to school to the filthy Canaanites, and educate themselves still more in the arts of iniquity." (Spurgeon)

c. **They even sacrificed their sons and their daughters to demons**: One of the worst examples of this evil influence was Israel's worship of *Molech*, a Canaanite god sometimes worshipped with child sacrifice.

> i. **To demons**: "They did not worship God, as they pretended and sometimes designed, but devils in their idols; and that those spirits which were supposed by the heathen idolaters to inhabit in their images, and which they worshipped in them, were not gods or good spirits, as they imagined, but evil spirits or devils." (Poole)

> ii. **Demons**: "The devils are here called *Shedim*, destroyers (in opposition to *Shaddai*, the Almighty), and worthily; for they make it their work to waste and spoil people of their dearest children." (Trapp)

d. **The land was polluted with blood**: Until justice prevails, the blood of innocents murdered cries out to God (Genesis 4:10) and pollutes a nation in the eyes of God (Numbers 35:33).

> i. "The promised land, the holy land, which was the glory of all lands, for God was there, was defiled…by the blood red hands of their parents, who slew them in order to pay homage to devils." (Spurgeon)

e. **Thus they were defiled by their own works**: In both the *atmosphere they allowed* and the *deeds they did*, the Israelites **defiled** themselves **by their own works**. The same statement could be said over many of God's people today.

10. (40-43) Because of their sin, God gave them to their enemies.

Therefore the wrath of the Lord was kindled against His people,
So that He abhorred His own inheritance.
And He gave them into the hand of the Gentiles,
And those who hated them ruled over them.
Their enemies also oppressed them,
And they were brought into subjection under their hand.
Many times He delivered them;
But they rebelled in their counsel,
And were brought low for their iniquity.

a. **Therefore the wrath of the** Lord **was kindled against His people**: God's wrath righteously burned against the Israelites for all the sins mentioned in this long psalm. In a sense, **He abhorred His own inheritance**, and gave them over to severe correction.

i. "How far the divine wrath can burn against those whom he yet loves in his heart [is] hard to say, but certainly Israel pushed [it] to the extreme." (Spurgeon)

b. **He gave them into the hand of the Gentiles**: This seems to be a psalm of exile (especially in light of verse 46), written after the conquest and forced exile of Judah. This giving of Israel **into the hand of the Gentiles** was not merely defeat in a few battles, but their complete conquest and virtual depopulation of the land – **those who hated them ruled over them**.

i. "In their God they had found a kind master, but in those with whom they had perversely sought fellowship they found despots of the most barbarous sort." (Spurgeon)

c. **Many times He delivered them**: Israel's basic *ingratitude* is once again considered. God **delivered**, but they **rebelled**. Such ingratitude could not go forever unanswered. In time – after much longsuffering from God – Israel was **brought low for their iniquity**.

C. God's great mercy to Israel.

1. (44-46) Because of His mercy, God heard their cry of affliction.

Nevertheless He regarded their affliction,
When He heard their cry;
And for their sake He remembered His covenant,
And relented according to the multitude of His mercies.
He also made them to be pitied
By all those who carried them away captive.

a. **Nevertheless He regarded their affliction**: After the description of God's correction of Israel in the previous lines, the word **nevertheless** comes as a wonderful, gracious reprieve. Despite the judgment they well deserved, God **regarded their affliction** and **remembered His covenant**.

i. "Although the people were unfaithful to him, God nevertheless was faithful to them, which is why a psalm dealing with the sins of God's people can end on a positive note." (Boice)

ii. "The covenant forgotten by men is none the less remembered by Him. The numberless number of His lovingkindnesses, greater than that of all men's sins, secures forgiveness after the most repeated transgressions." (Maclaren)

b. **Relented according to the multitude of His mercies**: It *might* have been different; God *could have* dealt with Israel only on the basis of their sin and His righteous judgment. While not ignoring their sin, God decided to deal with them **according to the multitude of His mercies**.

c. **He also made them to be pitied**: One aspect of God's mercy to Israel was in giving them favor with the nations where they suffered exile. **Those who carried them away captive** felt sorry for their Israelite captives and treated them accordingly.

i. "This was particularly true as to the Babylonian captivity; for *Cyrus* gave them their liberty; *Darius* favoured them, and granted them several privileges; and *Artaxerxes* sent back Nehemiah, and helped him to rebuild Jerusalem and the temple." (Clarke)

2. (47-48) Praying to and praising the God of great mercy.

Save us, O LORD our God,
And gather us from among the Gentiles,
To give thanks to Your holy name,
To triumph in Your praise.
Blessed *be* the LORD God of Israel
From everlasting to everlasting!
And let all the people say, "Amen!"
Praise the LORD!

a. **Save us, O LORD our God, and gather us from among the Gentiles**: This psalm seems to have been composed when the mercies of God to the Israelites in their captivity were just beginning to be seen. The author of the psalm rightly took those early, small mercies as the basis to boldly ask for greater mercies – that their captivity would be ended and they could return to the land.

b. **To give thanks to Your holy name**: The psalmist predicted that God's people would respond gratefully, breaking the previous pattern of ingratitude. They would not forget, but **triumph in Your praise**.

i. "Penitence is never out of place in praise, nor praise in an act of penitence." (Kidner)

c. **Blessed be the LORD God of Israel**: The psalmist would not *wait* for the asked-for mercies to be evident before he began to thank and praise God. The praise started immediately, and would be given to God **from everlasting to everlasting**. This was praise that **all the peoples** should join in, saying "Hallelujah!" to God.

i. "Verse 48 therefore makes a fitting crown to a psalm whose theme has been God's steadfastness even more than man's perversity, and a doxology to conclude Book four of the Psalter." (Kidner)

Psalm 107 – Learning from God's Deliverance to Returning Captives

This remarkable psalm praises God's deliverance in four wonderful pictures. Derek Kidner titled this psalm "God to the Rescue." The four pictures show that everyone's story is different, and yet everyone's story is the same.

"Consider the successive vignettes of this psalm. Love broods over the weary caravan that faints in the desert; visits the prison-house with its captives; watches by our beds of pain; notices each lurch of the tempest-driven vessel; brings the weary hosts from the wilderness into the fruitful soil." (F.B. Meyer)

A. Dedication of the song.

1. (1) Dedicated in gratitude to God.

Oh, give thanks to the LORD, for *He is* good!
For His mercy *endures* forever.

> a. **Oh, give thanks to the LORD**: With the word **Oh**, the exhortation is stated as an exclamation. The singer of the psalm passionately pleads with his readers to give thanks to God, and for good reason. This **thanks** is directed to God because **He is good**. His goodness will be revealed throughout the rest of this psalm.

> b. **For His mercy endures forever**: In the psalms as a whole, this phrase has almost a liturgical quality to it. It is used more than 30 times and is an appreciative declaration of God's people, praising the great lovingkindness –covenant love – of God.

> > i. "The word *endureth* has been properly supplied by the translators, but yet it somewhat restricts the sense, which will be better seen if we read it, '*for his mercy for ever*.' That mercy had no beginning, and shall never know an end." (Spurgeon)

2. (2-3) Dedicated in light of the gathering and return of God's people.

Let the redeemed of the LORD **say** *so,*
Whom He has redeemed from the hand of the enemy,
And gathered out of the lands,
From the east and from the west,
From the north and from the south.

> a. **Let the redeemed of the L**ORD **say so**: Specifically, the psalmist invited the people of God – those **redeemed** by His enduring mercy – to declare that they *are* redeemed. It would be ungrateful and wrong to be silent about so great a work. The psalmist will describe four distinct aspects of God's redemption rescue – to the lost, to the guilty, to the sick, and to the storm-tossed. These **redeemed of the L**ORD should **say so**.

> > i. "Moses has given us in the law a clear and full idea of what we are to understand by the word *goel,* here rendered '*redeemed.*' If any person was either sold for a slave, or carried away for a captive, then his kinsman, who was nearest to him in blood, had the right and equity of redemption." (Romaine, cited in Spurgeon)

> b. **Whom He has redeemed from the hand of the enemy**: We might be redeemed from the world, the flesh, the devil, or countless other snares. Here, the psalmist has in mind redemption from **the hand of the enemy**, probably connected with the exile of God's people.

> c. **And gathered out of the lands**: This would be a fitting statement in the mouth of Daniel, Ezra, or Nehemiah, who had occasion to thank God for gathering a remnant of God's people from their lands of captivity.

> > i. **From the south**: "Hebrew, *from the sea.*" (Poole)

B. God's goodness seen in His deliverance to returning captives.

1. (4-9) Deliverance for those lost in the wilderness.

They wandered in the wilderness in a desolate way;
They found no city to dwell in.
Hungry and thirsty,
Their soul fainted in them.
Then they cried out to the LORD **in their trouble,**
And **He delivered them out of their distresses.**
And He led them forth by the right way,
That they might go to a city for a dwelling place.
Oh, that *men* **would give thanks to the L**ORD **for His goodness,**
And *for* **His wonderful works to the children of men!**
For He satisfies the longing soul,
And fills the hungry soul with goodness.

a. **They wandered in the wilderness**: When God gathered His people (verses 2-3), they had to come to the Promised Land from every direction. Some came from the **wilderness**, and they **wandered** the **desolate** desert.

i. **Wandered**: "Their passage through the wilderness was not a journeying, such as when men pass on in a road to some inhabited place; but a *wandering* up and down away from all path and road, and so in an endless maze of desolation." (Hammond, cited in Spurgeon)

ii. "They were lost in the worst possible place, even as the sinner is who is lost in sin; they wandered up and down in vain searches and researches as a sinner does when he is awakened and sees his lost estate; but it ended in nothing." (Spurgeon)

b. **Hungry and thirsty, their soul fainted in them**: In the trouble of the wilderness, the redeemed **cried out to the LORD in their trouble**, and God answered (**He delivered them out of their distresses**).

c. **He led them forth by the right way**: Better than modern navigation systems, God **led** His redeemed to just the right place, **to a city for a dwelling place**.

i. "His deliverance is full of surprises, as he supplies all the needs of his people. He straightens the way; leads them into the city; and provides for their shelter, food, and drink." (VanGemeren)

d. **Oh, that men would give thanks**: God's goodness to those returning through the wilderness should give everyone reason to thank Him, **for His wonderful works to the children of men**. We should be able to thank God for more than just His work in our personal lives, but also for what He does for others.

e. **He satisfies the longing soul**: The psalm spoke of those **hungry and thirsty** in the wilderness, but there is also a **longing** in the **soul** of man. God's literal guidance and deliverance for His redeemed in the wilderness becomes a picture of how He delivers the lost, thirsty, and **hungry soul**, and fills it **with goodness**.

i. It seems that Mary, the mother of Jesus, quoted verse 9 (**and fills the hungry soul with goodness**) in her song: *He has filled the hungry with good things* (Luke 1:53). This is one of many scriptural quotations and allusions found in Mary's song recorded in Luke 1:46-55, showing that she was a woman who knew and loved God's word.

2. (10-16) Deliverance for the captives.

Those who sat in darkness and in the shadow of death,
Bound in affliction and irons—

Because they rebelled against the words of God,
And despised the counsel of the Most High,
Therefore He brought down their heart with labor;
They fell down, and *there was* none to help.
Then they cried out to the LORD in their trouble,
And He saved them out of their distresses.
He brought them out of darkness and the shadow of death,
And broke their chains in pieces.
Oh, that *men* would give thanks to the LORD for His goodness,
And *for* His wonderful works to the children of men!
For He has broken the gates of bronze,
And cut the bars of iron in two.

a. **Those who sat in darkness and in the shadow of death, bound in affliction and irons**: When God gathered His people (verses 2-3), they had to come to the Promised Land from every direction. Some came from prisons and chains.

i. **In affliction and iron**: "With afflicting or grievous irons. Or, *in the cords of affliction*, as they are called, Job 36:8, and particularly in iron fetters." (Poole)

b. **Because they rebelled against the words of God**: The psalmist understood that some were imprisoned because they had **rebelled against** God. This should not be understood to mean that the psalmist believed *every one* of God's imprisoned people were there because they **despised the counsel of the Most High**, but at least in a general sense it was true.

i. The Apostle Paul later referred to himself as *the prisoner of the Lord* (Ephesians 4:1). These people were also prisoners of the Lord, but in a very different sense.

ii. "He delivered them into the hands of their enemies, and, as they would not be under subjection to GOD, he delivered them into slavery to wicked men.... God had forsaken them because they had forsaken him." (Clarke)

c. **They fell down, and *there was* none to help**: Their imprisonment was difficult, with forced labor and hardship.

i. "In eastern prisons men are frequently made to labour like beasts of the field. As they have no liberty, so they have no rest. This soon subdues the stoutest heart, and makes the proud boaster sing another tune." (Spurgeon)

d. **They cried out to the LORD in their trouble**: In their chains and hardship, God's imprisoned people begged Him for help, and He answered.

He saved them out of their distresses and **broke their chains in pieces**. This was pure grace and mercy from God; these prisoners were under God's own discipline. Yet when they **cried out** to Him, He mercifully answered.

> i. "This is comfort to the greatest sinners; if they can but find a praying heart, God will find a pitying heart, and rebels shall be received with all sweetness, if at length they return, though brought in by the cross." (Trapp)

e. **Oh, that *men* would give thanks to the L**ORD** for His goodness**: The refrain is repeated (previously in verse 8). Seeing the gracious power of God in action should move men to **give thanks**. God has **cut the bars of iron in two** so that His people could return as He gathered them.

> i. "The Lord breaks the strongest gates and bars when the time comes to set free his prisoners: and spiritually the Lord Jesus has broken the most powerful of spiritual bonds and made us free indeed. Brass and iron are [quickly consumed] before the flame of Jesus' love. The gates of hell shall not prevail against us, neither shall the bars of the grave detain us." (Spurgeon)

3. (17-22) Deliverance for those sick and near death.

Fools, because of their transgression,
And because of their iniquities, were afflicted.
Their soul abhorred all manner of food,
And they drew near to the gates of death.
Then they cried out to the LORD** in their trouble,**
***And* He saved them out of their distresses.**
He sent His word and healed them,
And delivered *them* from their destructions.
Oh, that *men* would give thanks to the LORD** for His goodness,**
And *for* His wonderful works to the children of men!
Let them sacrifice the sacrifices of thanksgiving,
And declare His works with rejoicing.

a. **Fools, because of their transgression, and because of their iniquities, were afflicted**: When God gathered His people (verses 2-3), they had to come to the Promised Land from every direction. Some came from sickness and affliction, and God rescued and redeemed them – even though their trouble could be traced to their foolishness, **transgression**, and iniquity.

> i. **Were afflicted**: "The verb as well as its supporting phrases points to their trouble as self-inflicted. In such a context, verse 18 could well call to mind in modern times the drug-addict, but only as one example of man's perennial determination to get hurt." (Kidner)

ii. "Sin is at the bottom of all sorrow, but some sorrows are the immediate result of wickedness; men by a course of transgression afflict themselves and are fools for their pains." (Spurgeon)

b. **They drew near to the gates of death**: The psalmist described those who were very sick and near death. They had no appetite (**their soul abhorred all manner of food**) and wasted away.

i. "Their 'affliction' is a sickness to death, when food and pleasure are no longer relevant. They 'loathe' their 'food,' as they feel that death is nearby." (VanGemeren)

ii. By spiritual analogy, when a sick soul has no appetite for the milk or meat of God's word, it shows that spiritual death is near.

iii. "We may pray about our bodily pains and weaknesses, and we may look for answers too. When we have no appetite for meat we may have an appetite for prayer." (Spurgeon)

c. **Then they cried out to the LORD in their trouble**: This phrase is again repeated (before in verses 6 and 13). Even when God's people are in trouble because of their own wrongdoing, God answers when they cry out unto Him.

d. **He sent His word and healed them**: They were healed by the power of God's word, reminding us of the many times Jesus healed people simply by speaking a word. These sick and afflicted ones were **delivered** from **their destructions** by the powerful word of God.

i. "When George Wishart arrived at Dundee, where the plague was raging [1545], he caused intimation to be made that he would preach; and for that purpose chose his station upon the head of the East-gate, the infected persons standing without, and those that were whole within. His text was Psalm 107:20, '*He sent his word, and healed them,*' etc., wherein he treated of the profit and comfort of God's word, the punishment that comes by contempt of it, the readiness of God's mercy to such as truly turn to him, and the happiness of those whom God takes from this misery, etc. By which sermon he so raised up the hearts of those that heard him, that they regarded not death, but judged them more happy that should then depart, rather than such as should remain behind, considering that they knew not whether they should have such a comforter with them." (Samuel Clarke, cited in Spurgeon)

ii. "All that God has to do, in order to save us, is to send us his word. He has done that by sending his dear Son, who is the incarnate Word. He sends us the word in the shape of the Holy Scriptures; he sends us the word in the preaching of his servants; but what we want most of all is to have that word sent home by the power of the Holy Spirit." (Spurgeon)

e. **Oh, that *men* would give thanks to the L**ORD** for His goodness**: Once again the psalmist encourages all men to give thanks to God for His deliverance.

4. (23-32) Deliverance for those on dangerous seas.

Those who go down to the sea in ships,
Who do business on great waters,
They see the works of the LORD**,**
And His wonders in the deep.
For He commands and raises the stormy wind,
Which lifts up the waves of the sea.
They mount up to the heavens,
They go down again to the depths;
Their soul melts because of trouble.
They reel to and fro, and stagger like a drunken man,
And are at their wits' end.
Then they cry out to the LORD** in their trouble,**
And He brings them out of their distresses.
He calms the storm,
So that its waves are still.
Then they are glad because they are quiet;
So He guides them to their desired haven.
Oh, that *men* would give thanks to the LORD** for His goodness,**
And *for* His wonderful works to the children of men!
Let them exalt Him also in the assembly of the people,
And praise Him in the company of the elders.

a. **Those who go down to the sea in ships**: When God gathered His people (verses 2-3), they had to come to the Promised Land from every direction. Some came over the **sea in ships**.

b. **They see the works of the L**ORD**, and His wonders in the deep**: On the seas, the returning captives see the greatness of God. They also see the great storms that raise **the waves of the sea** as high as **the heavens**, and plunge down again **to the depths**. It is not surprising that the **soul** of the unfortunate traveler on the stormy sea **melts because of trouble**.

i. "I have been at sea in the storm, and in the circumstances I describe; and, having *cried to the Lord in my trouble*, I am spared to describe the storm, and recount the tale of his mercy. None but either a man inspired by God, who, in describing, will show things *as they are*, or one who has been actually in these circumstances, can tell you with what propriety the psalmist speaks, or utter the thousandth part of the dangers and fearful apprehensions of those concerned in a tempest at sea, where all the winds of heaven seem collected to urge an already crazy vessel among the most tremendous rocks upon a lee shore! God save the reader from such circumstances!" (Clarke)

ii. **Stagger like a drunken man**: "The violent motion of the vessel prevents their keeping their legs, and their fears drive them out of all power to use their brains, and therefore they look like intoxicated men." (Spurgeon)

iii. **Are at their wits' end**: "All their skills at navigation are ineffective so that they become desperate ('at their wit's end,' literally, 'all their wisdom was swallowed up')." (VanGemeren)

iv. Writing in the 17th century, Trapp described these **works** and **wonders**: "…in sea monsters, as whales and whirlpools, and sudden change of weather, and the like, not a few; ebbs and flows, pearls, islands, etc. These are just wonders, and may fully convince the most stubborn atheist that is."

c. **They cry out to the LORD in their trouble**: Once again, the psalmist described how God's people **cry out to the LORD**, and **He brings them out of their distress**.

i. "We cannot help reflecting, that there is a ship in which we are all embarked; there is a troubled sea on which we all sail; there are storms by which we are all frequently overtaken; and there is a haven which we all desire to behold and enter." (Horne)

d. **He calms the storm, so that its waves are still**: God does what only God can do – calm the stormy sea by His command. This reminds us again of what Jesus did to calm the stormy Sea of Galilee by His own word and will.

i. Wild as it is, the sea obeys God's command. Trapp observed that if we "…will not be pacified when the Lord saith unto us, 'Be still'; every drop of water in the sea will be a witness of our monstrous rebellion and disobedience."

e. **Oh, that men would give thanks to the LORD for His goodness**: For the fourth and final time, the psalmist encourages all men to give thanks to God for His deliverance. This time God's people are encouraged to **exalt Him also in the assembly of the people**, praising Him among the people of God.

i. **In the company of the elders**: "Let them not be ashamed nor afraid to speak of God's wonderful works and praises before the greatest of men." (Poole)

C. God's goodness seen in His transformations.

1. (33-38) God's work in transforming the earth.

He turns rivers into a wilderness,
And the watersprings into dry ground;
A fruitful land into barrenness,
For the wickedness of those who dwell in it.
He turns a wilderness into pools of water,
And dry land into watersprings.
There He makes the hungry dwell,
That they may establish a city for a dwelling place,
And sow fields and plant vineyards,
That they may yield a fruitful harvest.
He also blesses them, and they multiply greatly;
And He does not let their cattle decrease.

a. **He turns rivers into a wilderness**: The God who has authority over the stormy seas can also transform creation itself. The transformation can be from good to bad (**a fruitful land into barrenness**) if the goal is the judgment of the **wicked**.

i. "The plain of Jordan, which, before the overthrow of Sodom and Gomorrah, was well watered everywhere, 'like the garden of Jehovah,' Genesis 13:10, hath, since that overthrow, been a land of salt and sulphur, and perpetual sterility." (Horne)

ii. Charles Spurgeon wrote in the 19th century, before Israel was gathered again as a nation in their land: "This has been done in many instances, and notably in the case of the Psalmist's own country, which was once the glory of all lands and is now almost a desert." (Spurgeon)

b. **He turns a wilderness into pools of water**: God's power to transform can also be used to transform from bad to good. **Dry land** can be turned into **watersprings**, into places of fruitfulness and civilization.

i. "The hymn of praise ascribes to the Lord the power to change things. His authority is limitless…. He can reverse the condition of anything and therefore the way of life of everybody!" (VanGemeren)

c. **He also blesses them, and they multiply greatly**: The psalmist relied upon God not only for the gathering of God's people from the captivity, but for His blessing and good transformation of the land when they returned to it. It had to be God's blessing *continually*.

i. "Things which appear contradictory are seen as evidences of consistency. Jehovah turns fruitful places into a wilderness; He turns the wilderness into a fruitful place.... He blesses and multiplies a people." (Morgan)

2. (39-42) God's work in transforming those oppressed and afflicted.

When they are diminished and brought low
Through oppression, affliction and sorrow,
He pours contempt on princes,
And causes them to wander in the wilderness *where there is* **no way;**
Yet He sets the poor on high, far from affliction,
And makes *their* **families like a flock.**
The righteous see *it* **and rejoice,**
And all iniquity stops its mouth.

a. **He pours contempt on princes**: In the same way that God can turn a river into a dry wilderness, He can take the **princes** of this world and bring them low, causing them **to wander in the wilderness**. This is especially true of those rulers who subject God's people under **oppression, affliction, and sorrow**.

b. **Yet He sets the poor on high**: In the same way that God can turn a wilderness into pools of water, He can also lift up the **poor**, setting them up **far from affliction** and making **their families like a flock**.

i. "The final section reflects in a distant, settled way on God's sovereign workings by which his people are sometimes lifted up and sometimes brought low." (Boice)

c. **The righteous see it and rejoice**: God's righteous ones are happy that He knows how to bring low the proud and oppressive, and that He knows how to lift up the poor and afflicted. When the judgments of God operate this way, people notice and **all iniquity stops its mouth**.

i. **All iniquity stops its mouth**: As it says in Job 5:16, *injustice shuts her mouth*. It will be a wonderful day when **iniquity** and injustice are silent.

3. (43) Conclusion: wisdom and understanding.

Whoever *is* **wise will observe these** *things,*
And they will understand the lovingkindness of the Lord.

a. **Whoever is wise will observe these things**: The psalmist invited us to look at the way God works in the world, both in responding to those who cry out to Him and in His ability to bring low and raise high. Wisdom tells us to take notice.

i. "It is himself that the reader is to recognize in the fourfold picture of plight and salvation, and it is the steadfastness of God that he is now to praise with new insight." (Kidner)

ii. "It is a great song of the mercy of God. Let its message be heeded, then shall we cry unto God in our distress, and finding deliverance through His goodness, we shall give Him thanks and praise Him." (Morgan)

iii. "The conclusion to this psalm transforms the hymn of thanksgiving and praise to a wisdom psalm. The righteous will become wise by studying the acts of the Lord in the affairs of man." (VanGemeren)

b. **And they will understand the lovingkindness of the Lord**: We understand the *hesed* (**lovingkindness**, loyal love, covenant love) of God by the statements and promises of His word. But we also understand it by how He acts among men and in history – *if* we have the wisdom to see it. With this wisdom, we **will understand the lovingkindness of the Lord**.

i. **And they will understand**: "'All things work together for good to them that love God'; and the more they love Him, the more clearly will they see, and the more happily will they feel, that so it is. How can a man contemplate the painful riddle of the world, and keep his sanity, without that faith? He who has it for his faith will have it for his experience." (Maclaren)

Psalm 108 – Praise and Trust from the Past for Today

This psalm is titled **A Song. A Psalm of David**. *It is actually a compilation of sections from two other psalms. Psalm 108:1-5 is very similar to Psalm 57:7-11, and Psalm 108:6-13 is almost identical to Psalm 60:5-12. These are David's words, by the inspiration of the Holy Spirit, taken and applied to a present challenge. The enemies specified in Psalm 108:9-13 are Moab, Edom, and Philistia (with the emphasis on Edom). It may be that the old foe, subdued earlier in David's day, rose again and Israel must defeat her again.*

Psalm 108 shows us that we can and should use the words of Scripture as our present prayers and praises, suitable to our present situation.

"This is not a new song, save in its arrangement." (G. Campbell Morgan)

"The Holy Spirit is not so short of expressions that he needs to repeat himself, and the repetition cannot be meant merely to fill the book: there must be some intention in the arrangement of two former divine utterances in a new connection." (Charles Spurgeon)

A. The declaration of God's praise.

1. (1-2) The earnest nature of David's praise to God.

O God, my heart is steadfast;
I will sing and give praise, even with my glory.
Awake, lute and harp!
I will awaken the dawn.

> a. **My heart is steadfast**: As in Psalm 57:7, David sang of the strength of his heart in God. His **steadfast** confidence in God gave him a fixed point from which he could and would **sing and give praise**.

> b. **Even with my glory**: David praised God with the best of his being. Whatever **glory** belonged to David, he directed it toward God in praise.

c. **Awake, lute and harp**: The earnest praise offered to God was *musical*. David was a skilled musician (1 Samuel 16:18), and it could be said that this skill was part of his **glory** – so he offered it to God in praise.

i. **Lute and harp**: "The *Psaltery* [**lute**] was a stringed instrument, usually with twelve strings, and played with the fingers. The *harp* or lyre was a stringed instrument, usually consisting of ten strings. Josephus says that it was struck or played with a key. It appears, however, that it was sometimes played with the fingers." (Barnes, cited in Spurgeon)

d. **I will awaken the dawn**: David was determined to give God the best in praise, so he gave unto God the choice part of the day. David let the sound of his praise greet the **dawn** as it rose in the early morning hours.

I, David was awake, so he could **awaken the dawn**. "Some singers had need to awake, for they sing in drawling tones, as if they were half asleep; the tune drags wearily along, there is no feeling or sentiment in the singing, but the listener hears only a dull mechanical sound…. Oh, choristers, wake up, for this is not a work for dreamers, but such as requires your best powers in their liveliest condition." (Spurgeon)

2. (3-4) The wide audience of David's praise.

I will praise You, O LORD, among the peoples,
And I will sing praises to You among the nations.
For Your mercy *is* great above the heavens,
And Your truth *reaches* to the clouds.

a. **I will praise You, O LORD, among the peoples**: David directed his praise to Yahweh, the covenant God of Israel. Yet he was praising Yahweh in the presence of the people of Israel (**the peoples**) or **among the nations**. His praise was not secret, but open and public.

b. **For Your mercy is great above the heavens**: The large audience was appropriate because of the large nature of God's great **mercy** (*hesed*, lovingkindness, loyal love, or covenant love). David understood that the **mercy** of God was so great that if it were to be measured, it would extend **above the heavens**, and His **truth** would reach **to the clouds**.

i. "God *is* exalted above the heavens. His glory *does* fill the earth. The goal of history is that God might be known as God and be honored for it." (Boice)

3. (5-6) A cry of exaltation to God.

Be exalted, O God, above the heavens,
And Your glory above all the earth;

That Your beloved may be delivered,
Save *with* Your right hand, and hear me.

a. **Be exalted, O God**: If the measure of God's mercy and truth are high above the heavens and the clouds, then the honor and recognition to God should also be that great. A God of great mercy and truth is worthy of great praise and recognition of **glory**.

b. **That Your beloved may be delivered**: David's praise transformed into a prayer, asking that he would be rescued from his present distress. The opening of Psalm 108 is so filled with praise that we didn't even know David was in trouble. He only mentioned his distress after setting his heart and mind right with praise from his entire being.

c. **Your beloved**: David understood that God loved him, and he appealed to God on that basis. David's mind understood that there were many others that God loved, but his heart came to God as if he were the only one, not one of many. **Beloved** (Hebrew, *yadid*) was the meaning David's own name – *dawid*, which means *beloved*.

i. **Beloved**: "The Hebrew word belongs to the language of love poetry; it appeals to the strongest of bonds, the most ardent of relationships." (Kidner)

d. **Save with Your right hand**: The **right hand** is regarded as the hand of skill and strength. God's rescue could not come through half measures. David called upon God to bring all His skill and strength into his resuce.

B. The declaration of God's victory.

1. (7-8) God's dominion over Israel and its land.

God has spoken in His holiness:
"I will rejoice;
I will divide Shechem
And measure out the Valley of Succoth.
Gilead *is* Mine; Manasseh *is* Mine;
Ephraim also *is* the helmet for My head;
Judah *is* My lawgiver.

a. **God has spoken in His holiness**: David was a prophet (Acts 2:30) and was about to prophesy of Yahweh's ultimate victory over all nations. He began by noting that this proclamation came from God's **holiness** – His quality and character of being separate and set apart from all His creation.

b. **I will rejoice**: God's victory over all nations will make Him happy. He will not perform this reluctantly.

c. **I will divide Shechem and measure out the Valley of Succoth**: These verses refer to both a city and a region in Israel. God declared His sovereignty over the land; He would **divide** and **measure** it as He pleased. Comprehensively, the regions of greater Israel (including **Gilead** and **Manasseh** on the east side of the Jordan River, and the central sections of **Judah** and **Ephraim**) were under His dominion.

d. **Ephraim also is the helmet for My head**: The tribe of **Ephraim** descended from Joseph and was one of the prominent tribes of Israel. Sometimes the northern tribes were collectively called **Ephraim**, after this large and influential tribe. **Ephraim** was like a **helmet**, expressing God's strength and security.

> i. "As *Ephraim* was the most populous of all the tribes, he appropriately terms it *the strength of his head,* that is, of his dominions." (Calvin, cited in Spurgeon)

e. **Judah is My lawgiver**: If Ephraim expressed God's strength, the tribe of Judah expressed His *rule* and *government*, as a **lawgiver**. **Judah** was the tribe of King David and later of Jesus the Messiah.

2. (9) God's dominion over the nations.

Moab *is* My washpot;
Over Edom I will cast My shoe;
Over Philistia I will triumph."

a. **Moab is My washpot**: Yahweh was not merely a local deity with authority over Israel alone. He was the God of all the nations, and David recognized that by mentioning three neighboring kingdoms. God would use **Moab** as it pleased Him, and if it were for humble service like a pot for washing feet, then so be it. David did conquer Moab (2 Samuel 8:2).

> i. Both Moab and Edom were noted for their pride (Isaiah 16:6, Obadiah 3). Here God gives them places of humble service. "The picture of Moab coming with a washbasin for the warrior to wash his feet represents her subjugation to servant status." (VanGemeren)

b. **Over Edom I will cast My shoe**: In a day when roads and paths were dirty and covered with refuse of all kinds, a person's shoes were regarded with contempt. If God wanted to throw a dirty **shoe** over **Edom** as an expression of His contempt, He had the power and right to do it. With God's power, David did conquer Edom (2 Samuel 8:14).

> i. "*Will I cast out my shoe,* i.e. I will use them like slaves; either holding forth my shoes, that they may pluck them off; or throwing my shoes at them, either in anger or contempt, as the manner of many masters was and is in such cases." (Poole)

c. **Over Philistia I will triumph**: God's dominion would also be expressed over these long and bitter enemies of Israel. God helping, David did conquer the Philistines (2 Samuel 8:1).

3. (10-13) Trust in God and the help He will bring.

Who will bring me *into* the strong city?
Who will lead me to Edom?
***Is it* not *You,* O God, *who* cast us off?**
And *You,* O God, *who* did not go out with our armies?
Give us help from trouble,
For the help of man is useless.
Through God we will do valiantly,
For *it is* He *who* shall tread down our enemies.

a. **Who will bring me into the strong city?** This psalm appears to have been composed and sung on the eve of battle. Before David confronted a **strong city** of Edom, he praised God and expressed his total confidence in God's dominion over Israel *and* the pagan nations.

b. **The strong city**: The most notable **strong city** among the Edomites was the famous Petra. We have no record of David attacking or conquering that city. If **the strong city** refers to Petra, perhaps David did conquer it, but it is not in the Biblical record. Or, David may mean Petra as simply an example of what seemed to be an unconquerable city that could not resist God's power if He willed it.

i. "There were a number of well-fortified cities in Edom, the source of the country's strength and great pride, but when the psalm speaks of *the* fortified city it can only mean Petra, the legendary, inaccessible, and apparently impregnable mountain stronghold of Edom." (Boice)

ii. This is an important and eternal principle: That which seems unconquerable can be overcome by the power of God.

c. **Is it not You, O God, who cast us off?** David prayed this prayer in light of recent defeats, recognizing that those defeats came because God's favor did not shine upon Israel's armies. If God **did not go out with our armies**, there was no hope for victory – **for the help of man is useless**.

i. **The help of man is useless**: David had seen many brave men accomplish great things on the field of battle. Yet for David and for Israel, the help of man was not enough; indeed, it was **useless**. God's help would lead them to victory.

ii. "The king is not looking for a military solution to his problems, such as alliances with other kings, because he knows that their 'help is worthless'." (VanGemeren)

iii. "We ought to pray with all the more confidence in God when our confidence in man is altogether gone. When the help of man is vain, we shall not find it vain to seek the help of God." (Spurgeon)

d. **Through God we will do valiantly**: David's formula was simple. Without God, they could do nothing. With and **through God**, they could win great victories and accomplish great things. The victory belonged to God (**it is He who shall tread down our enemies**); it was Israel's place to praise God and bring themselves into right relationship with Him. This was the goal of this psalm, and we can suppose that it accomplished its purpose and the battle David faced was won.

i. David understood that it was not for Israel to avoid fighting and passively see what God would do. Instead, they would fight, but fight **through God**. Their fighting through God would be brave and valiant, and in it they would see God **tread down our enemies**.

ii. **We will do valiantly**: "Divine working is not an argument for human inaction, but rather it is the best excitement for courageous effort." (Spurgeon)

iii. **Through God we will do valiantly**: "What, then, is the meaning of this word? That God will overcome Edom? By no means. Rather that the people who are of fixed heart in God will themselves do the valiant deed, but that they will do it through Him. This is ever the way of victory." (Morgan)

iv. **It is He who shall tread down our enemies**: "Faith is neither a coward nor a sluggard she knows that God is with her, and therefore she does valiantly; she knows that he will tread down her enemies, and therefore she arises to tread them down in his name." (Spurgeon)

Psalm 109 – A Prophecy of Vengeance Against Hateful Enemies

Psalm 109 is titled **To the Chief Musician. A Psalm of David.** *Some think the* **Chief Musician** *was the choirmaster for King David; others think it was a poetic reference to God Himself, the author of music itself.*

This is a **Psalm of David,** *and is thought to be the strongest of what are known as the imprecatory psalms, David's songs that call down curses upon his enemies. It is important to remember that these are prayers, committing vengeance unto God. With the greater revelation of grace and truth that came by Jesus Christ, we understand that we are to pray for the good of our enemies, and not for their ruin.*

Yet, we remind ourselves that David refused to act upon these curses; he left vengeance up to God. This is especially relevant regarding David, who knew what it was to take life with the sword. When David withheld vengeance, it was because he chose to, not because he lacked the opportunity, skill, or courage.

A. A prayer for deliverance.

1. (1-3) Deliverance from the hatred of enemies.

> **Do not keep silent,**
> **O God of my praise!**
> **For the mouth of the wicked and the mouth of the deceitful**
> **Have opened against me;**
> **They have spoken against me with a lying tongue.**
> **They have also surrounded me with words of hatred,**
> **And fought against me without a cause.**

> a. **Do not keep silent, O God of my praise**: David was once again in trouble, beset by many enemies. The **mouth of the wicked** spoke against him, so he prayed that God would not be **silent**. He did not want the **mouth of the deceitful** to have the last word.

i. **O God of my praise**: "A resolute stand taken before the troubled thoughts surge in. The psalm will feel its way back to this vantage point, but only regain it in the last two verses." (Kidner)

b. **Fought against me without a cause**: David was confident in his own innocence in reference to his enemies. Their harsh words were spoken **with a lying tongue**, and their **words of hatred** were **without a cause**.

i. "There is nothing more easy than to wag a wicked tongue." (Trapp)

ii. "In all Satan's armoury there are no worse weapons than deceitful tongues." (Spurgeon)

2. (4-5) Deliverance from the ingratitude of those who hate.

In return for my love they are my accusers,
But I *give myself to* **prayer.**
Thus they have rewarded me evil for good,
And hatred for my love.

a. **In return for my love they are my accusers**: In the previous lines David insisted that the hatred of his enemies against him was without cause. Here he further explained that he extended **love** to these adversaries, but they gave David **evil for good, and hatred for...love**.

i. **Accusers** is the same basic Hebrew word that we also translate *Satan* – the accuser. "Hebrew, they satanically hate me. To render evil for evil is brutish, but to render evil for good is devilish." (Trapp)

b. **But I give myself to prayer**: David's response was proper, even using a New Testament understanding. The following lines are filled with bitter wishes that form something of a prophecy of doom against these enemies. Yet David *did* nothing to bring this doom against these enemies. That was God's work, not his own. As for David, he would **give** himself **to prayer** and leave it with the LORD.

i. "The Hebrew is more abrupt and therefore even stronger. It says literally, 'But I prayer.' That is, 'I am all prayer or characterized by prayer. While my enemies are uttering false words about me to other people, trying to do me harm, I am speaking to God. I am praying to God always.'" (Boice)

ii. "He did nothing else but pray. He became prayer as they became malice. This was his answer to his enemies, he appealed from men and their injustice to the Judge of all the earth, who must do right." (Spurgeon)

B. A prophecy of doom.

1. (6-13) Destruction upon the enemy's family.

Set a wicked man over him,
And let an accuser stand at his right hand.
When he is judged, let him be found guilty,
And let his prayer become sin.
Let his days be few,
And let another take his office.
Let his children be fatherless,
And his wife a widow.
Let his children continually be vagabonds, and beg;
Let them seek *their bread* also from their desolate places.
Let the creditor seize all that he has,
And let strangers plunder his labor.
Let there be none to extend mercy to him,
Nor let there be any to favor his fatherless children.
Let his posterity be cut off,
And in the generation following let their name be blotted out.

a. **Set a wicked man over him**: David now speaks of his enemy in the singular, either having in mind the leader of the larger group mentioned in verses 1-5, or making a single target out of many. When David prophesied doom over his enemy, he began with the wish that in judgment his enemies would be ruled by a **wicked man**. Ungodly leadership is a form of God's judgment upon a people.

i. This begins a long and intense set of curses that David pronounced against his enemy. There are some who think that verses 6-20 describe the lying words that David's enemies spoke against *him*, and that the use of the singular in that section proves it – as well as later in verse 20. Morgan had this opinion: "I entirely agree with those expositors who treat this passage as the singer's quotation of the language of his enemies against him."

ii. The main argument *against* this approach is how Peter, in Acts 1:20, quoted Psalm 109:8, applying the verse to an evil man rightly condemned (Judas) and not to an innocent man wrongly condemned.

iii. "We therefore take these words to be David's own, and while giving due weight to the element of righteous anger and of rhetorical hyperbole, we see them as comparable to the outbursts of Jeremiah and Job: recorded for our learning, not for our imitation; yet voicing the cry of innocent blood which God is pledged to hear." (Kidner)

iv. It is fair to note that the tone of these curses are generally in the form of *prophecies* rather than immediate curses. David predicted the righteous judgment to come rather than pronouncing it – though, he certainly wished for this judgment.

v. "David was well known, even praised, for being a nonvindictive, long-suffering, and merciful man. We have only to think of the two occasions when David could have killed his archenemy King Saul if he had wanted to (1 Sam. 24, 26). David did not even think of killing Saul. He said instead, 'I will not lift my hand against my master, because he is the Lord's anointed' (1 Sam. 24:10). All the imprecatory psalms have the flavor of Romans 12:19: '"It is mine to avenge; I will repay," says the Lord.' They leave the execution of justice in God's hands." (Boice)

b. **Let an accuser stand at his right hand**: The curse David had in mind was of an **accuser** or adversary standing in the place of aid and help; the guilty one would be left without help and instead would have *Satan* **at his right hand** (considering that the Hebrew word for **accuser** is *Satan*).

c. **When he is judged, let him be found guilty**: David thought of every possible calamity that could come upon his enemy. In the court of law, he would be **guilty**. When he prayed, the **prayer** itself would **become sin**. His life would be short and another would occupy **his office**.

i. The phrase **let another take his office** was, by the inspiration of the Holy Spirit, quoted by Peter to determine that the apostles should replace Judas in their apostolic number (Acts 1:20). The hateful enemy described by David was certainly a preview of Judas, who fought against Jesus without cause (Psalm 109:3) and rewarded the good Jesus did to him with evil (as in verse 5).

d. **Let his children be fatherless**: David prophesied that the doom to come upon this hateful enemy would extend to his families. His short life meant his children would be orphans **and his wife a widow**. His orphan children would suffer great poverty and themselves have cursed lives (**in the generation following let their name be blotted out**).

i. "Psalm 109:10-15 extend the maledictions to the enemy's children and parents, in accordance with the ancient strong sense of family solidarity, which was often expressed in practice by visiting the kindred of a convicted criminal with ruin, and levelling his house with the ground." (Maclaren)

ii. "We are staggered to find the children included in the father's sentence, and yet as a matter of fact children do suffer for their father's sins, and, as long as the affairs of this life are ordered as they are, it must be so." (Spurgeon)

iii. "A breach of the covenant resulted in the execution of the curses, including famine, sickness, exile, and death (Lev 26:14-39). Thus the psalmist prays that the Lord's word will be fulfilled with regard to the profligate." (VanGemeren)

2. (14-20) Destruction against the enemy's many sins.

Let the iniquity of his fathers be remembered before the LORD**,**
And let not the sin of his mother be blotted out.
Let them be continually before the LORD**,**
That He may cut off the memory of them from the earth;
Because he did not remember to show mercy,
But persecuted the poor and needy man,
That he might even slay the broken in heart.
As he loved cursing, so let it come to him;
As he did not delight in blessing, so let it be far from him.
As he clothed himself with cursing as with his garment,
So let it enter his body like water,
And like oil into his bones.
Let it be to him like the garment which covers him,
And for a belt with which he girds himself continually.
Let **this** *be* **the L**ORD**'s reward to my accusers,**
And to those who speak evil against my person.

a. **Let the iniquity of his fathers be remembered before the L**ORD: David hoped that the sins of his enemy's ancestors would also be held against his enemy, and that the remembrance of those sins would be **continually before the L**ORD.

b. **Because he did not remember to show mercy**: This enemy and his companions despised the goodness David extended to them (verse 5). Yet the hateful ways went beyond the wrong done to David; he also **persecuted the poor and needy**.

i. Matthew Poole thought that the **poor and needy man** was David himself, "who was desolate and miserable, who required pity, and not additions of cruelty." (Poole)

c. **That he might even slay the broken in heart**: This merciless cruelty to the **broken in heart** was completely contrary to the nature of God. *The* L*ORD is near to those who have a broken heart* (Psalm 34:18); God never despises a broken heart (Psalm 51:17).

d. **As he loved cursing, so let it come to him**: David's prayer was rooted in simple justice. He wanted God to do to this enemy what that guilty man had done to others. David wanted the man to be clothed with curses.

i. "The wicked's love for cursing became so much a part of him that the psalmist describes it as if 'he wore cursing as his garment'." (VanGemeren)

ii. "Retaliation, not for private revenge, but as a measure of public justice, is demanded by the Psalmist and deserved by the crime. Surely the malicious man cannot complain if he is judged by his own rule, and has his corn measured with his own bushel." (Spurgeon)

e. **Let this be the LORD's reward to my accusers**: This emphasizes that this is a *prayer* from David. As he said in verse 4, he would pray and leave the matter to the Lord. David wished and prophesied this doom; but it would be God's job to perform it.

i. "All these maledictions shall be fulfilled on my enemies; they shall have them for their reward." (Clarke)

C. A plea for help.

1. (21-25) Help requested because of weakness.

But You, O GOD the Lord,
Deal with me for Your name's sake;
Because Your mercy *is* good, deliver me.
For I *am* poor and needy,
And my heart is wounded within me.
I am gone like a shadow when it lengthens;
I am shaken off like a locust.
My knees are weak through fasting,
And my flesh is feeble from lack of fatness.
I also have become a reproach to them;
When they look at me, they shake their heads.

a. **Deal with me for Your name's sake**: David understood that it wasn't enough to have his enemy judged. David needed help from God, from Yahweh Adonai. David asked on the basis of God's **name** and **mercy**, not on the basis of his own righteousness.

b. **My heart is wounded within me**: David was **poor and needy**, and shows that he was the one *broken in heart* mentioned in verse 16.

c. **I am gone like a shadow when it lengthens**: David's misery was also physical. He felt his life was wasting away, complaining that his **flesh** was **feeble from lack of fatness**. The hateful enemy either caused this physical weakness or took advantage of it.

d. **When they look at me, they shake their heads**: People looked at David in his sorry condition and despised him (**become a reproach**), shaking their heads in both pity and disgust.

2. (26-29) Help requested with a heart for God's glory.

Help me, O LORD my God!
Oh, save me according to Your mercy,
That they may know that this *is* Your hand—
***That* You, LORD, have done it!**
Let them curse, but You bless;
When they arise, let them be ashamed,
But let Your servant rejoice.
Let my accusers be clothed with shame,
And let them cover themselves with their own disgrace as with a mantle.

a. **Help me, O LORD my God**: David's plea was straightforward and simple. Like the woman of Canaan with the demon-possessed daughter (Matthew 15:21-25), he asked God for **help**. As in verse 21, he asked for it on the basis of God's **mercy**, not his own merit.

b. **That they may know that this is Your hand**: It was very important to David that his enemies and all who looked on him knew that his rescue was from God's **hand**; the LORD had **done it**. He didn't want deliverance only for his own sake, but also for the glory of God.

i. **That this is Your hand**: "Ungodly men will not see God's hand in anything if they can help it, and when they see good men delivered into their power they become more confirmed than ever in their atheism; but all in good time God will arise and so effectually punish their malice and rescue the object of their spite that they will be compelled to say like the Egyptian magicians, '*this* is the finger of God.'" (Spurgeon)

c. **Let them curse, but You bless**: David understood that the curses of his enemies could never triumph over the blessings of God in his life. This would make David **rejoice** and his enemies **be clothed with shame**, wearing their **disgrace** as if it were a **mantle**.

3. (30-31) Confidently praising God for His answer.

I will greatly praise the LORD with my mouth;
Yes, I will praise Him among the multitude.
For He shall stand at the right hand of the poor,
To save *him* from those who condemn him.

a. **I will greatly praise the LORD with my mouth**: David's heart was to see God honored in this deliverance. He would praise God vocally and publicly (**among the multitude**).

> i. "The psalm began with addressing 'the God of my praise'; it ends with the confidence and the vow that the singer will yet praise Him. It painted an adversary standing at the right hand of the wicked to condemn him; it ends with the assurance that Jehovah stands at the right hand of His afflicted servant, as his advocate to protect him." (Maclaren)

b. **He shall stand at the right hand of the poor**: God is to be praised for His love and care for **the poor** and for those oppressed by such hateful enemies who **condemn** the righteous.

> i. The One who **shall stand** is "…replacing the figure of the accuser, who stands at the right hand of his victim, by the figure of God who *stands at the right hand of the needy* in a very different sense. It is the complete answer." (Kidner)

Psalm 110 – Messiah, Priest, Conquering King

*This psalm carries the title **A Psalm of David**. Strangely, some scholars and commentators deny David's authorship. Yet as Derek Kinder noted: "Our Lord gave full weight to David's authorship and David's words, stressing the former twice by the expression 'David himself', and the latter by the comment that he was speaking 'in the Holy Spirit' (Mark 12:36f.)."*

This remarkable psalm is one of the Old Testament portions most quoted in the New Testament. James Montgomery Boice counted 27 direct quotations or indirect allusions to Psalm 110 in the New Testament.

A. The character of the Messiah.

1. (1-2) Appointed and honored by Yahweh.

The LORD said to my Lord,
"Sit at My right hand,
Till I make Your enemies Your footstool."
The LORD shall send the rod of Your strength out of Zion.
Rule in the midst of Your enemies!

a. **The LORD said to my Lord**: David prophetically revealed the words of Yahweh (**the LORD**) to the Messiah, David's **Lord**. This is clear not only from the context, but especially by how this verse is quoted in the New Testament.

i. The first verse of this psalm is one of the Old Testament verses most quoted in the New Testament.

- Jesus quoted it in Matthew 22:43-45 (also Mark 12:36-37), showing how David called the Messiah "Lord" – recognizing that the Messiah was greater than David himself.

- Peter quoted it on Pentecost, explaining how David prophesied the deity and ascension of Jesus (Acts 2:34-35).

249

- Paul referred to it in 1 Corinthians 15:25, explaining the rule and dominion of Jesus the Messiah.

- The author of Hebrews quotes it in Hebrews 1:13, referring to the superiority of Jesus the Messiah over any angel.

- The author of Hebrews referred to it in Hebrews 10:13, explaining the rule and dominion of Jesus the Messiah.

ii. "How condescending on Jehovah's part to permit a mortal ear to hear, and a human pen to record his secret converse with his co-equal Son! How greatly should we prize the revelation of his private and solemn discourse with the Son, herein made public for the refreshing of his people!" (Spurgeon)

b. **The LORD said to my Lord**: The fact that Yahweh – the LORD, the covenant God of Israel – spoke to one that David himself called **Lord** (*Adonai*) demonstrates that both Yahweh and Adonai mentioned in this verse are God.

i. Specifically speaking, we would say that Yahweh is the Triune God, with references to the persons of the Father, Son, and Holy Spirit each being Yahweh. Normally, when Yahweh is mentioned without specific connection to the person of the Son or the Holy Spirit, we assume it refers to God the Father. Therefore, here God the Father is speaking to the Messiah, God the Son.

ii. "*Adonai* refers to an individual greater than the speaker. Here is a case of David's citing God's words in which God tells another personage, who is greater than David, to sit at God's right hand until God makes the person's enemies a footstool for the person's feet. This person can only be a divine Messiah, who is Jesus Christ." (Boice)

c. **Sit at My right hand, till I make Your enemies Your footstool**: Yahweh (specifically, God the Father) spoke to the Messiah (specifically, God the Son), telling Him to take His enthroned place (Ephesians 1:20, Hebrews 8:1) until the Father provided the victory for the Son.

i. **Sit at My right hand**: "His work is done, and he may sit; it is well done, and he may sit at his right hand; it will have grand results, and he may therefore quietly wait to see the complete victory which is certain to follow." (Spurgeon)

ii. **Your footstool**: "Thy slaves and vassals to be put to the meanest and basest services, as this phrase implies, 1 Kings 5:3, Psalms 18:39, 91:13; being taken from the manner of Eastern princes, who used to tread upon the necks of their conquered enemies, as we read, Joshua 10:24." (Poole)

d. The LORD shall send the rod of Your strength out of Zion: The Messiah's authority would not be limited to Israel. It would extend to the entire world, dominating all the kings and nations of the earth, giving Him **rule** over all **enemies**.

i. Adam Clarke is among those who think **the rod of Your strength** represents the Gospel: "*The Gospel* – the *doctrine of Christ crucified*; which is the powerful sceptre of the Lord that bought us; is *quick and powerful, sharper than any two-edged sword*; and is the power of God to salvation to all them that believe."

2. (3) Recognized and honored by His people.

Your people *shall be* volunteers
In the day of Your power;
In the beauties of holiness, from the womb of the morning,
You have the dew of Your youth.

a. **Your people shall be volunteers in the day of Your power**: When the people of God see and experience the victory of their Messiah, they will gladly give themselves to His work. They are willing in **the day** of His **power**. Since the Hebrew word translated **power** is the word for a *host* or *army*, the idea is that the Messiah's people are gathered together as a willing army.

i. **Be volunteers**: "Heb. *willingnesses*, i.e. most willing, as such plural words are frequently used." (Poole)

ii. "There are no mercenaries in this battle, no slaves pressed into the ranks of Jesus' soldiers. This army is composed entirely of volunteers." (Boice)

iii. "Whensoever the Holy Spirit is supreme in a church there will be a free-will offering of young hearts and lives…. There are no pressed men in our Master's army – all are volunteers. Offer your will to God; say you are willing to be made willing." (Meyer)

b. **You have the dew of Your youth**: The people of God praise the victorious Messiah, and are noted for their beautiful **holiness**, their radiant being (**the womb of the morning**), and their ageless strength (**dew of Your youth**).

i. "But the reference of the expression is to the army, not to its leader. '*Youth*' here is a collective noun, equivalent to 'young *men*.' The host of his soldier-subjects is described as a band of young warriors, whom he leads, in their fresh strength and countless numbers and gleaming beauty like the dew of the morning." (Maclaren, cited in Spurgeon)

3. (4) Established as an eternal priest.

The Lord has sworn
And will not relent,
"You *are* a priest forever
According to the order of Melchizedek."

a. **The Lord has sworn and will not relent**: This puts the statement which follows in the most solemn and strong context possible. Yahweh (specifically, God the Father) made an oath that would never be annulled.

i. "God, as it were, pledges His own name, with its fulness of unchanging power, to the fulfilment of the word; and this irrevocable and omnipotent decree is made still more impressive by the added assurance." (Maclaren)

b. **You are a priest forever according to the order of Melchizedek**: This is the oath of Yahweh (specifically, God the Father) regarding the Messiah, God the Son. He vowed that the Messiah had an eternal priesthood, and that it was after the pattern (**order**) of **Melchizedek**, who is mentioned in a single account in the Old Testament (Genesis 14).

i. The Genesis 14 account is brief, but densely packed with information about **Melchizedek**.

- After Abraham defeated the confederation of kings who took his nephew Lot captive, Abraham met with a mysterious priest named Melchizedek, whose name means *king of righteousness* and who was also king over the city of Salem (an ancient name for the city of Jeru*salem*), which made him the *king of peace*.

- Melchizedek was not merely a worshipper of the true God. He had the honored title *priest of the Most High God.* The greatness of God magnified the greatness of Melchizedek's priesthood.

- Melchizedek blessed Abraham, demonstrating his greatness over the patriarch.

- Abraham gave Melchizedek a tithe, which is a tenth part of all (all the spoils of battle, as mentioned in Genesis 14:20).

- There is no mention of any father or mother of Melchizedek, and he appears without any genealogy.

c. **You are a priest forever according to the order of Melchizedek**: With this oath, God revealed that there is *another* order of priesthood, *apart* from the priestly order of Aaron. The Israelite priests were all descended from Aaron and served in the tabernacle (later the temple), offering sacrifices and conducting ceremonies according to God's law. Here we see that God established another priestly **order**, after the pattern of **Melchizedek**.

d. **You are a priest forever according to the order of Melchizedek**: This oath was so important that the author of Hebrews refers to it five times (Hebrews 5:6, 5:10, 6:20, 7:17, and 7:21).

- Hebrews 5:5-6 and 5:10 emphasize that this was *Yahweh's declaration*, not something that the Messiah claimed for Himself.

- In Hebrews 6:20, the emphasis is on the idea that Jesus the Messiah serves now and forever as a living, active High Priest for His people.

- Hebrews 7:17 emphasizes that the priesthood of Jesus the Messiah according to the **order of Melchizedek** is better than the priestly order of Aaron, because it is eternal and will never end.

- Hebrews 7:21 emphasizes that the priesthood of Jesus the Messiah according to the **order of Melchizedek** is better than the priestly order of Aaron because it was founded on a direct **oath** of Yahweh, unlike the priestly order of Aaron.

  i. "His priesthood is not, like that of Aaron, figurative, successive, and transient, but real and effectual, fixed and incommunicable, eternal and unchangeable." (Horne)

  ii. "The Church is collected and conserved not only by Christ's kingly power, but also by his priestly mediation." (Trapp)

B. The conquest of the Messiah.

1. (5) The Messiah contends with the kings of the nations.

The Lord *is* at Your right hand;
He shall execute kings in the day of His wrath.

a. **The Lord is at Your right hand**: The favor and strength of the Messiah (**Your right hand**) is aligned with, and an instrument of, the strength of God (**the Lord**).

  i. "The second part of the psalm carries the King into the battlefield. He comes forth from the throne, where He sat at Jehovah's right hand, and now Jehovah stands at His right hand." (Maclaren)

  ii. "Now the Lord (i.e. Yahweh) and his King act as one, and the army of volunteers which was seen in verse 3 is no longer in the picture. The battle is the Lord's, yet he and his King are so united." (Kidner)

b. **He shall execute kings**: With the authority mentioned in verse 2, the strength of the Messiah extends out of Zion and brings the righteous judgment of God against even the greatest **kings**.

2. (6-7) The Messiah judges all nations.

He shall judge among the nations,
He shall fill *the places* with dead bodies,
He shall execute the heads of many countries.
He shall drink of the brook by the wayside;
Therefore He shall lift up the head.

a. **He shall judge among the nations**: In His conquest, the Messiah will exercise His authority over all **nations**, bringing His judgment.

b. **He shall fill the places with dead bodies**: This seems to anticipate the slaughter at the Battle of Armageddon (Revelation 16:16, 19:11-21).

i. "The choice for every man is being crushed beneath His foot, or being exalted to sit with Him on His throne. 'He that overcometh, to him will I give to sit down with Me on My throne, even as I also overcame, and am set down with My Father on His throne.' It is better to sit on His throne than to be His footstool." (Maclaren)

c. **Therefore He shall lift up the head**: While the rebellious nations of the world receive their judgment, the Messiah Himself is refreshed (**drink of the brook**) and exalted (**lift up the head**).

i. **He shall drink**: Curiously, many commentators take this as a reference to the Messiah's *humiliation*. It is better to see it as His refreshment on the day of battle. "Psalm 110:7 is usually taken as depicting the King as pausing in His victorious pursuit of the flying foe to drink, like Gideon's men, from the brook, and then with renewed vigour pressing on." (Maclaren)

ii. **He shall lift up the head**: "…i.e. shall be delivered from all his sorrows and sufferings, and exalted to great glory, and joy, and felicity, as this phrase usually signifies, as Psalms 3:3, 27:6, Jeremiah 52:31, and oft elsewhere; as, on the contrary, to *hang down the head*, is a signification of great grief and shame, as Lamentations 2:10." (Poole)

iii. "His own head shall be lifted high in victory, and his people, in him, shall be upraised also." (Spurgeon)

Psalm 111 – The Greatness of God's Works

This is another of the acrostic psalms, arranged according to the Hebrew alphabet. Except for the opening line of "Praise the Lord" (Hallelujah), each of the 22 lines of Psalm 111 begins with a successive letter of the Hebrew alphabet.

"The great art used in the composure of this and some other psalms (after the order of the Hebrew alphabet) serveth both to set forth their excellence and for the help of memory." (John Trapp)

Many commentators note the connection between Psalms 111 and 112. James Montgomery Boice observed, "The two psalms are an obviously matched pair. The first is an acrostic poem about God; the second is an acrostic poem about the godly man."

A. Thinking about the great works of God.

1. (1) The declaration and the decision to give God praise.

Praise the LORD!
I will praise the LORD with *my* whole heart,
In the assembly of the upright and *in* the congregation.

a. **Praise the LORD**: Psalm 111 begins with the simple declaration, *Hallelujah!* It was as if the psalmist thought, *Before I describe how I will praise Him, let me simply declare His praise.* The declaration also has the idea of encouraging others to do the same – I will praise the LORD, and you should also.

b. **I will praise the LORD with my whole heart**: The proclamation came after the declaration. There would be nothing held back in his praise; it would be given to God with his **whole heart**.

i. "If we want other people to praise God, we must praise God first. If we want them to love God, we must love him too. If we want others to serve God, we must serve him. We must set an example." (Boice)

255

ii. **My whole heart**: "God cannot be acceptably praised with a divided heart, neither should we attempt so to dishonour him; for our whole heart is little enough for his glory, and there can be no reason why it should not all be lifted up in his praise." (Spurgeon)

c. **In the assembly of the upright**: The praise would be wholehearted, but it would also be *public*. Praising God with others showed that the psalmist gloried in the praises of God; praising God with others was also a help and encouragement to praise Him.

i. The word for **assembly** and the word for **congregation** indicate different size groups. **Assembly** refers to a smaller, private group – something like our modern small group. **Congregation** refers to the larger gatherings of God's people.

ii. "*Company* [**assembly**] is that intimate word *sôd*, which has the connotation of a circle of friends or advisers." (Kidner)

2. (2-3) The study of God's great works.

The works of the LORD are great,
Studied by all who have pleasure in them.
His work *is* honorable and glorious,
And His righteousness endures forever.

a. **The works of the LORD are great**: God should be praised for who He is, but what He has done is also worthy of praise. Here the emphasis is on His work in creation, and these **works** are **great** in their number and in their significance.

i. Kidner comments on the specific Hebrew word translated **works** in verse 2: "In the Psalms, the Lord's *works* (*maasim*) are sometimes his deeds, as in verse 6, but more often the things he has made (e.g., the heavens, 8:3; 19:1; 102:25; and the populous earth, 104:24)."

ii. "No small things are done by so great a hand." (Trapp)

iii. "In design, in size, in number, in excellence, all the works of the Lord are great. Even the little things of God are great." (Spurgeon)

b. **Studied by all who have pleasure in them**: The greatness of God's work invites close study by the scientist, the historian, and the theologian. Their findings will lead them to do their work with all their strength and take **pleasure** in how God's wisdom and power are revealed through His **honorable and glorious** works.

i. **Studied**: "The more one gazes, the more one sees." (Maclaren)

ii. "There is a science laboratory in Cambridge, England, called the Cavendish Laboratory, named after the eighteenth-century English chemist and physicist Sir Henry Cavendish (1731–1810). It is distinguished by having the words of Psalm 111:2 inscribed over the entrance to its building as a charter for every believing scientist: *Great are the works of the Lord; they are pondered by all who delight in them.*" (Boice)

iii. "Kepler, when he first turned his telescope to clustered worlds, exclaimed, 'I am thinking over again the first thoughts of God.' Would that the ecstasy of the ardent student of nature might fill our hearts as we direct our thought to the great works of our Saviour-God." (Meyer)

iv. "Happy are they who, with humility and diligence, with faith and devotion, give themselves to the contemplation of these works, and take 'pleasure' and delight therein. To them shall the gate of true science open; they shall understand the mysteries of creation, providence, and redemption; and they who thus 'seek,' shall find the treasures of eternal wisdom." (Horne)

v. "But while this verse is well taken as God's charter for the scientist and artist, verse 10 must be its partner, lest 'professing to be wise' we become fools, like the men of Romans 1:18-23." (Kidner)

vi. This **pleasure** can be ours forever. "Probably this will be our employment in eternity; ever passing into deeper and fuller appreciation of the works of God, and breaking into more rapturous songs." (Meyer)

c. **His work is honorable and glorious**: Not only are God's works in creation great, but so is His **work** of guiding and arranging all things, His **work** of *providence*.

i. Kidner notes that a different Hebrew word is translated **work** in verse 3: "Here God's *work* (*poal*) is more likely to mean his providential acts, as in, e.g., Deuteronomy 32:4 [*His work is perfect*]."

B. Describing the great works of God.

1. (4-6) Remembering God's great works.

He has made His wonderful works to be remembered;
The Lord is gracious and full of compassion.
He has given food to those who fear Him;
He will ever be mindful of His covenant.
He has declared to His people the power of His works,
In giving them the heritage of the nations.

a. **He has made His wonderful works to be remembered**: God designed His saving acts to **be remembered** among His people. It is a dishonor to him and a failure of man that the miracles of His redemption are forgotten, or worse yet *denied.*

> i. Kidner points out that still a third Hebrew word is translated **wonderful works**: "The expression *wonderful works* opens up another line of thought. It is a single word, 'wonders', and refers most often to the great saving acts of God."

> ii. **To be remembered**: "The word *zeker*…is a noun in Hebrew. It connotes the act of 'proclamation.' Israel not only remembered but proclaimed what God had done." (VanGemeren)

b. **The LORD is gracious and full of compassion**: First in the mind of the psalmist was God's great work of grace and love. He is **full** of these qualities in His being, and expresses them in his great works.

> i. "**Is gracious and full of compassion** towards his people, as appears from his works and carriage towards us, in sparing, and pardoning, and restoring, and preserving us when we have deserved to be utterly destroyed." (Poole)

c. **He has given food to those who fear Him**: Perhaps the psalmist had in mind God's provision for Israel through the wilderness, or the more general principle David wrote of in Psalm 37:25, that he had never seen the descendants of the righteous begging bread.

> i. **Food**: "The word signifies what is taken in *hunting* – wild beasts, venison, or *fowls* of any kind; particularly such as were proper for food. It also signifies *spoil* taken from enemies." (Clarke)

d. **He will ever be mindful of His covenant**: God will never forget the covenant He made with Abraham and his descendants (Genesis 12) or the covenant He made with Israel at Mount Sinai (Exodus 24).

e. **He has declared to His people the power of His works**: God did not hide His greatness, but **declared** it to **His people** – *if they would pay attention!* This declaration of His great works brought Israel into the land of Canaan (**giving them the heritage of the nations**).

> i. "…two standing proofs of Divine kindness are the miraculous provision of food in the desert and the possession of the promised land." (Maclaren)

2. (7-9) The nature of God's great works.

The works of His hands *are* verity and justice;
All His precepts *are* sure.
They stand fast forever and ever,
***And are* done in truth and uprightness.**

He has sent redemption to His people;
He has commanded His covenant forever:
Holy and awesome *is* His name.

a. **The works of His hands are verity and justice**: What God does is true and fair, and what He commands is settled (**His precepts are sure**). This is seen in God's great works in creation and in history.

i. "Thus the inspired author brings out the coherence between the Lord's acts and words. They all reflect his divine nature as a Father-King in relationship to his children-subjects. The precepts with their encouragements, promises, threats, blessings, and curses are true!" (VanGemeren)

ii. **His precepts are sure**: "He is no fickle despot, commanding one thing one day and another [on a different day], but his commands remain absolutely unaltered, their necessity equally unquestionable, their excellence permanently proven, and their reward eternally secure." (Spurgeon)

b. **He has sent redemption to His people**: One of God's greatest works is rescuing His people from their oppression and sin, and doing it in the context of **His covenant**. The psalmist likely had the exodus in mind.

i. The King James Version translates the phrase, **holy and awesome is His name** as *holy and reverend is his name*. Adam Clarke comments on the word *reverend* from the King James Version: "The word *reverend* comes to us from the Latins, *reverendus*, and is compounded of *re*, intensive, and *vereor*, to be *feared*; and *most* or *right* reverend, *reverendissimus*, signifies *to be greatly feared*. These terms are now only titles of ecclesiastical respect, especially in the *Protestant* ministry; but there was a time in which these were no empty titles. Such was the power of the clergy, that, when they walked not in the fear of the Lord, they caused the *people to fear*, and *they themselves* were to *be feared*; but, when the *secular power* was added to the *spiritual*, they were then truly *reverendi* and *reverendissimi, to be feared* and *greatly to be feared.*"

3. (10) What should be learned from God's great works.

The fear of the LORD is the beginning of wisdom;
A good understanding have all those who do *His commandments*.
His praise endures forever.

a. **The fear of the LORD is the beginning of wisdom**: Recognizing the greatness of God's works, one should appropriately **fear** Him. God should be regarded with respect, reverence, and awe. This proper attitude of the creature toward the Creator is **the beginning of wisdom**. Wisdom cannot advance further until this starting point is established.

i. The idea that the fear of the Lord is the beginning of wisdom is also found in Job 28:28; Proverbs 1:7; 9:10; and Ecclesiastes 12:13.

ii. "It is probably a safe bet to say that most people today are not much interested in wisdom. They are interested in making money and in having a good time. Some are interested in knowing something, in getting an education. Almost everyone wants to be well liked. But wisdom? The pursuit of wisdom is not a popular ideal." (Boice)

iii. "It is not only the beginning of wisdom, but the middle and the end. It is indeed the Alpha and Omega, the essence, the body and the soul, the sum and substance. He that hath the fear of God is truly wise." (de Superville, cited in Spurgeon)

b. **A good understanding have all those who do His commandments**: Taking into account the greatness of God's works, one should obey God – that is, **do His commandments**. A life of obedience reveals that one has a **good understanding** of the greatness of God's works.

i. "Obedience to God proves that our judgment is sound." (Spurgeon)

ii. "The Psalm closes with words which prepare for the next, as they declare that the fear of Jehovah is the beginning of wisdom, and that such as act according to that fear have good understanding." (Morgan)

c. **His praise endures forever**: Taking into account the greatness of God's works, one should **praise** Him and never stop praising Him. The angels surrounding God's throne see His greatness and the greatness of His works, and they never stop praising Him (Revelation 4:8).

Psalm 112 – The Blessings Upon Those Who Fear the LORD

Like Psalm 111 before it, Psalm 112 is an acrostic psalm. James Montgomery Boice commented on the similarities between Psalms 111 and 112: "They are the same length, fall into identical stanzas, and even have identical or similar phrases occurring at the same places in each. Both are precise acrostics; that is, they have twenty-two lines each of which begins with a successive letter of the Hebrew alphabet."

Charles Spurgeon wrote this regarding the connection between Psalms 111 and 112: "It bears the same relation to the preceding which the moon does to the sun; for, while the first declares the glory of God, the second speaks of the reflection of the divine brightness in men born from above."

A. The blessed man and his family.

1. (1) The blessed life of the man who fears the LORD.

Praise the LORD!
Blessed *is* the man *who* fears the LORD,
***Who* delights greatly in His commandments.**

> a. **Praise the LORD:** Like several others in this section of the psalms, Psalm 112 begins with *Hallelujah!* This was both the personal praise of the psalmist and an exhortation to others to praise Him.

> > i. "The Psalm cannot be viewed as the extolling of man, for it commences with 'Praise ye the Lord;' and it is intended to give to God all the honour of his grace which is manifested in the sons of God." (Spurgeon)

> b. **Blessed is the man who fears the LORD:** Psalms 111 and 112 may have been composed together; they are certainly set together in the collection on purpose. Psalm 111 ended with the idea that the fear of the LORD is the

beginning of wisdom; now the psalmist explains the blessedness of the one who does fear the LORD.

> i. "The fear the Bible is talking about is best described as a profound reverence; that is, we are to revere God, or stand in awe of him." (Boice)

c. **Who delights greatly in His commandments**: This blessed one does not fear God in a sense of misery and reluctant obligation. This psalm speaks of one who **delights greatly** in God's commandments.

> i. "There is a deliberate echo of the previous psalm here. Psalm 111:2 spoke of delight in God's *works*. In Psalm 112:1 we are told that God's people also delight in God's *words* (commands)." (Boice)

> ii. "To this man God's word is as fascinating as are his works to the naturalist; and the term used for it, *his commandments*, implies that his interest is practical. What grips him is God's will and call." (Kidner)

> iii. "The man who duly 'feareth God,' is delivered from every other fear; the man who 'delighteth in God's commandments,' is freed from every inordinate desire of earthly things." (Horne)

> iv. "It is not enough to *fear God*, we must also *love him: fear* will deter us from *evil; love* will lead us to *obedience*." (Clarke)

> v. Think of the great measure of blessedness upon Jesus. No one revered God the Father as Jesus did; no one delighted in the Father's commandments as much as Jesus did.

2. (2-3) The household of the blessed man.

His descendants will be mighty on earth;
The generation of the upright will be blessed.
Wealth and riches *will be* in his house,
And his righteousness endures forever.

a. **His descendants will be mighty on earth**: The one who *fears the LORD* and *delights greatly in His commandments* (verse 1) has God's blessing on his family. The psalmist pronounced blessing on the **descendants** of this man, the one who is **upright**.

> i. "'Mighty' here means being of recognized stature or standing rather than being physically strong." (Boice)

> ii. "If any one should desire to leave behind him a flourishing posterity, let him not think to accomplish it by accumulating heaps of gold and silver, and leaving them behind him; but by rightly recognising God and serving Him; and commending his children to the guardianship and protection of God." (Mollerus, cited in Spurgeon)

b. **Wealth and riches will be in his house**: The psalmist also pronounced a blessing on the economic life of the one who fears the LORD. Their life of obedience and honor to God means God's blessing will also come to their financial dealings.

> i. "Such promises are expected to be fulfilled in general; it is not required by any proper rules of interpreting language that this should be universally and always true." (Barnes, cited in Spurgeon)

> ii. "The prosperity promised in the present verses may be largely material, but a closer look reveals the moral and spiritual terms which make it an instrument of good." (Kidner)

> iii. "Understood literally this is rather a promise of the old covenant than of the new, for many of the best of the people of God are very poor; yet it has been found true that uprightness is the road to success, and, all other things being equal, the honest man is the rising man." (Spurgeon)

> iv. "It sometimes pleaseth God to bestow on his servants, as he did on Israel of old, the good things of this world. And a rich man is therefore happier than a poor man, because 'it is more blessed to give than to receive.'" (Horne)

c. **His righteousness endures forever**: This blessed man's good works and right standing with God are lasting. They will not fade in this world or the world to come.

> i. "He is not the worse for his wealth, nor drawn aside by the deceitfulness of riches." (Trapp)

> ii. Adam Clarke had an interesting idea: **righteousness** here and in verse 9 refer to the generous giving of the man who fears the LORD. Clarke stated that the both the Hebrew and Greek words normally translated **righteousness** "...are often used to signify, not only *justice* and *righteousness*, but also *beneficence* and *almsgiving*; and this is most probably the meaning here."

B. The contrast between the upright and the wicked.

1. (4-8) The upright are established.

Unto the upright there arises light in the darkness;
***He is* gracious, and full of compassion, and righteous.**
A good man deals graciously and lends;
He will guide his affairs with discretion.
Surely he will never be shaken;
The righteous will be in everlasting remembrance.

He will not be afraid of evil tidings;
His heart is steadfast, trusting in the LORD.
His heart *is* established;
He will not be afraid,
Until he sees *his desire* upon his enemies.

a. **Unto the upright there arises light in the darkness**: The psalmist recognized the **darkness** that often fills the world, but the **upright** one who fears the LORD will be blessed with **light** in the midst of the darkness.

> i. "God himself is the light which arises in darkness for those who are sincere in their dealings with him." (Delitzsch, cited in Boice)

> ii. "The relationship of God to the godly person is like the relationship of the sun to the moon. The sun shines by its own glorious light. The moon does not, but still it shines, and the way it shines is by reflecting the light coming to it from the sun." (Boice)

> iii. "While we are on earth, we are subject to a threefold 'darkness;' the darkness of error, the darkness of sorrow, and the darkness of death." (Horne)

> iv. "The psalm gives a realistic portrayal of wisdom as it brings out, not only the blessings of honor, children, and riches, but also the reality of adversities." (VanGemeren)

b. **He is gracious, and full of compassion, and righteous**: The light received from God shines through the righteous one, and he displays to others the grace, **compassion**, righteousness, and generosity God has granted to him.

> i. Verse 3 referred to the *wealth and riches* that often come to those who fear the Lord. Kidner observed, "The psalm deals realistically with the temptations that go with the possession of money." These include abuse to power, refusing to lend, fear, rivalry, and lack of generosity.

> ii. **And lends**: "Finding himself in circumstances which enable him to spare a little of his wealth he lends judiciously where a loan will be of permanent service. Providence has made him able to lend, and grace makes him willing to lend. He is not a borrower, for God has lifted him above that necessity; neither is he a hoarder, for his new nature saves him from that temptation; but he wisely uses the talents committed to him." (Spurgeon)

c. **He will guide his affairs with discretion**: The one who fears the LORD is blessed with wisdom (Psalm 111:10) that flows from his godly character.

i. "**With discretion,** Heb. *with judgment*; so as is fit and meet, and as God requires, not getting his estate unjustly, nor casting it away prodigally or wickedly, nor yet withholding it uncharitably from such as need it." (Poole)

d. **He will never be shaken**: Because of His character and wisdom, the one who fears the LORD will be firmly established. His **remembrance** will last, with nothing to fear from **evil tidings**. As he trusts in the LORD, **his heart is established** and in the end, he will see victory over his enemies.

i. "He who builds his transient life on and into the Rock of Ages wins rocklike steadfastness…. Lives rooted in God are never uprooted." (Maclaren)

ii. **Everlasting remembrance**: "The righteous are worth remembering, their actions are of the kind which record themselves, and God himself takes charge of their memorials." (Spurgeon)

e. **He will not be afraid of evil tidings**: Evil tidings are all around us, and come to us every day. Evil tidings may come to us from our family, from our health, from business, from the unfaithful, from the culture around us, or from politics. Yet the one who fears the LORD **will not be afraid**.

i. "There cannot be evil tidings to the soul which has fixed its trust in the Lord…. If tidings were to come to you today of disease, loss, bereavement, death, they could not be evil if your heart dares to maintain a fixed trust in God; for such trust robs death of its sting, and the grave of its victory. I cannot understand, but I can trust Him." (Meyer)

ii. **His heart is established**: "'His heart is propped up;' he is *buttressed up* by the strength of his Maker." (Clarke)

iii. "He is neither fickle nor cowardly; when he is undecided as to his course he is still fixed in heart: he may change his plan, but not the purpose of his soul." (Spurgeon)

2. (9-10) The grief of the wicked.

He has dispersed abroad,
He has given to the poor;
His righteousness endures forever;
His horn will be exalted with honor.
The wicked will see *it* and be grieved;
He will gnash his teeth and melt away;
The desire of the wicked shall perish.

a. **He has dispersed**: This psalm has much to say about the *generosity* of the one who fears the LORD. Since he is blessed in regard to material things (verse 3), it is important that he is generous with his blessings. He is also *wise*; **dispersed** implies a wise and thoughtful distribution as part of the *discretion* that guides his affairs (verse 5).

> i. Paul quoted verse 9 in 2 Corinthians 9:9 to encourage Christians to be generous: *As it is written: "He has dispersed abroad, He has given to the poor; His righteousness endures forever."*

> ii. This generosity is not "…given indiscriminately and at random, but 'dispersed,' like precious seed, with prudence and discretion, according to the nature of the soil, and in proper season, so as to produce the most plentiful harvest." (Horne)

b. **His righteousness endures forever**: The profile of this man (or woman) who fears the LORD is remarkable. It is a reflection of the character of God Himself, even as the moon reflects the sun's light. It is partially fulfilled in the godly man or woman, and perfectly fulfilled in the man Jesus Christ.

- He is a God-fearing man (*who fears the LORD*).
- He is a lover of God's word (*delights greatly in His commandments*).
- He is a prosperous man (*wealth and riches*).
- He is a man who makes a home for his family (*his descendants…his house*).
- He is a loving and kind man (*gracious, and full of compassion*).
- He is a helping man (*deals graciously and lends*).
- He is a wise man (*will guide his affairs with discretion*).
- He is a strong man (*not afraid of evil tidings*).
- He is a generous man (*he has dispersed abroad*).
- He is a man who does not abuse power (*his horn will be exalted with honor*).
- He is a hated man (*the wicked will see it and be grieved*).

> i. **Endures forever**: "Wise living is characterized by lasting success, unlike many human endeavors that fail or are short-lived." (VanGemeren)

> ii. "When all the flashes of sensual pleasure are quite extinct, when all the flowers of secular glory are withered away; when all earthly treasures are buried in darkness; when this world, and all the fashion of it, are utterly vanished and gone, the bountiful man's state will be

still firm and flourishing, and '*his righteousness shall endure for ever.*'" (Barrow, cited in Spurgeon)

iii. **His horn will be exalted with honor**: "His power and authority *shall be exalted with honour*. He shall rise to influence only through his own worth, and not by extortion or flattery." (Clarke)

iv. "Let it now be read again in close connection with the preceding one [Psalm 111], and it will be seen that the supreme fact about this man is that he has indeed become like the God Whom he fears and obeys. The very things celebrated in the praise of Jehovah are those which constitute the excellencies of this man who fears Him." (Morgan)

c. **The wicked will see it and be grieved**: In contrast to the enduring blessing upon the upright man, the wicked man will **melt away**. His misery will be all the worse as his **desire** is frustrated and he sees the blessings that come to those who fear the LORD.

i. The wicked may not gnash their teeth in this life, but they certainly will in the age to come (Luke 13:28).

ii. "The covetous wretch who sat a brood upon his bags, and befooled the bountiful man, shall himself come to beggary, which he so much feared, and be ready to eat his own nails through envy at the other's prosperity." (Trapp)

Psalm 113 – Praise to the LORD Who Lifts the Lowly

The book of Psalms contains three collections titled Hallel, with Psalms 113-118 known as the Egyptian Hallel, mainly because of their connection with Passover celebrations, commemorating Israel's deliverance from Egypt. The psalms of the Egyptian Hallel were sung as part of the Passover ceremony, with 113-114 sung before the meal and 115-118 after the meal.

"This group is necessarily of special interest to us because in all probability, these psalms were sung by our Lord and His disciples on that dark night in which He was betrayed." (G. Campbell Morgan)

"To these reference is made by the evangelists, Matthew 26:30, and Mark 14:26, there called the hymn which Jesus and his disciples sung at the passover." (Adam Clarke)

A. Calling God's servants to continually praise Him.

1. (1) A call to praise the LORD.

Praise the LORD!
Praise, O servants of the LORD,
Praise the name of the LORD!

> a. **Praise the LORD:** This is the third consecutive psalm to begin with the exclamation, *Hallelujah!* As in Psalms 111 and 112, it is both a personal statement of praise and an encouragement for others to do the same.

> b. **Praise, O servants of the LORD:** God's **servants** have special reason to praise Him. They have the honor of sharing in His great work, and they are promised eternal reward for doing so. Everyone has reason for praise; **servants of the LORD** have many more reasons.

> c. **Praise the name of the LORD:** This means honoring and exalting Yahweh Himself and His character, which are represented by His **name**.

268

i. "There is a point in specifying the Lord's *servants* and his *name*, since worship to be acceptable must be more than flattery and more than guess-work. It is the loving homage of the committed to the Revealed." (Kidner)

ii. "In the case of God 'the name of the Lord' is all important, for it has to do with the revelation of who God is. In other words, it is not just any God we are to worship. We are to praise the one true 'Lord,' who has revealed himself in creation, on Sinai, and more recently in the person of his only Son, Jesus of Nazareth." (Boice)

2. (2-3) The lasting nature of God's praise.

Blessed be the name of the LORD
From this time forth and forevermore!
From the rising of the sun to its going down
The LORD's name *is* to be praised.

a. **From this time forth and forevermore**: In verse 1 we were encouraged to praise the name of Yahweh. In this next verse we are encouraged to do it **forevermore**. The unchanging God never becomes unworthy of our praise. For the child of God with open eyes, time only reveals more reasons to praise Him.

i. **Blessed be the name of the LORD**: "Praise him with utmost intention and extension of spirit and of speech. God is therefore called, by an appellative proper, The Blessed One." (Trapp)

b. **From the rising of the sun to its going down**: Using the Hebrew pattern of repetition, the psalmist emphasized the idea that God's is worthy of *continual* praise.

B. Reasons to praise God continually.

1. (4-6) The greatness of God's glory.

The LORD is high above all nations,
His glory above the heavens.
Who *is* like the LORD our God,
Who dwells on high,
Who humbles Himself to behold
***The things that are* in the heavens and in the earth?**

a. **His glory above the heavens**: Yahweh is not only greater than all the heathen **nations**, but His glory extends **above the heavens**. The covenant God of little Israel is greater than everything in creation.

i. "Though the Gentiles knew him not, yet was Jehovah their ruler: their false gods were no gods, and their kings were puppets in his hands." (Spurgeon)

b. **Who is like the LORD our God**: His exaltation above everything on earth or heaven shows that Yahweh is incomparable. Nothing exists that is greater than He **who dwells on high**.

c. **Who humbles Himself to behold**: When we understand the greatness of God, His interest and care for creation (especially mankind) is remarkable. Here the psalmist shared the idea of David in Psalm 8:4: *What is man that You are mindful of him, and the son of man that You visit him?* Psalm 144:3 has a similar sense of amazement.

i. "God's loftiness can never be adequately measured, unless His condescension is taken into account; and His condescension never sufficiently wondered at, unless His loftiness is felt." (Maclaren)

ii. "What amazes the psalmist is that God is exalted so high that he has to stoop low to see not only the earth but also the heavens, and yet at the same time he cares for the lowly." (Boice)

iii. "Heathen philosophers could not believe that the great God was observant of the small events of human history; they pictured him as abiding in serene indifference to all the wants and woes of his creatures." (Spurgeon)

iv. "If it be such condescension for God to behold things in heaven and earth, what an amazing condescension was it for the Son of God to come from heaven to earth and take our nature upon him, that he might seek and save them that were lost! Here indeed he humbled himself." (Henry, cited in Spurgeon)

2. (7-9) God's care for the lowly.

He raises the poor out of the dust,
***And* lifts the needy out of the ash heap,**
That He may seat *him* with princes—
With the princes of His people.
He grants the barren woman a home,
Like a joyful mother of children.
Praise the LORD!

a. **He raises the poor out of the dust**: When God in heaven beholds the things on earth (verse 6), He sees the **poor** down in the **dust** and the **needy** in the **ash heap** – and He **raises** them up.

i. "When no hand but his can help he interposes, and the work is done. It is worthwhile to be cast down to be so divinely raised from the dust." (Spurgeon)

ii. When Jesus sang these words on the night of His betrayal and arrest, it must have occurred to Him that in a sense *He* was the one who would be lifted from the **dust** of the grave to the highest place.

b. **That He may seat him with princes**: God lifts the poor and needy *from* the depths *up to* the heights. In light of the new covenant, we can make the connection with God's work in the life of the believer as described in Ephesians 2:5-6: *…even when we were dead in trespasses, [He] made us alive together with Christ (by grace you have been saved), and raised us up together, and made us sit together in the heavenly places in Christ Jesus.*

i. While these words look forward to Ephesians 2:5-6, they also look back. "Consciously, however, these verses look back to the song of Hannah, which they quote almost exactly (cf. 7, 8a with 1 Sam. 2:8). Hence the sudden reference to the childless woman who becomes a mother (9), for this was Hannah's theme." (Kidner)

c. **He grants the barren woman a home**: The psalmist illustrated one way the work of lifting the poor and needy to a high and honored place might work. The picture is of a woman **barren** of children becoming **a joyful mother**.

i. "The afflicted man will receive recognition and the oppressed woman will receive honor in being a woman. In the ancient Near East, and especially in Israel, motherhood was a crowning achievement of any woman. A barren woman was a social outcast; she was a disappointment to her husband, to other women, and especially to herself." (VanGemeren)

ii. "Sarah, Rachel, the wife of Manoah, Hannah, Elizabeth, and others were all instances of the miraculous power of God in literally fulfilling the statement of the Psalmist." (Spurgeon)

iii. "This psalm ends by saying that the great exalted God of the Bible is not only concerned about needy people in general but also with the individual. He cares about you. He cares for you and me personally." (Boice)

iv. It is significant to remember that Jesus sang these words on the night He was betrayed and arrested, the night before His crucifixion. "As he approached the ultimate depths in this stooping, He sang the song which offers praise to God for this condescending grace." (Morgan)

d. **Praise the LORD**: The caring, loving God who comes from the highest heaven to help the humble of the earth is worthy of praise – Hallelujah!

    i. "The music concludes upon its key-note. The Psalm is a circle, ending where it began, praising the Lord from its first syllable to its last. May our life-psalm partake of the same character, and never know a break or a conclusion. In an endless circle let us bless the Lord, whose mercies never cease." (Spurgeon)

Psalm 114 – The Mighty Presence of God Delivers His People from Egypt

Charles Spurgeon had high praise for Psalm 114, the second in the series of psalms known as the Egyptian Hallel and sung as part of Israel's Passover ceremony: "This sublime SONG OF THE EXODUS is one and indivisible. True poetry has here reached its climax: no human mind has ever been able to equal, much less to excel, the grandeur of this psalm."

A. Introduction: God's deliverance of Israel from Egypt.

1. (1) Delivered from a foreign land.

When Israel went out of Egypt,
The house of Jacob from a people of strange language,

> a. **When Israel went out of Egypt**: Israel's deliverance from **Egypt** was the central act of redemption under the Old Covenant. It was to be constantly remembered and celebrated, and this song joins in the celebration.

> > i. For those who are under the New Covenant in Jesus, the work of Jesus at the cross and empty tomb becomes the central act of redemption. We are likewise called to constantly remember and celebrate what God did to set us free by dying on the cross for us.

> b. **The house of Jacob from a people of strange language**: The emphasis is on the idea that Israel did not *belong* in Egypt. Though they lived there for some 400 years, it was never their home. In a similar way, this world is a place of **a people of strange language** for all whom God redeems.

> > i. "The reference to the 'foreign tongue' evokes the association with oppression (cf. Isaiah 28:11; Jeremiah 5:15) and is synonymous with 'the house of bondage' (cf. Exodus 20:2)." (VanGemeren)

2 (2) Delivered to be His dwelling place and His servants.

Judah became His sanctuary,
And Israel His dominion.

> a. **Judah became His sanctuary**: The leading tribe of Israel (**Judah**) represented the whole nation which became the dwelling place of God (**His sanctuary**). The godly in Israel always understood that God's dwelling in the tabernacle or temple was only symbolic of His presence in His people.

> > i. "There is a dramatic change of status between the first verse and the second. The group of aliens, their isolation increased by the *strange language* that surrounded them, is now viewed in relation not to man but to God." (Kidner)

> > ii. "Judah he mentions as the chief of all the tribes, not only in number and power, but also in dignity, in which the kingdom was to be seated, Genesis 49:10, etc., as at this time it actually was, and from which the Messias was to spring." (Poole)

> > iii. "They are two names [**Judah** and **Israel**] for the one people that came out of Egypt at the exodus. This one people is declared to be both God's sanctuary and God's kingdom." (Boice)

> b. **And Israel His dominion**: Any place God dwells, He dominates. God's desire to make Israel His **sanctuary** was so they could honor Him as Lord and Master, not merely as a helper or mascot.

B. The great works of God in delivering Israel from Egypt.

1. (3-6) God's authority over the waters and the mountains.

The sea saw *it* and fled;
Jordan turned back.
The mountains skipped like rams,
The little hills like lambs.
What ails you, O sea, that you fled?
O Jordan, *that* you turned back?
O mountains, *that* you skipped like rams?
O little hills, like lambs?

> a. **The sea saw it and fled**: As in other places in Hebrew poetry, the psalmist personified nature and described it as responding to God in fear or reverence. Here he mentioned the parting of waters at both the Red Sea and the **Jordan** River, at the beginning and end of Israel's journey to the Promised Land.

> > i. "Nature recognised His presence and obeyed His will. The sea fled, Jordan was driven back, mountains and little hills were moved." (Morgan)

ii. "If the divine presence hath such an effect upon inanimate matter, how ought it to operate on rational and accountable beings?" (Horne)

b. **Jordan turned back**: The psalmist gives a beautiful and powerful picture. When these waters divided, they simply responded to the awesome presence of the Lord. The sense is, "What else could they do?"

i. "The poet does not sing of the suspension of natural laws, or of a singular phenomenon not readily to be explained; but to him the presence of God with his people is everything, and in his lofty song he tells how the river was driven back because the Lord was there." (Spurgeon)

ii. "It is noticeable that the Exodus is thought of in its completeness; not only escape from Egypt, but entrance to the land, for both Sea and Jordan are seen as passed." (Morgan)

iii. Spurgeon saw spiritual significance in this combination of the start of the Exodus and the end of it: "The division of the sea and the drying up of the river are placed together though forty years intervened, because they were the opening and closing scenes of one great event. We may thus unite by faith our new birth and our departure out of the world into the promised inheritance.... It is all one and the same deliverance, and the beginning ensures the end."

c. **The mountains skipped like rams**: This probably has reference to the strong earthquakes and similar phenomena that happened at Mount Sinai (Exodus 19:16-20) when God manifested His presence there. They shook and "**skipped**" like sheep.

i. "Men fear the mountains, but the mountains tremble before the Lord." (Spurgeon)

ii. The idea of **skipped like rams** carries also the thought of *joy*. We might say creation was *happy* God brought this deliverance to His people. "Truly Yahweh appeared to Israel and established his kingdom in Israel. That is why nature as it were responded with a twofold response: fear and great joy." (VanGemeren)

d. **What ails you, O sea**: The psalmist challenged both the **sea** and the **mountains**. *They* were powerless to stand against the mighty presence of God. It's even more foolish to think that mankind (either individually or together) can stand against God's mighty presence.

i. "Such speeches directed to [inanimate objects] are very frequent, both in Scripture and in other authors, and especially in poetical writings, such as this." (Poole)

ii. "God has come nearer to us than ever he did to Sinai, or to Jordan, for he has assumed our nature, and yet the masses of mankind are neither driven back from their sins, nor moved in the paths of obedience." (Spurgeon)

2. (7-8) Calling the earth to honor the Lord.

Tremble, O earth, at the presence of the Lord,
At the presence of the God of Jacob,
Who turned the rock *into* a pool of water,
The flint into a fountain of waters.

a. **Tremble, O earth, at the presence of the Lord**: The psalmist called upon *all* the **earth** to honor *Adonai* in His mighty **presence**. The **God of Jacob** is more than a local deity; He is God of all the earth.

i. Verse 7 is the first time in this psalm that God is referred to by any name or title (**Lord** [*Adonai*] and **God of Jacob**). Up to this point, the psalmist has asked questions: Who is it? What did it? "The author must have been having fun as he wrote, knowing the answer and knowing we know the answer too, but holding it off. What could have caused the sea to part, the river to turn back, and the hills to tremble? he asks. For twelve lines he has allowed our interest to build for dramatic effect." (Boice)

ii. Morgan linked the idea of **tremble** to labor pains in birth. "When Jehovah, acting as Sovereign Lord, and in His might thus convulsed Nature, it was that a nation might be born." (Morgan)

b. **Who turned the rock into a pool of waters**: The psalmist remembered one more event which demonstrated God's power over creation during the Exodus years – when God brought forth water for His people from **the rock** and the hardened **flint**. This assured the people of God that His mighty presence works *for* them, not against them.

i. As Psalm 113 closed with God's compassion on the barren woman, this psalm closes with God's compassion on thirsty Israel. His great power and might are not merely for the dividing of waters and the shaking of mountains. His majestic might brings blessing to His people one by one.

ii. **The flint into a fountain of waters**: "This is a miracle which we all need to have wrought in our experience. Our heart is flint, our eyes are dry, our souls fail to respond with tears and regrets to the love of the Pierced One, and to the indictment that charges us with His death." (Meyer)

iii. Psalm 114 ends without giving any specific instruction to the people of God, but simply declares His great works. "He has no word of 'moral,' no application, counsel, warning, or encouragement to give. Whoso will can draw these. Enough for him to lift his soaring song, and to check it into silence in the midst of its full music." (Maclaren)

iv. We again remind ourselves that Jesus probably sang this psalm together with His disciples on the night He was betrayed and arrested (Matthew 26:30 and Mark 14:26). He would grant the people of God a greater deliverance than Israel out of Egypt. In that work all nature would be shaken (Matthew 27:45, 51).

Psalm 115 – The LORD Our Help and Shield

Psalm 115 is a continuation of the collection of the Egyptian Hallel psalms (Psalms 113-118) sung by the Jews during their Passover celebrations. It therefore makes up part of the hymns which would have been sung by Jesus and His disciples on the night He was betrayed and arrested, the night before His crucifixion (Matthew 26:30 and Mark 14:26). It is especially meaningful to consider this psalm in the heart and on the lips of Jesus during those great moments.

Regarding the structure of this psalm, James Montgomery Boice observed: "The opinion of the majority of scholars is that the psalm is liturgical, intended to be sung by alternating groups of worshipers: the priests, the high priest, the people, and so on."

A. The LORD exalted above all idols.

1. (1-2) Praise and a subtle prayer.

Not unto us, O LORD, not unto us,
But to Your name give glory,
Because of Your mercy,
Because of Your truth.
Why should the Gentiles say,
"So where *is* their God?"

> a. **Not unto us, but to Your name give glory**: The singer of this psalm understood that when God did wonderful things, the glory should be given to God – not to God's people (**not unto us**), even if they are in some sense active in the work. The **glory** should go unto God and His holy **name**.

> > i. "This is the godly man's motto, and his daily practice." (Trapp)

> > ii. "Not first for the welfare of the people does [the psalmist] care, but for the vindication of his God. This is a deep note, and all too rare in our music. We are ever in danger of putting the welfare of man before the glory of God." (Morgan)

iii. "The repetition of the words, 'Not unto us,' would seem to indicate a very serious desire to renounce any glory which they might at any time have proudly appropriated to themselves, and it also sets forth the vehemence of their wish that God would at any cost to them magnify his own name." (Spurgeon)

iv. "Adoniram Judson, full of ambition, seeking a great name, met with this text, and rebelled against it; but he says that all his bright visions for the future seemed to vanish as these words sounded in his soul, 'Not unto us, O Lord, not unto us, but unto thy name give glory.'" (Spurgeon)

v. These verses were likely in the mind and heart of Jesus on the night before His crucifixion. Singing these words must have moved Him in a way beyond our comprehension. "No soul – neither that of the composer of the song, nor that of anyone who employs it – ever entered so completely into all its deep spiritual significance, as did the soul of Jesus, as, before passing out to Olivet, to Gethsemane, to Calvary, He sang it with that little group of men." (Morgan)

b. **Because of Your mercy, because of Your truth**: The **mercy** of God alone means that He is worthy of praise and glory – not His people who receive His **mercy**. We may add to that His **truth**, because truth is *grounded* in Him and not in His people.

i. **Mercy** translates the great Hebrew word *hesed*, which may be understood as Yahweh's grace, His loyal love, His covenant love unto His people. When John later wrote *grace and truth came through Jesus Christ* (John 1:17), he wrote with the same idea of the psalmist and saw it perfectly fulfilled in Jesus.

ii. "Thy mercy gave thy promise, thy truth fulfilled it." (Clarke)

c. **Why should the Gentiles say, "So where is their God?"** This is a skillfully formed prayer. The request is made subtly but powerfully. The psalmist asked God to deliver His people so that He would be glorified among the nations, and the Gentiles would have no reason to think God had forsaken them.

i. "It was very natural that the heathen should say, 'Where is their God?' because they had no outward emblem, no visible image, no tangible token; whereas the heathen had their gods many, such as they were, made of wood and stone; so that they asked, 'Where is their God?'" (Spurgeon)

2. (3-8) Yahweh's exaltation over the idols of the nations.

But our God *is* in heaven;
He does whatever He pleases.
Their idols *are* silver and gold,
The work of men's hands.
They have mouths, but they do not speak;
Eyes they have, but they do not see;
They have ears, but they do not hear;
Noses they have, but they do not smell;
They have hands, but they do not handle;
Feet they have, but they do not walk;
Nor do they mutter through their throat.
Those who make them are like them;
So is everyone who trusts in them.

a. **But our God is in heaven**: At best, nations worshipped imaginary beings and the projections of their own lusts and longing. At worst, the nations worshipped demonic spirits. Yet Yahweh, the covenant **God** of Israel is different. He lives and reigns **in heaven**, and sovereignly **does whatever He pleases**.

i. **Our God is in heaven**: "Where he should be; above the reach of mortal sneers, over-hearing all the vain janglings of men, but looking down with silent scorn upon the makers of the babel." (Spurgeon)

b. **They have mouths, but they do not speak**: The psalmist exposed the folly of idolatry. Men worshipped statues of **silver and gold** that they themselves made (**the work of men's hands**). The idols were fashioned with human body parts (**mouths, eyes, ears, noses, hands, feet,** and a **throat**). Yet they couldn't do with those body parts what their makers could – **speak, see, hear, smell, handle, walk,** or even **mutter**. Men worship things so obviously *below* them!

i. "The tone of the description is like that of the manufacture of an image in Isaiah 44:9-20." (Maclaren)

ii. "It is one of the places where Scripture, like the child in the story of the Emperor's New Clothes, takes a cool stare at what the world does not care to admit. What the psalm does to the gods, Ecclesiastes will do supremely to man and his ambitions." (Kidner)

iii. **Eyes they have, but they do not see**: "Certain idols have had jewels in their eyes more precious than a king's ransom, but they were as blind as the rest of the fraternity. A god who has eyes, and cannot see, is a blind deity; and blindness is a calamity, and not an attribute of godhead. He must be very blind who worships a blind god: we *pity* a blind man, it is strange to *worship* a blind image." (Spurgeon)

iv. **They do not smell**: "In sacred scorn he mocks at those who burn sweet spices, and fill their temples with clouds of smoke, all offered to an image whose nose cannot perceive the perfume." (Spurgeon)

v. **They do not walk**: John Trapp related how an ancient city, under siege, put a chain on their idol statue of Hercules, so he would not abandon them in their time of need. Hercules did not go anywhere, but they were still conquered. "The [smallest] insect has more power of [movement] than the greatest heathen god." (Spurgeon)

vi. **Nor do they mutter**: "*Mutter*, or *make a noise*, as this word signifies, Isaiah 10:14. They are so far from speaking with their throat and other instruments of speech as men do, that they cannot make such an inarticulate and senseless sound with them as the beasts do." (Poole)

vii. "A beautiful contrast is formed between the God of Israel and the heathen idols. He made everything, they themselves are made by men; he is in heaven, they are upon earth; he doeth whatsoever he pleaseth, they can do nothing; he seeth the distress, heareth and answereth the prayers, accepteth the offerings, cometh to the assistance, and effecteth the salvation of his servants; they are blind, deaf, and dumb senseless, motionless, and impotent." (Horne)

ix. Boice quoted Augustine's sharp addition to the indictment of idols and their worshippers: "Even the dead surpass a deity who neither lives nor has lived."

c. **Those who make them are like them**: The psalmist understood that when men worship things beneath them, it brings them lower. They begin to lose the strength of their own ability to perceive and interact with the world. All who **make** or all who trust in idols will have this as their destiny, and false gods draw men down, never up.

i. **Those who make them are like them** is virtually a spiritual law: *we become like what we worship*. When we worship the true God who reigns in righteousness, the God perfectly revealed in Jesus Christ, we become like Him. When we worship false and vain idols, we become like them.

ii. "False worship is not innocent but demoralizing, and ultimately the worshipers will perish together with their perishable idols." (VanGemeren)

iii. "Worship is sure to breed likeness. A lustful, cruel god will make his devotees so. Men make gods after their own image, and, when made, the gods make men after theirs. The same principle which degrades the idolater lifts the Christian to the likeness of Christ." (Maclaren)

iv. F.B. Meyer observed how this principle worked among those who worship idols: "Men first impute to their deities their own vices, as the Greeks and Romans to the gods and goddesses of their Pantheon; and then endeavor to honor them by imitation." He then noted how it worked in a positive sense among the disciples of Jesus: "This is the Divine method: look and live; trust and be transfigured; abide in Him, and He shall abide in you."

B. Israel called to trust in the LORD and to receive His blessing.

1. (9-11) A call to trust in the LORD.

O Israel, trust in the LORD;
He *is* their help and their shield.
O house of Aaron, trust in the LORD;
He *is* their help and their shield.
You who fear the LORD, trust in the LORD;
He *is* their help and their shield.

a. **O Israel, trust in the LORD**: Knowing the folly of idolatry should renew our trust in the true God and compel us to look to Him as our **help** and **shield**. In this we have something of Peter's heart when he said, *Lord, to whom shall we go? You have the words of eternal life* (John 6:68).

i. We see the singer's exhortation was not merely to *trust the LORD*, but to **trust in** Him. This goes beyond regarding Him as trustworthy, and actually placing our trust, our confidence, our reliance in Him and not in self or any idol.

ii. Despite our many disappointments when we look to other places for a **help** and a **shield**, we often repeat the mistake. We need to hear the commonsense exhortation to look nowhere else for help and protection.

iii. "He is the succour, support, guardian, and defence of all who put their confidence in him." (Clarke)

iv. We can imagine an idolater having to help and shield the idol he made or bought. It's much better to have a God who can be *your* help and shield.

b. **O house of Aaron, trust in the LORD**: If God's people as a whole should trust God, then those who are His appointed servants should trust Him even more. It was right and good for all the priesthood, all the **house of Aaron**, to regard the God of Israel as **their help and their shield**.

i. "Ministers must be patterns to others of depending upon God, and living by faith." (Trapp)

ii. "You who are nearest to him, trust him most; your very calling is connected with his truth and is meant to declare his glory, therefore never entertain a doubt concerning him, but lead the way in holy confidence." (Spurgeon)

c. **You who fear the LORD, trust in the LORD**: Those who truly respect and reverence Yahweh should take the logical step of putting their **trust in the LORD**. This third group (**you who fear the LORD**) may refer to Gentiles who loved and honored the God of Israel yet did not become Jews.

i. In the New Testament such people are known as *God fearers* (Acts 10:1-2, 13:16, 13:26), and the title may have come from such Old Testament passages as these. The Old Testament writers recognized Gentiles who honored the God of Israel (1 Kings 8:41, Isaiah 56:6).

ii. **You who fear the LORD**: "These are most naturally understood as proselytes, and, in the prominence given to them we see the increasing consciousness in Israel of its Divine destination to be God's witness to the world." (Maclaren)

iii. The thought of encouraging those who **fear the LORD** – God-fearers, Gentiles who honor the God of Israel – to trust in God must have sounded especially sweet to Jesus on the night of the last supper, knowing how great the harvest among the Gentiles would soon be.

2. (12-13) The confident assurance of those who make the LORD their help and shield.

The LORD has been mindful of *us;*
He will bless us;
He will bless the house of Israel;
He will bless the house of Aaron.
He will bless those who fear the LORD,
***Both* small and great.**

a. **The LORD has been mindful of us; He will bless us**: The psalmist drew upon God's past faithfulness and used it as confidence in God's future blessing. He has not forgotten us in the past and He will not forget to **bless** us in the future.

i. "God hath, and therefore God will, is an ordinary Scripture argument." (Trapp)

ii. **He will bless us**: "It is his nature to bless, it is his prerogative to bless, it is his glory to bless, it is his delight to bless; he has promised to bless, and therefore be sure of this, that he will bless and bless and bless without ceasing." (Spurgeon)

b. **He will bless the house of Israel**: Blessings were pronounced upon all those who were called to trust in the Lord in verses 9-11. All who trust Him will be blessed, **both small and great**.

i. We take comfort that the **small** are mentioned first, meaning they will not be forgotten. "God's blessing is for you, whoever you may be, if you will only stop trusting in yourself and your own devices and instead begin to trust God." (Boice)

3. (14-15) A blessing pronounced.

May the Lord give you increase more and more,
You and your children.
May **you** *be* **blessed by the Lord,**
Who made heaven and earth.

a. **May the Lord give you increase more and more**: In the world of ancient Israel, many looked to the idols of the nations for fertility and the prosperity of their fields, their flocks, and their families. In giving this blessing to those of us who fear and trust the Lord, the psalmist recognized Yahweh as the true source of such blessing, extending even to our **children**.

b. **May you be blessed by the Lord, who made heaven and earth**: Once again in this psalm, Yahweh is exalted above the idols of the nations. He alone has **made heaven and earth**.

i. "If he blesseth, poverty cannot starve thee, sickness cannot kill thee, toil cannot wear thee out, sorrow cannot consume thee, life cannot allure thee, death cannot slay thee, hell cannot enclose thee." (Spurgeon)

4. (16-18) Heaven, earth, and praise forevermore.

The heaven, *even* **the heavens,** *are* **the Lord's;**
But the earth He has given to the children of men.
The dead do not praise the Lord,
Nor any who go down into silence.
But we will bless the Lord
From this time forth and forevermore.
Praise the Lord!

a. **The heaven, even the heavens, are the Lord's**: The psalmist recognized God's authority as creator over both heaven and earth (verse 15). Here he acknowledged God's continuing dominion over **the heavens**, probably in all three senses (the blue sky, the starry sky, and the heaven where God dwells).

b. **The earth He has given to the children of men**: Though God has authority over earth as the Creator, He has **given** a significant dominion on the earth to **the children of men**. The psalmist must have had in mind God's grant to Adam (and his descendants) of dominion over the earth (Genesis 1:26-30).

i. This dominion **given** by God means that men and women should use the earth and its resources for the good of humanity, as wise and thoughtful stewards. We can use, but we should not waste and destroy.

ii. "The earth is man's, but by Jehovah's gift. Therefore its inhabitants should remember the terms of their tenure, and thankfully recognise His giving love." (Maclaren)

iii. "All is his, but we are his substantial heirs and trustees. There is generosity in the phrase, 'the earth he has given'; there is responsibility as well, for we are not its makers, nor is it simply 'there' as meaningless matter to exploit. Behind the gift is the Giver." (Kidner)

c. **The dead do not praise the** Lord: Their voice is no longer heard *among* the living. Whatever heavenly choir they may join, they are absent from an earthly choir, and their praise will no longer testify to those who resist and reject the true God.

i. When Jesus sang this with His disciples (Matthew 26:30, Mark 14:26), He sang knowing that He would not sing among His disciples on earth anymore. Consider the depth of feeling in Jesus that would bring!

d. **From this time forth and forevermore**: Given the perceived uncertainty of praise in the life to come, the greatness of God, and the astounding blessing He has given to humanity, He is worthy to be praised **forevermore**. This is something to which God's people can say *Hallelujah!* (**Praise the** Lord!)

i. **From this time forth and forevermore** may have the sense, *in this life and the life to come*. There are only two times we should **praise the** Lord – *now* and *forever*.

ii. "We who are still living will take care that the praises of God shall not fail among the sons of men. Our afflictions and depressions of spirit shall not cause us to suspend our praises." (Spurgeon)

iii. If the praise is to last **forevermore**, then it *does* extend into the world to come, even when the voice of praise is no longer heard on earth.

iv. "Though the dead cannot, and the wicked will not, and the careless do not praise God, yet we will shout 'Hallelujah' for ever and ever. Amen." (Spurgeon)

v. "And again the thought reverts to the upper room, and the Singer Whose deepest passion was ever the will of God and the glory of His name; to the One Who was soon going into the silence where no note of praise would be heard; and yet to the One Who would turn the silence into song forevermore." (Morgan)

Psalm 116 – Paying the Vow of Gratitude

As another one of the Egyptian Hallel Psalms (Psalms 113-118), sung by Jesus with His disciples on the night of His betrayal and arrest (Matthew 26:30 and Mark 14:26), we can say with G. Campbell Morgan: "Whatever the local circumstances which gave rise to this song, it is evident that all its rich meaning was fulfilled, when in the midst of that little company of perplexed souls, the shadows of the One Death already on Him, Jesus sang this song of prophetic triumph over the sharpness of the hour of passion to which He was passing. He has made it over to all His own as their triumph song over death."

A. A life rescued.

1. (1-2) Loving the LORD who answers prayer.

I love the LORD, because He has heard
My voice *and* my supplications.
Because He has inclined His ear to me,
Therefore I will call *upon Him* as long as I live.

a. **I love the LORD, because He has heard my voice**: The psalmist began his song with the most simple expression of grateful love. He had a great love for Yahweh because He answered prayer in a desperate season.

> i. "How vain and foolish is the *talk*, 'To love God for his benefits to us is mercenary, and cannot be pure love!' Whether pure or impure, there is no other love that can flow from the heart of the creature to its Creator." (Clarke)

> ii. "They say that love is blind; but when we love God our affection has its eyes open and can sustain itself with the most rigid logic. We have reason, superabundant reason, for loving the Lord." (Spurgeon)

b. **I will call upon Him as long as I live**: The singer vowed to never call upon any other supposed deity. His allegiance, love, and prayer would always be to the One who **inclined His ear to me**.

i. "It is a resolve to trust God exclusively…and worship him explicitly." (Kidner)

2. (3-4) Prayer from one in the pains of death.

The pains of death surrounded me,
And the pangs of Sheol laid hold of me;
I found trouble and sorrow.
Then I called upon the name of the LORD:
"O LORD, I implore You, deliver my soul!"

a. **The pains of death surrounded me**: In the painful grip of death, the psalmist knew nothing but **trouble and sorrow**. This death crisis may have come from sickness, injury, or persecution.

i. **Pains of death…pangs of Sheol**: "In Old Testament poetry *death* and *Sheol* are aggressive, clutching at the living to waste them with sickness or crush them with despondency; so the singer's plight may equally have been a desperate illness or (as verse 11 suggests) a wounding and disillusioning experience. Like Job's, it could well have been both together." (Kidner)

ii. Many centuries later Peter used the phrase **the pains of death** to describe the peril from which God the Father delivered Jesus Christ through His resurrection (Acts 2:24). It adds a powerful prophetic and messianic meaning to the psalm, since this was one of the psalms Jesus would have sung with His disciples at the last supper (Matthew 26:30, Mark 14:26).

iii. Perhaps while singing this phrase Jesus considered the linen windings that would soon be wrapped around His dead body. "…the *cables* or *cords of death*; alluding to their bonds and fetters during their captivity; or to the cords by which a criminal is bound who is about to be led out to execution; or to the bandages in which the dead were enveloped, when head, arms, body, and limbs were all *laced down* together." (Clarke)

b. **Then I called upon the name of the LORD**: In his deadly danger, the psalmist cried out to God in light of of all He is and represents (**the name of the LORD**). His cry was:

• Delivered straight to God: **O LORD**.

• Deeply felt: **I implore You**.

• Directly stating the need: **Deliver my soul**.

i. "This form of petition is short, comprehensive, to the point, humble, and earnest. It were well if all our prayers were moulded upon this model; perhaps they would be if we were in similar circumstances to those of the Psalmist, for real trouble produces real prayer." (Spurgeon)

3. (5-7) Praising the God who preserves us.

Gracious *is* the Lord, and righteous;
Yes, our God *is* merciful.
The Lord preserves the simple;
I was brought low, and He saved me.
Return to your rest, O my soul,
For the Lord has dealt bountifully with you.

a. **Gracious is the Lord, and righteous**: In light of his deliverance through answered prayer, the psalmist praised the **gracious**, **righteous**, and **merciful** character of God.

i. Before His obedient surrender to the ordeal of His suffering and crucifixion, Jesus sang these words with His disciples (Matthew 26:30, Mark 14:26). He testified to the truth that God was **gracious**, **righteous**, and **merciful** before, during, and after His ordeal.

b. **The Lord preserves the simple**: In humility, the psalmist counted himself as one who did not exalt himself above others and who might be considered **simple**. He didn't have to exalt himself, because when he **was brought low**, God brought His salvation.

i. "**The simple;** sincere and plain-hearted persons, who dare not use those frauds and crafty and wicked artifices in saving themselves or destroying their enemies, but wait upon God with honest hearts in his way and for his time of deliverance. Such persons he calls *simple* or *foolish*, as this word is commonly rendered, not because they are really so, but because the world esteems them so." (Poole)

ii. **The simple**: "It is humble of the psalmist to identify with them; it is humble of God to have time for them." (Kidner)

iii. In its messianic aspect, we consider these words sung and spoken by Jesus among His disciples. He was far from a **simple** man, but was considered so by the proud and arrogant religious hierarchy, who despised His lack of formal credentials and training.

iv. "Not only is God gracious, he is also gracious to the little people, to the plain, to commoners, to the everyday person on the bus or in the shop – to people like the psalmist. That is one of the great glories of our God. When Jesus called his disciples, he called fishermen and tax collectors. When the angels announced the birth of Jesus, they appeared to shepherds." (Boice)

v. **He saved me**: "The knowledge that David had of God's goodness was experiential…. A carnal man knoweth God's excellencies and will revealed in his word only, as we know far countries by maps; but an experienced Christian, as one that hath himself been long there." (Trapp)

vi. "Happy the man who, like the psalmist, can give confirmation from his own experience to the broad truths of God's protection to ingenuous and guileless souls!" (Maclaren)

c. **Return to your rest, O my soul**: For a season, the death-like crisis had troubled the soul of the psalmist. Now he could reflect on how God had **dealt bountifully** with him, and he had come back to a previous standing of **rest**. There is true **rest** for our soul in God's bounty.

i. "The word '*rest*' is put in the plural, as indicating complete and entire rest, at all times, and under all circumstances." (Edersheim, cited in Spurgeon)

ii. "Oh, learn this holy art; acquaint thyself with God, acquiesce in him, and be at peace; so shall good be done unto thee." (Trapp)

iii. "Whenever a child of God even for a moment loses his peace of mind, he should be concerned to find it again, not by seeking it in the world or in his own experience, but in the Lord alone." (Spurgeon)

4. (8-11) The testimony of the one delivered.

For You have delivered my soul from death,
My eyes from tears,
And my feet from falling.
I will walk before the LORD
In the land of the living.
I believed, therefore I spoke,
"I am greatly afflicted."
I said in my haste,
"All men _are_ liars."

a. **You have delivered my soul from death**: The crisis was deep, even unto death. The deliverance was great, bringing comfort to tearful eyes and strength to falling feet. This powerful praise matched the greatness of the deliverance.

i. "He is recalling the agitation which shook him, but feels that, through it all, there was an unshaken centre of rest in God. The presence of doubt and fear does not prove the absence of trust." (Maclaren)

ii. Once again we are moved by the thought that Jesus sang these words with His disciples on the night of His betrayal and arrest. Knowing all the suffering set before Him, Jesus sang with confidence of deliverance from His coming **death**, His coming **tears**, and **falling** under the weight of the cross soon to come.

b. **I will walk before the LORD in the land of the living**: These were the grateful words of the psalmist *after* his deliverance. They were also the confident words, sung in faith, by Jesus before every agony of the coming cross. He could go to the cross with full confidence that having been rescued from falling feet, He would once again walk **in the land of the living**.

i. "To *walk before the Lord*, like the New Testament expression to 'walk in the light', is both demanding and reassuring, since…one is wholly exposed but wholly befriended." (Kidner)

ii. "By a man's walk is understood his way of life: some men live only as in the sight of their fellow men, having regard to human judgment and opinion; but the truly gracious man considers the presence of God, and acts under the influence of his all-observing eye." (Spurgeon)

c. **I believed, therefore I spoke**: Full of faith, the psalmist trusted God in the depth of his distress. He was a shadowy preview of the greatest faith, demonstrated by Jesus among His disciples before the cross.

i. The Apostle Paul took this line (**I believed, therefore I spoke**) and applied the principle to his own times of trusting God and speaking from the experience of that trust, even in trying times (2 Corinthians 4:13-14).

ii. "Paul quotes the LXX [Septuagint] form of the verse: 'I believed, and so I spoke' (2 Cor. 4:13), which is stronger than our Hebrew text. But the latter agrees in making faith the underlying attitude of the speaker, even though it is faith hard-pressed." (Kidner)

iii. "Walter Kaiser remarks from Paul's quotation of Psalm 116:10 in 2 Corinthians 4:13 that it was the same Holy Spirit who worked in the psalmist, Paul, and all other Christians to believe." (VanGemeren)

d. **All men are liars**: The bitter experience of the psalmist made this seem like a logical statement, but that was a hasty conclusion. Though forsaken by all His disciples (and partners in song), Jesus would not come to this hasty conclusion.

i. There is one way in which the statement is true, because "…all men will prove to be liars if we unduly trust in them; some from want of truthfulness, and others from want of power" (Spurgeon). Yet the phrasing makes it clear that the psalmist understood that he was wrong at this time in saying so. The judgment was too harsh in his present circumstances.

ii. **I said in my haste**: "Speaking in haste is generally followed by bitter repentance. It is much better to be quiet when our spirit is disturbed and hasty, for it is so much easier to say than to unsay; we may repent of our words, but we cannot so recall them as to undo the mischief they have done." (Spurgeon)

B. A life of gratitude.

1. (12-14) Thankfully receiving and responding.

What shall I render to the LORD
***For* all His benefits toward me?**
I will take up the cup of salvation,
And call upon the name of the LORD.
I will pay my vows to the LORD
Now in the presence of all His people.

a. **What shall I render to the LORD?** Gratitude drove the psalmist to consider what return he could make to the God who had so generously shared **His benefits**, making the psalmist like the one grateful leper among the ten Jesus healed (Luke 17:12-19).

i. The psalmist wisely considered *why God had been so good to him* instead of *why he had problems at all*. He knew that problems were common to all men, but the benefits often only belonged to those who trusted God.

ii. **All His benefits**: "His benefits are so many, so various, so minute, that they often escape our observation while they exactly meet our wants." (Spurgeon)

b. **I will take up the cup of salvation**: Gratitude drove the psalmist to *receive* from God. Before we can do anything for Him, we begin by gratefully receiving.

i. "It is a profound insight: The only way we can repay God from whom everything comes is by taking even more from him." (Boice)

ii. "We can do this figuratively at the sacramental table, we can do it spiritually every time we grasp the golden chalice of the covenant, realizing the fulness of blessing which it contains, and by faith receiving its divine contents into our inmost soul." (Spurgeon)

iii. There is a connection between the phrases, **I will take up the cup of salvation** and **call upon the name of the LORD**. "The cup of salvation is the cup of blessing, which is given to the soul. Let the soul take it and drink it, but let him remember that the very partaking is in itself of the nature of a pledge of loyalty; it is the oath of allegiance in which he calls upon the Name of Jehovah." (Morgan)

iv. We continue to marvel at how significant it is that Jesus sang *these words* on the night of His betrayal and arrest, having instituted the **cup of salvation** under the New Covenant with His apostles (Luke 22:20). Jesus *received* that **cup of salvation** from His Father and gave it unto His people.

v. "Within a very little while after this singing, He, in Gethsemane, spoke of a cup, and in complete surrender to His Father's will, consented to drink it. That was the cup of sorrows, of bitterness, of cursing. Having emptied it, He filled it with joy, with sweetness, with blessing. When we take that cup let us never forget the cost at which He so filled it for us." (Morgan)

c. **I will pay my vows to the LORD now in the presence of all His people**: The singer publically declared – perhaps in a sacrificial ritual of gratitude at the temple's altar – God's greatness and faithfulness. He would complete what he had determined to do before God.

i. "He presently resolveth to make the only return in his power, namely, to acknowledge and declare before men the goodness of Jehovah, ascribing all the glory where it is all due." (Horne)

ii. "This word 'pay' importeth that vows lawfully made are due debt; and debt, till paid, is a disquieting thing to an honest mind." (Trapp)

iii. How *moving* it was for Jesus to sing these words, when *He Himself* was about to become that sacrifice!

iv. "Foxe, in his Acts and Monuments, relates the following concerning the martyr, John Philpot: He went with the sheriffs to the place of execution…coming into Smithfield, he kneeled down there, saying these words, 'I will pay my vows in thee, O Smithfield.'" (Spurgeon)

2. (15-17) A life gratefully pledged.

Precious in the sight of the LORD
***Is* the death of His saints.**
O LORD, truly I *am* Your servant;
I *am* Your servant, the son of Your maidservant;
You have loosed my bonds.
I will offer to You the sacrifice of thanksgiving,
And will call upon the name of the LORD.

a. **Precious in the sight of the L**ORD **is the death of His saints**: This psalm celebrates the deliverance from death, but the singer knew that death is still a reality for every one of God's **saints**. When that day comes, God holds the **death** of His people as a **precious** thing.

i. "The more usual form of expression for the idea in Psalms 116:15 is 'their blood is precious'. [Psalm 72:14] The meaning is that the death of God's saints is no trivial thing in God's eyes, to be lightly permitted." (Maclaren)

ii. "God is particularly close to his people when they stand at death's door. God watches over his people when they are sick or dying, coming close to them and making his presence known so that they have comfort in death's hour. He also frequently intervenes and does not allow them to perish. In either case, the Lord does what is best." (Boice)

iii. God regards the death of His martyrs as especially **precious**. "Though they have been cast to the beasts in the amphitheatre, or dragged to death by wild horses, or murdered in dungeons, or slaughtered amongst the snows of the Alps, or made to fatten Smithfield with their gore, precious has their blood been, and still is it in his sight." (Spurgeon)

iv. Though death is a curse and an enemy, it is still precious because it removes the remaining barriers between God and His saints, and is the doorway to an eternity of perfect fellowship. "Death to the saints is not a penalty, it is not destruction, it is not even a loss." (Spurgeon)

v. "When Baxter lay a dying, and his friends came to see him, almost the last word he said was in answer to the question, 'Dear Mr. Baxter, how are you?' 'Almost well,' said he, and so it is. Death cures; it is the best medicine, for they who die are not only almost well, but healed for ever." (Spurgeon)

vi. As Jesus sang these words with His disciples on the night before His own death (Matthew 26:30, Mark 14:26), the words were powerful and prophetic. Jesus was the ultimate holy one and His death **precious** beyond all reckoning.

b. **O L**ORD**, truly I am Your servant**: The singer dedicated himself to God's service on the basis of **loosed** bonds. Set free by God's great work, both honor and gratitude led him to forever be Yahweh's **servant**.

i. Adam Clarke saw here the words of a bondservant, as in Exodus 21:5-6: "I am a *servant*, son of *thy servant*, made free by thy kindness; but, refusing *to go out*, I have had my *ear bored to thy door-post*, and am to continue by *free choice* in thy house for ever."

ii. **The son of Your maidservant**: "Bless God for the privilege of being the children of godly parents. Better be the child of a godly than of a wealthy parent. I hope none of you are of so vile a spirit as to contemn your parents because of their piety." (Manton, cited in Spurgeon)

iii. **The son of Your maidservant**: "Alas, there are many who are the sons of the Lord's handmaids, but they are not themselves his servants. They give sad proof that grace does not run in the blood." (Spurgeon)

c. **I will offer to You the sacrifice of thanksgiving**: Once again (before in verse 14) we find ourselves at the altar of sacrifice with the singer. He was happy and duty-bound to proclaim his gratitude to God and to **call upon** Him alone.

3. (18-19) Vows gratefully paid.

I will pay my vows to the LORD
Now in the presence of all His people,
In the courts of the LORD's house,
In the midst of you, O Jerusalem.
Praise the LORD!

a. **I will pay my vows to the LORD**: The repetition of this phrase (before in verse 14) keeps us at the altar with a public sacrifice of thanksgiving. There, **in the courts of the LORD's house**, the psalmist would proclaim his praise and gratitude toward God.

i. **Now in the presence of all His people**: "Once more the lonely suppliant, who had waded such deep waters without companion but Jehovah, seeks to feel himself one of the glad multitude in the courts of the house of Jehovah, and to blend his single voice in the shout of a nation's praise. We suffer and struggle for the most part alone. Grief is a hermit, but Joy is sociable; and thankfulness desires listeners to its praise." (Maclaren)

b. **Praise the LORD**: The psalm ends with *Hallelujah*, both as a declaration of personal praise and a call to God's people to join with the proclamation.

Psalm 117 – Calling All Peoples to Praise the LORD

"This is the shortest song in the whole collection, but there is none greater or grander in its expression of praise." (G. Campbell Morgan)

"Martin Luther devoted thirty-six pages to this psalm, expounding it in four important categories: (1) prophecy (the Gentiles will participate in gospel blessings), (2) revelation (the kingdom of Christ is not earthly and temporal but rather heavenly and eternal), (3) instruction (we are saved by faith alone and not by works, wisdom, or holiness), and (4) admonition (we should praise God for such a great salvation)." (James Montgomery Boice)

A. The call to praise.

1. (1) Gentiles called to praise the LORD.

Praise the LORD, all you Gentiles!
Laud Him, all you peoples!

a. **Praise the LORD:** Previous psalms called on Israel to give **praise** to Yahweh, but here **all** the **Gentiles** are called to praise Him. This showed a largeness of heart that God intended Israel to have from the beginning, pointing to the truth that in Abraham all the peoples of the world were to be blessed (Genesis 12:3).

i. "For the most part the Jews looked with little sympathy on their Gentile neighbors, and had no desire that they should laud Jehovah, save as they became proselytes of Judaism. But where the love of God is strong in the heart, it overleaps the bounds of custom and racial prejudice, and yearns that all the world should know and love the Saviour." (Meyer)

ii. "The Psalm was an intimation to Israel that the grace and mercy of their God were not to be confined to one nation, but would in happier days be extended to all the race of man." (Spurgeon)

iii. Since this is one of the five Egyptian Hallel Psalms (113-118), sung as part of the Passover service, Jesus would have sung Psalm 117 with His disciples (Matthew 26:30, Mark 14:26). Therefore, on the eve of His crucifixion, we *know* that Jesus had all the peoples, all the Gentiles in mind. Through His work on the cross and victory over death at the empty tomb, God would call a people to Himself from every tribe and tongue.

iv. "The historical limitations of God's manifestation to a special nation were means to its universal diffusion. The fire was gathered in a grate, that it might warm the whole house. All men have a share in what God does for Israel." (Maclaren)

b. **Laud Him, all you peoples**: To **laud** is to say praiseworthy things about a person. The psalmist called upon **all peoples** to praise God intelligently, and he provided reasons why He is worthy of worship.

i. "Inasmuch as the matter is spoken of twice, its certainty is confirmed, and the Gentiles must and shall extol Jehovah." (Spurgeon)

ii. Some suggest that **all you peoples** refers to the Jewish people, but Paul's quotation of Psalm 117:1 in Romans 15:11 leads us to believe that this is a call to the nations.

iii. The word for **peoples** suggests all the *tribes* of the earth. "The very diversity of God's subjects comes out in the expressions *all nations... all tribes*." (Kidner)

iv. "Here then is a true Christian universalism, not that all people will be saved regardless of the god they believe in, but rather that all people may be saved through Jesus Christ." (Boice)

v. The call to **all you peoples** makes this a strong missionary psalm. "Are we doing all we can to kindle the nations to praise? They cannot praise Him whom they do not know. It is mere hypocrisy to bid them praise Him, if we have never sought to spread, by lip or gift, the mercy and truth revealed in Jesus our Lord." (Meyer)

B. The reasons for praise.

1. (2) Praising God for His mercy and truth.

For His merciful kindness is great toward us,
And the truth of the Lord endures forever.
Praise the Lord!

a. **For His merciful kindness is great**: In thinking of reasons to praise God, the psalmist first lists, because of His **great** *hesed* (**merciful kindness**). The

Hebrew actually has *His hesed hesed*, with the idea of God's loyal, covenant love repeated twice for emphasis.

i. **Is great**: The Hebrew word doesn't have the thought of *exceedingly large*, but as something that is mighty and prevails. "*Gabar*, is *strong*: it is not only *great* in *bulk* or *number*, but it is *powerful*; it *prevails* over *sin, Satan, death*, and *hell*." (Clarke)

ii. "…lovingkindness is 'mighty over us' – the word used for being mighty has the sense of prevailing, and so 'where sin abounded, grace did much more abound.'" (Maclaren)

b. **Great toward us**: This is further reason for praise; not only does God have **great** lovingkindness, but that **merciful kindness** is **toward us**. By **us** the psalmist has in mind Israel and the *all peoples* as mentioned in the previous verse.

i. "Towards all of us, all the children of Abraham, whether carnal or spiritual, who were to be incorporated together, and made one body and one fold by and under the Messias, John 10:16, Ephesians 2:14, which mystery seems to be insinuated by this manner of expression." (Poole)

ii. "It may also be that the 'us' of verse 2 has already found room for the 'you' implied in verse 1, by seeing Israelites and Gentiles as one people under God." (Kidner)

c. **The truth of the LORD endures forever**: God is to be praised not only for His loyal love, but also for His **truth**. His ever-enduring truth means that He will not change in His love and goodness to us.

i. When mercy and truth are praised together like this, it reminds us that *the law was given through Moses, but grace and truth came through Jesus Christ* (John 1:17).

ii. "If God stood for truth alone, there would be no hope for us. On the other hand, if the grace of God could act apart from truth, we should equally be without hope." (Morgan)

iii. "Once again we can imagine with what perfect joy our Lord sang this song, as He moved to the uttermost in His sorrows; for He did so in full and perfect apprehension of the union of lovingkindness and truth in God." (Morgan)

iv. **Endures forever**: "Not only is his love so great in depth and height (cf. Rom 5:20; 1 Tim 1:14), it is also lasting ('endures forever')." (VanGemeren)

d. **Praise the LORD**: Once again, all peoples are called to say, *Hallelujah!*

i. "By the union of grace and truth, in and through Jesus, the call to praise went out to all nations and peoples." (Morgan)

ii. "Let the hallelujahs of the redeemed be suitable to that 'mercy,' and co-eternal with that 'truth.'" (Horne)

iii. "In God's worship it is not always necessary to be long; few words sometimes say what is sufficient, as this short Psalm giveth us to understand." (Dickson, cited in Spurgeon)

Psalm 118 – The Chief Cornerstone

Psalm 118 does not name an author in its title, but there is reason to believe it was King David, the Sweet Psalmist of Israel. Ezra 3:10-11 suggests that Psalm 118 was sung at the founding of the second temple, and when they sang it, they attributed it to David ("according to the ordinance of David king of Israel," Ezra 3:10).

"Most probably David was the author of this psalm.... It partakes of David's spirit, and everywhere shows the hand of a master. The style is grand and noble; the subject, majestic." (Adam Clarke)

Though this was likely David's psalm, it was also Jesus' psalm. "This is pre-eminently the triumph song of the Christ, He the ideal Servant, He the perfect Priest, He the Leader of the people. How much all these words meant to Him as He sang them on that night in the upper room." (G. Campbell Morgan)

Though this was likely David's psalm, it was also Luther's psalm. "This is my own beloved psalm. Although the entire Psalter and all of Holy Scripture are dear to me as my only comfort and source of life, I fell in love with this psalm especially. Therefore I call it my own. When emperors and kings, the wise and the learned, and even saints could not aid me, this psalm proved a friend and helped me out of many great troubles. As a result, it is dearer to me than all the wealth, honor, and power of the pope, the Turk, and the emperor. I would be most unwilling to trade this psalm for all of it." (Martin Luther, cited by Boice)

A. Praising God for His great mercy and deliverance.

1. (1-4) Calling a congregation to declare Yahweh's never-ending mercy.

Oh, give thanks to the LORD, for *He is* good!
For His mercy *endures* forever.
Let Israel now say,
"His mercy *endures* forever."
Let the house of Aaron now say,
"His mercy *endures* forever."

Let those who fear the LORD now say,
"His mercy *endures* forever."

a. **Give thanks to the LORD, for He is good**: Many of the psalms call upon God's people to thank Him. Psalm 118 opens with an *emphatic* call, indicated by the word **Oh**. God's goodness is so great and apparent that it deserves emphatic thanks.

> i. **For He is good**: "This is reason enough for giving him thanks; goodness is his essence and nature, and therefore he is always to be praised whether we are receiving anything from him or not. Those who only praise God because he *does* them good should rise to a higher note and give thanks to him because he *is* good." (Spurgeon)

b. **For His mercy endures forever**: This psalm begins and ends with this declaration. It is a statement of fact and of gratitude, noting that God's *hesed* – His loyal covenant love, His lovingkindness – will never be taken from His people.

> i. **For His mercy endures forever**: In the psalms, this phrase has almost a liturgical quality to it. It is used 34 times and is an appreciative declaration of God's people, praising the great lovingkindness or covenant love of God.

> ii. "Other psalms confirm the familiarity of this call to worship (106:1; 136:1), and show the opportunity it gave to cantor and congregation to rehearse the great acts of God together (136:1–26)." (Kidner)

> iii. "The word *endureth* has been properly supplied by the translators, but yet it somewhat restricts the sense, which will be better seen if we read it, '*for his mercy for ever.*' That mercy had no beginning, and shall never know an end." (Spurgeon)

> iv. This psalm is the last of the five Egyptian Hallel Psalms, sung in Jesus' day as part of the Passover ritual. When Matthew 26:30 and Mark 14:26 tell us that Jesus sang a hymn with His disciples at the last supper, it refers to these Hallel Psalms. As Jesus sang the words **for His mercy endures forever**, He did it with complete knowledge that the endurance of God's mercy would be tested to the utmost in the work to come the next day at the cross.

c. **Let Israel now say**: The psalmist invited the people of **Israel**, the priests of **the house of Aaron**, and even Gentiles who honored God (**those who fear the LORD**) to join in the emphatic chorus, **His mercy endures forever**.

> i. "Three classes are called on: the whole house of Israel, the priests, and 'those who fear Jehovah' – *i.e.,* aliens who have taken refuge beneath the wings of Israel's God" (Maclaren). This suggests that the

song was written with distinct parts meant for different groups in the congregation.

ii. **The house of Aaron**: "If this Psalm refers to David, the priests had special reason for thankfulness on his coming to the throne, for Saul had made a great slaughter among them, and had at various times interfered with their sacred office." (Spurgeon)

2. (5-9) A testimony to His enduring mercy.

I called on the LORD in distress;
The LORD answered me *and set me* in a broad place.
The LORD is on my side;
I will not fear.
What can man do to me?
The LORD is for me among those who help me;
Therefore I shall see *my desire* on those who hate me.
***It is* better to trust in the LORD**
Than to put confidence in man.
***It is* better to trust in the LORD**
Than to put confidence in princes.

a. **I called on the LORD in distress**: The never-ending mercy of God was shown when **the LORD answered** the singer's cry of distress. God answered by setting the psalmist in a secure, **broad place** where he could confidently stand.

i. **I called on the LORD**: "Thou must learn to call, and not to sit there by thyself, and lie on the bench, hang and shake thy head, and bite and devour thyself with thy thoughts; but come on, thou indolent knave, down upon thy knees, up with thy hands and eyes to heaven, take a Psalm or a prayer, and set forth thy distress with tears before God." (Luther, cited in Spurgeon)

ii. "The true value of every deliverance is to be estimated by the nature of the 'distress' which required it." (Horne)

iii. It is wonderful to think of Jesus confidently singing these words with His disciples on the night of His betrayal and arrest, and before His suffering and crucifixion. Like none other ever, Jesus would call **on the LORD in distress** and see God's faithful answer.

b. **The LORD is on my side**: The never-ending mercy of God was shown by God's open favor and help to the one who called upon Him. Knowing God was on his side, he could live free from the **fear** of man, knowing **what can man do to me?**

i. **The LORD is on my side**: "We know very well the great anxiety shown by men, in all their worldly conflicts, to secure the aid of a powerful ally; in their lawsuits, to retain the services of a powerful advocate; or, in their attempts at worldly advancement, to win the friendship and interest of those who can further the aims they have in view.... If such and such a person be on their side, men think that all must go well. Who so well off as he who is able to say, '*The Lord is on my side*'?" (Power, cited in Spurgeon)

ii. **I will not fear**: "He does not say that he should not suffer, but that he would not fear: the favour of God infinitely outweighed the hatred of men, therefore setting the one against the other he felt that he had no reason to be afraid." (Spurgeon)

c. **The LORD is for me**: Hundreds of years before the book of Romans was written, the psalmist understood the principle of Romans 8:31: *If God is for us, who can be against us?* The psalmist had nothing to fear, even from **those who hated** him.

d. **It is better to trust in the LORD than to put confidence in man**: The psalmist knew it to be true, no doubt learned through the experience of bitter disappointments. Neither the common **man** or even **princes** among men could help the way God can help. It **is better to trust** Him!

i. **It is better to trust in the LORD than to put confidence in man**: Spurgeon suggested many reasons why this is true.

- It is better because it is wiser.
- It is better morally, fulfilling the duty of the creature to the Creator.
- It is better because it is safer.
- It is better in its direction, lifting us up instead of bowing us down.
- It is better in its outcome.

ii. Jesus knew this by His own experience as each of His disciples forsook Him at the cross, and even leaders who were sympathetic to Him (such as Joseph of Arimathea and Nicodemus) did not give their help to Jesus during His suffering and crucifixion.

iii. **Than to put confidence in princes**: "Men of high estate are generally *proud, vain-glorious, self-confident*, and *rash*: it is better to trust in God than in them. Often they *cannot* deliver, and often they *will not* when they *can*. However, in the concerns of our *salvation*, and in matters which belong to *Providence*, they can do nothing." (Clarke)

iv. Spurgeon observed, "They are noblest in rank and mightiest in power, and yet as a rule, princes are not one whit more reliable than the rest of mankind." He also noted that a weathervane covered with gold turns in the wind just as easily as a weathervane made of tin.

v. Boice on Psalm 118:8-9: "It is reported by people who count such things that there are 31,174 verses in the Bible, and if that is so, then these verses, the 15,587[th] and the 15,588[th], are the middle verses. That position should be reason enough to give them prominence."

3. (10-14) Surrounded by enemies but helped by God.

All nations surrounded me,
But in the name of the LORD I will destroy them.
They surrounded me,
Yes, they surrounded me;
But in the name of the LORD I will destroy them.
They surrounded me like bees;
They were quenched like a fire of thorns;
For in the name of the LORD I will destroy them.
You pushed me violently, that I might fall,
But the LORD helped me.
The LORD is my strength and song,
And He has become my salvation.

a. **All nations surrounded me**: In the pattern of Hebrew poetry, the idea is repeated for emphasis. The singer knew what it was to be trapped by enemies who swarmed **like bees**.

i. **I will destroy them**: "There is a grand touch of the *ego* in the last sentence, but it is so over-shadowed with the name of the Lord that there is none too much of it." (Spurgeon)

ii. We picture Jesus singing these words, knowing that only a few hours later He would be truly surrounded by those who would mock, torture, and kill Him – with, no doubt, a multitude of **nations** surrounding Him.

iii. **They surrounded me like bees**: "Christ's enemies are so spiteful, that in fighting against his kingdom, they regard not what become of themselves, so they may hurt his people; but as the bee undoeth herself in stinging, and loseth her life or her power with her sting, so do they." (Dickson, cited in Spurgeon)

iv. **They were quenched like a fire of thorns**: "But the Hebrew text looks beyond the 'blaze' of this *fire of thorns* to its extinction…for such a fire burns out as suddenly as it flares up, and the power of evil will turn out to be as short-lived as it was fierce." (Kidner)

b. **In the name of the LORD I will destroy them**: The psalmist understood that the power for victory was not in Himself, but only in the name of God. He would be rescued as **the LORD helped** him.

c. **The LORD is my strength and my song**: Quoting Miriam's song (Exodus 15:2), the singer knew not only that God could *bring* **strength** and a **song**, but that Yahweh Himself *became* their **strength** and the **song** of those who put their trust in Him. Going even further, the psalmist understood that Yahweh had **become** his **salvation**. Yahweh *is* these things for His people.

i. When the LORD is our **strength**, it means that He is our resource and our refuge. We look to Him for our needs, and we are never unsatisfied.

ii. When the LORD is our **song**, it means that He is our joy and our happiness. We find our purpose and life in Him, and He never disappoints.

iii. When the LORD is our **salvation**, it means we put our trust for help and deliverance in none other. He is our rest and rescue.

iv. With all this true, it emphasizes the importance of seeking God Himself when we need **strength**, a **song**, or **salvation**. Often we seek the things themselves, sometimes as even detached from God Himself. To seek God and to receive Him is to receive all these profound gifts.

v. "Good songs, good promises, good proverbs, good doctrines are none the worse for age. What was sung just after the passage of the Red Sea, is here sung by the prophet, and shall be sung to the end of the world by the saints of the Most High." (Plumer, cited in Spurgeon)

vi. "Thus delivered, the singer breaks into the ancient strain, which had gone up on the shores of the sullen sea that rolled over Pharaoh's army, and is still true after centuries have intervened: '*Jah* is my strength and song, and He is become my salvation.' Miriam sang it, the restored exiles sang it, tried and trustful men in every age have sung and will sing it, till there are no more foes; and then, by the shores of the sea of glass mingled with fire, the calm victors will lift again the undying 'song of Moses and of the Lamb.'" (Maclaren)

4. (15-18) Rejoicing in deliverance from death.

The voice of rejoicing and salvation
Is **in the tents of the righteous;**
The right hand of the LORD does valiantly.
The right hand of the LORD is exalted;

The right hand of the LORD does valiantly.
I shall not die, but live,
And declare the works of the LORD.
The LORD has chastened me severely,
But He has not given me over to death.

a. **The voice of rejoicing and salvation is in the tents of the righteous**: Having received God's wonderful rescue, God's people give **voice** to their joy. It would be wrong for those who have received so much to be silent about it.

i. "'The tents of the righteous' may possibly allude to the 'tabernacles' constructed for the feast, at which the song was probably sung." (Maclaren)

ii. "Apart from its use during the Passover Seder, Psalm 118 was also sung during the Feast of Tabernacles, according to the Talmud (b. *Sukkoth* 45a-b)." (VanGemeren)

b. **The right hand of the LORD does valiantly**: Repeatedly (for emphasis), the singer praises the **right hand** of God, recognizing it as the hand of skill and strength. God will not use lesser measures to rescue His people.

c. **I shall not die, but live**: The psalmist was confident that God would keep him from death in the present crisis. As Jesus sang this song at the last supper with His disciples, He could proclaim this confidently – that death would keep no hold upon Him, but He would **live, and declare the works of the LORD.**

i. **I shall not die, but live**: Verse 17 was precious to John Wycliffe: "John Wycliffe, the Protestant Reformer, fell sick at one point as the result of his incessant labors for the gospel. The friars heard that their enemy was dying and hastened to his bedside. Surely Wycliffe would be overcome with remorse for his Protestant heresies. Surely he would renounce his views and ask for God's forgiveness and the friars' blessing. A crowd of monks representing four major orders of the friars gathered around him. They began by wishing him health, then quickly changed their tune and urged him to make a full confession since he would soon have to give an accounting of himself to God. Wycliffe waited patiently until they had ended. Then, asking his servant to raise him a little so he could speak better, Wycliffe fixed his keen eyes on them and said in a commanding voice, 'I shall not die but live and proclaim...*the evil deeds of the friars.*'" (Boice)

ii. **I shall not die, but live**: Verse 17 was also precious to Martin Luther, who faced threats on his life due to his reformation efforts.

"According to Matthesius, Luther had this verse written against his study wall." (Spurgeon)

d. **The LORD has chastened me severely**: The singer understood that God had a training and corrective purpose in allowing the present crisis, but God would not allow it to destroy him. Rather, the crisis would be of benefit.

i. These words had great meaning for Jesus before the cross, where He would endure the Father's purposeful suffering, yet not be **given…over to death**.

B. The Song of the Great Deliverer.

1. (19-20) The open gates of righteousness.

Open to me the gates of righteousness;
I will go through them,
And **I will praise the LORD.**
This is the gate of the LORD,
Through which the righteous shall enter.

a. **Open to me the gates of righteousness**: The psalmist probably had in mind a triumphal entry into the holy city. With those gates **open**, he would **go through them**, full of **praise** to **the LORD**.

i. In the song Jesus sang, He proclaimed His entrance into the ultimate reality of heaven, of which Jerusalem was only a representation. After His completed work on the cross, after His deliverance from death in the resurrection, He would be received in glory at the ascension.

ii. In that Jesus is a forerunner for His people, **open to me the gates of righteousness** can also be said by His people. "We may extend our ideas much further, and consider the whole company of the redeemed, as behold the angels ready to unbar the gates of heaven, and throw open the doors of the eternal sanctuary, for the true disciples of the risen and glorified Jesus to enter in. 'Open ye,' may believers exclaim in triumph, to those celestial spirits who delight to minister to the heirs of salvation." (Horne)

iii. "Alas, there are multitudes who do not care whether the gates of God's house are opened or not; and although they know that they are opened wide they never care to enter, neither does the thought of praising God so much as cross their minds. The time will come for them when they shall find the gates of heaven shut against them, for those gates are peculiarly the gates of righteousness through which there shall by no means enter anything that defileth." (Spurgeon)

b. **This is the gate of the** Lord: Now we picture the singer actually passing through the open gate, declaring God's great works for **the righteous**.

2. (21-24) The chief cornerstone.

I will praise You,
For You have answered me,
And have become my salvation.
The stone *which* **the builders rejected**
Has become the chief cornerstone.
This was the Lord's **doing;**
It *is* **marvelous in our eyes.**
This *is* **the day the** Lord **has made;**
We will rejoice and be glad in it.

a. **I will praise You**: Having passed into the holy city, the singer openly praised God for the answer and the salvation previously mentioned in this psalm.

b. **The stone which the builders rejected has become the chief cornerstone**: We don't know what personal experience the psalmist might have had that led to these words. Perhaps it was purely a prophetic statement, because it certainly *was* fulfilled in the work of Jesus.

i. "And these master-builders rejected David as an obscure, and treacherous, and rebellious person, fit to be not only laid aside and thrown away, but also to be crushed to pieces. And so their successors rejected Christ as an enemy to Moses, a friend to sinners, and a blasphemer against God, and therefore deserving death and damnation." (Poole)

ii. This is a strong and important statement in the New Testament understanding of the person and work of Jesus. Jesus quoted this of Himself in Matthew 21:42, Mark 12:10-11, and Luke 20:17. Peter quoted it in reference to Jesus in Acts 4:11. Paul alluded to this verse in Ephesians 2:20, and Peter also referred to it in 1 Peter 2:7-8. No text in the Old Testament is quoted more in the New Testament.

iii. Boice noted something interesting about Peter's quotation of Psalm 118 in Acts 4:11: "In quoting from the Septuagint at this point Luke varied the quotation slightly, adding the word 'you.' The Septuagint says, 'The stone the builders rejected has become the capstone.' Luke changes it to say, 'The stone *you* builders rejected' (italics added), undoubtedly because that is what Peter said. Peter used the text to reinforce what he had been teaching about the guilt of Israel's leaders."

c. **The stone which the builders rejected**: It was true of Jacob, Joseph and David – each were rejected and then raised high. It was most certainly true of Jesus.

- They didn't approve of His origin (John 7:52).
- They didn't approve of His lack of formal education (John 7:15).
- They didn't approve of His disregard for religious traditions (Luke 6:2).
- They didn't approve of His choice of friends (Matthew 9:11).

  i. "Still do the builders refuse him: even to this day the professional teachers of the gospel are far too apt to fly to any and every new philosophy sooner than maintain the simple gospel, which is the essence of Christ: nevertheless, he holds his true position amongst his people, and the foolish builders shall see to their utter confusion that his truth shall be exalted over all." (Spurgeon)

d. **Has become the chief cornerstone**: This was also most certainly true. Fulfilled in Jesus, we see that even though the religious leaders (**the builders**) of His day **rejected** Him, God established Jesus as the **chief cornerstone** of His great plan of the ages, that all things would be founded and fulfilled in Him.

  i. **Chief cornerstone**: "The 'capstone' was an important stone that held two rows of stones together in a corner ('cornerstone') or stabilized the stones at the foundation or elsewhere (cf. Isa 28:16)." (VanGemeren)

  ii. "Now he is the bond of the building, holding Jew and Gentile in firm unity. This precious cornerstone binds God and man together in wondrous amity, for he is both in one. He joins earth and heaven together, for he participates in each. He joins time and eternity together, for he was a man of few years, and yet he is the Ancient of Days. Wondrous cornerstone!" (Spurgeon)

  iii. Jesus was and will be exalted. "It would be far better for Jesus to be exalted by your praise of his great grace and mercy in saving you than to be exalted in his power as he judges you justly for your sin." (Boice)

  iv. It is hard to imagine Jesus singing this the night before His great rejection, leading to His suffering and crucifixion, *without* tears in His eyes. He would be **rejected**, and He would **become the chief cornerstone**.

  v. "That these verses belong, in a full, proper sense, to Messiah, is confessed by the rabbis, and acknowledged by all." (Horne)

e. **This was the LORD's doing; it is marvelous in our eyes**: The psalmist spoke here on behalf of those redeemed by the Lord and whose life and future is built upon that **chief cornerstone**. *They* rejoice in God's **marvelous** work, despite the rejection of the builders.

i. **This is the LORD's doing**: The exaltation of Jesus from the cross to the resurrection to the right hand of God on high is the work of God *alone*. Who lifted Jesus high again, exalting Him above all?

- Not the religious leaders – they rejected Him.
- Not the Roman leaders – they crucified Him.
- Not the Jewish multitudes – they chose another.
- Not the disciples – they cowered in fear.
- Not His influential followers – they buried Him.
- Not the devoted women – they were beset by grief.
- *Only* God the Father Himself could lift Jesus high.

ii. "What can be more truly marvelous, that a person, put to death as a malefactor, and laid in the grave, should from thence arise immortal, and become the head of an immortal society; should ascend into heaven, be invested with power, and crowned with glory; and should prepare a way for the sons of Adam to follow him into those mansions of eternal bliss?" (Horne)

iii. "What astonishment will then take hold upon those who refused his righteous claims. Then will they know that this is the Lord's doing; though it will be terrible in their eyes. All intelligent beings, even down to the blackest devil of hell, shall at the second advent of our Lord be obliged to confess that the stone which the builders refused hath become the head stone of the corner." (Spurgeon)

f. **This is the day that the LORD has made; we will rejoice and be glad in it**: When Jesus quoted verse 22 (at Matthew 21:42, Mark 12:10-11, and Luke 20:17), He did so in response to the praise and hosannas given to Him at what is commonly called the triumphal entry. Since this psalm is prophetically connected with that event, **the day** mentioned here can be prophetically understood as the day Jesus formally entered Jerusalem as Messiah and King.

i. It is true in a *general* sense that the LORD makes every day, and there is reason to **rejoice and be glad** in every day. Yet specifically, the **day** the LORD made to rejoice and be glad in was the day Jesus entered Jerusalem with hosannas welcoming Him as Israel's Savior. If on that day human voices failed to **rejoice and be glad**, Jesus said that the very stones would cry out their praises and hosannas (Luke 19:40).

ii. There is also reason to believe, based on the chronology of Sir Robert Anderson, that the particular day of the triumphal entry was prophesied in Daniel's prophecy of the Seventy Weeks (Daniel 9:24-26). Anderson's chronology is controversial and rejected by some, but as John Walvoord noted, "No one today is able dogmatically to declare that Sir Robert Anderson's computations are impossible."

3. (25-29) The sacrifice bound to the altar.

Save now, I pray, O Lord;
O Lord, I pray, send now prosperity.
Blessed *is* he who comes in the name of the Lord!
We have blessed you from the house of the Lord.
God *is* the Lord,
And He has given us light;
Bind the sacrifice with cords to the horns of the altar.
You *are* my God, and I will praise You;
***You are* my God, I will exalt You.**

a. **Save now, I pray, O Lord**: The context of the open gates (verse 19) and the coming into the city, as well as the arrangement of this psalm give the sense that these are words from different speakers or parts of a chorus.

i. **Save**: "With the Hebrews salvation is a wide word, comprising all the favours of God that may lead to preservation." (Hall, cited in Spurgeon)

b. **Blessed is he who comes in the name of the Lord**: The main point of this ceremony of song is to welcome God's deliverer through the open gates into the holy city. This deliverer received a blessing from the singers as he approached the **house of the Lord**.

i. Matthew 21:9 (along with Mark 11:9 and John 12:13) quote this phrase as spoken by those who welcomed Jesus at His triumphal entrance into Jerusalem, when He formally presented Himself to Israel as their Messiah and King. The words **save now** are in Hebrew *hosanna*, which is exactly what the crowd at the triumphal entry cried out.

ii. We have a strange prediction that was fulfilled precisely. This deliverer was to be welcomed with open gates (verse 19), hosannas (verse 25), and blessings (verse 26). Yet He is and was the same chief cornerstone that would be rejected (verse 22). Exactly according to the words and spirit of this psalm, Jesus was welcomed as deliverer and

Messiah on Palm Sunday, and rejected and crucified only a few days later.

iii. **We have blessed you from the house of the** LORD: "We can glimpse two companies at this point: one already in the temple court, greeting another which is arriving with the king. *Blessed be he who enters* is an individual welcome, but *We bless you* is addressed to the many who are with him." (Kidner)

iv. **We have blessed you from the house of the** LORD: "Thus say the priests to the people. Ministers must bless those that bless Christ, saying, 'Grace be with all them that love our Lord Jesus Christ in sincerity,' Ephesians 6:24." (Trapp)

c. **God is the** LORD: There is a brief but important focus on Yahweh as the true God, above all idols.

d. **Bind the sacrifice with cords to the horns of the altar**: In view of the greatness of Yahweh and the light He gives, the sacrifice is willingly given. This was fulfilled in a way that the psalmist likely never expected – that the deliverer of the previous verses would *Himself* be the sacrifice, **bound** to an **altar**.

i. It is remarkable to consider and understand that *Jesus sang these words with His disciples a few hours before His crucifixion*. He invited God the Father to **bind** Him to the cross in making a holy sacrifice for sins at God's appointed **altar**. "How significant that before the final note of praise these words should occur!" (Morgan)

ii. Hebrews 13:10 makes reference to the sacrifice of Jesus at an **altar**, probably speaking of the cross.

iii. As we follow Jesus our forerunner, we also **bind** ourselves **with cords to the horns of the altar** of living sacrifice to Jesus (Romans 12:1-2). "It is well to be bound. Wilt Thou bind us, most blessed Spirit, and enamor us with the Cross, and let us never leave it? Bind us with the scarlet cord of redemption, and the golden cord of love, and the silver cord of Advent-hope." (Meyer)

iv. "How precious are the last lines that David Livingstone penned in his diary, before his boys found him kneeling beside his bed, dead, though in the attitude of prayer, the candle burning beside him: 'My Jesus, my King, my Life, my All; to Thee I again dedicate myself.' So bind each of us with the cords of love, and the bands of a man." (Meyer)

e. **You are my God, and I will praise You**: We take these words to be in the mouth of the deliverer who arrived through the open gates. He rightly surrendered Himself to God, filled with praise in view of the ultimate triumph. The voice of Jesus singing this praise and exaltation of God echoed through the upper room as evidence of His submission and obedience.

4. (29) Ending with praise.

Oh, give thanks to the Lord, for *He is* good!
For His mercy *endures* forever.

a. **Oh, give thanks to the Lord**: This psalm began with exuberant and heartfelt praise, and it ends with the same – recognizing once again the goodness of God at the end of it all. If we start with praise, we are in a much better position to end with praise, despite all we go through.

b. **For His mercy endures forever**: Jesus Himself believed in and received this unending mercy and proclaimed it in song with His disciples in the upper room. The same **mercy**, that loyal love, covenant love, and lovingkindness that never ended for Him, is also given to His people.

i. "What better close could there be to this right royal song? The Psalmist would have risen to something higher, so as to end with the climax, but nothing loftier remained. He had reached the height of his grandest argument, and there he paused." (Spurgeon)

Psalms 81-118 – Bibliography

Boice, James Montgomery *Psalms, Volume 2 – Psalms 42-106* (Grand Rapids, Michigan: Baker Books, 1996)

Boice, James Montgomery *Psalms, Volume 3 – Psalms 107-150* (Grand Rapids, Michigan: Baker Books, 1999)

Chappell, Clovis G. *Sermons from the Psalms* (Nashville, Tennessee: Cokesbury Press, 1931)

Clarke, Adam *The Holy Bible, Containing the Old and New Testaments, with A Commentary and Critical Notes, Volume III – Job to Song of Solomon* (New York: Eaton and Mains, 1827?)

Harris, Arthur Emerson *The Psalms Outlined* (Philadelphia: The Judson Press, 1925)

Horne, George *Commentary on the Psalms* (Audubon, New Jersey: Old Paths Publications, 1997 reprint of a 1771 edition)

Kidner, Derek *Psalms 73-150, A Commentary* (Leicester, England: Inter-Varsity Press, 1975)

Maclaren, Alexander *The Psalms, Volume II – Psalms 39-89* (London: Hodder and Stoughton, 1892)

Maclaren, Alexander *The Psalms, Volume III – Psalms 90-150* (London: Hodder and Stoughton, 1892)

Meyer, F.B. *Our Daily Homily* (Westwood, New Jersey: Revell, 1966)

Morgan, G. Campbell *Searchlights from the Word* (New York: Revell, 1926)

Morgan, G. Campbell *An Exposition of the Whole Bible* (Old Tappan, New Jersey: Revell, 1959)

Poole, Matthew *A Commentary on the Holy Bible, Volume 2* (London: The Banner of Truth Trust, 1968)

Spurgeon, Charles Haddon *The Treasury of David, Volume 2 – Psalms 58-110* (Peabody, Massachusetts: Hendrickson, 1988)

Spurgeon, Charles Haddon *The Treasury of David, Volume 3 – Psalms 111-150* (Peabody, Massachusetts: Hendrickson, 1988)

Spurgeon, Charles Haddon *The New Park Street Pulpit, Volumes 1-6* and *The Metropolitan Tabernacle Pulpit, Volumes 7-63* (Pasadena, Texas: Pilgrim Publications, 1990)

Trapp, John *A Commentary on the Old and New Testaments, Volume 3 – Proverbs to Daniel* (Eureka, California: Tanski Publications, 1997)

VanGemeren, Willem A. "Psalms," *The Expositor's Bible Commentary, Volume 5: Psalms-Song of Songs* (Grand Rapids, Michigan: Zondervan, 1991)

As the years pass I love the work of studying, learning, and teaching the Bible more than ever. I'm so grateful that God is faithful to meet me in His Word.

Mary Osgood is doing a wonderful work in proofreading and with editorial suggestions for these volumes of commentary on Psalms. Mary, thank you for helping me to write clearer and better!

Thanks to Brian Procedo for the cover design and the graphics work.

Most especially, thanks to my wife Inga-Lill. She is my loved and valued partner in life and in service to God and His people.

David Guzik

David Guzik's Bible commentary is regularly used and trusted by many thousands who want to know the Bible better. Pastors, teachers, class leaders, and everyday Christians find his commentary helpful for their own understanding and explanation of the Bible. David and his wife Inga-Lill live in Santa Barbara, California.

You can email David at
david@enduringword.com

For more resources by David Guzik,
go to www.enduringword.com

www.ingramcontent.com/pod-product-compliance
Lightning Source LLC
Chambersburg PA
CBHW021217090426
42740CB00006B/257